ALLEN CARR'S
EASY WAY TO
STOP
SMOKING

ALLEN CARR'S
EASY WAY TO
STOP
SMOKING

BARNES
&NOBLE
BOOKS
NEW YORK

To the smokers I have failed to cure,
I hope it will help them to get free.

And to Sid Sutton

But most of all to Joyce

This edition published by Barnes & Noble, Inc.,
by arrangement with Allen Carr's Easyway (International) Ltd.

1999 Barnes & Noble Books

ISBN 0-7607-1200-X

Book design by Jim Sarfati, Rocket Design

Printed and bound in the United States of America

99 00 01 02 03 M 9 8 7 6 5 4 3 2 1

FG

Contents

Preface

At last the miracle cure all smokers have been waiting for:

- Instantaneous
- Equally effective for the heavy smoker
- No bad withdrawal pangs
- Needs no willpower
- No shock treatment
- No aids or gimmicks required
- You will not even put on weight
- Permanent

Perhaps you are somewhat apprehensive about reading this book. Perhaps, like the majority of smokers, the mere thought of stopping fills you with panic and although you have every intention of stopping one day, it is not today.

If you are expecting me to inform you of the terrible health risks that smokers run, that smokers spend a small fortune during their smoking lives, that it is a filthy, disgusting habit and that you are a stupid, spineless, weak-willed jellyfish, then I must disappoint you. Those tactics never helped me to quit and if they were going to help you, you would already have quit.

My method, which I shall refer to as EASYWAY, doesn't work that way. Some of the things that I am about to say, you might find difficult to believe. However by the time you've finished the book, you'll not only believe them, but wonder how you could ever have been brainwashed into believing otherwise.

There is a common misapprehension that we choose to smoke. Smokers no more choose to smoke than alcoholics choose to become alcoholics, or heroin addicts choose to become heroin addicts. It is true that we choose to light those first experimental cigarettes. I occasionally choose to go to the cinema, but I certainly didn't choose to spend my whole life in a cinema.

Please reflect on your life. Did you ever make the positive decision that at certain times in your life, you couldn't enjoy a meal or a social occasion without smoking, or that you couldn't concentrate or handle stress without a cigarette? At what stage did you decide that you needed cigarettes, not just for social occasions, but that you needed to have them permanently in your presence, and felt insecure, even panic-stricken without them?

Like every other smoker, you have been lured into the most sinister, subtle trap that man and nature have combined to devise. There is not a parent on this planet, whether smoker or non-smoker, that likes the thought of his or her children smoking. This means that all smokers wish they had never started. Not surprisingly really, no one needs cigarettes to enjoy meals or cope with stress before he or she gets hooked.

At the same time all smokers wish to continue to smoke. After all, no one forces us to keep lighting up; whether we understand the reason or not, it is only smokers themselves that decide to light up.

If there were a magic button that smokers could press to wake up the following morning as if they had never lit that first cigarette, the only smokers there would be tomorrow morning would be the youngsters who are still at the experimental stage. The only thing that prevents us from quitting is: **FEAR!**

Fear that we will have to survive an indeterminate period of misery, deprivation and unsatisfied craving in order to be free. Fear that a meal or social occasion will never be quite as enjoyable without a cigarette. Fear that we'll never be able to concentrate, handle stress or be as confident without our little crutch. Fear that our personality and character will change. But most of all, the fear of 'once a smoker—always a smoker,' that we will never be completely free and spend the rest of our lives at odd times craving the occasional cigarette. If, as I did, you have already tried all the conventional ways to quit and been through the misery of what I describe as the willpower method of stopping, you will not only be affected by that fear, but convinced you can never quit.

If you are apprehensive, panic-sticken or feel that the time is not right for you to give up, then let me assure you that your apprehension or panic is caused by fear. That fear is not relieved by cigarettes but created by them. You didn't decide to fall into the nicotine trap. But like all traps, it is designed to ensure that you remain trapped. Ask yourself, when you lit those first experimental cigarettes, did you decide to remain a smoker as long as you have? So when are you going to quit? Tomorrow?

Next year? Stop kidding yourself! The trap is designed to hold you for life. Why else do you think all these other smokers don't quit before it kills them?

This book was first published by Penguin a decade ago and has been a bestseller every year since then. I now have ten years' feedback. As you will soon be reading, the feedback has revealed information that has exceeded my wildest aspirations of the effectiveness of my method. It has also revealed two aspects of EASYWAY that have caused me concern. The second I will be covering later. The first arose from the letters that I have received. I give three typical examples:

'I didn't believe the claims you made and I apologize for doubting you. It was just as easy and enjoyable as you said it would be. I've given copies of your book to all my smoking friends and relatives, but I can't understand why they don't read it.'

'I was given your book eight years ago by an ex-smoking friend. I've just got around to reading it. My only regret is that I wasted eight years.'

'I've just finished reading EASYWAY. I know it has only been four days, but I feel so great, I know I'll never need to smoke again. I first started to read your book five years ago, got halfway through and panicked. I knew that if I went on reading I would have to stop. Wasn't I silly?'

No, that particular young lady wasn't silly. I've referred to a magic button. EASYWAY works just like that magic button. Let me make it quite clear, EASYWAY isn't magic, but for me and the hundreds of thousands of ex-smokers who have found it so easy and enjoyable to quit, it seems like magic!

This is the warning. We have a chicken and egg situation. Every smoker wants to quit and every smoker can find it easy and enjoyable to quit. It's only fear that prevents smokers from trying to quit. The greatest gain is to be rid of that fear. But you won't be free of that fear until you complete the book. On the contrary, like the lady in the third example, that fear might increase as you read the book and this might prevent you from finishing it.

You didn't decide to fall into the trap, but be clear in your mind, you won't escape from it unless you make a positive decision to do so. You might already be straining at the leash to quit. On the other hand you might be apprehensive. Either way please bear in mind: **YOU HAVE ABSOLUTELY NOTHING TO LOSE!**

If at the end of the book you decide that you wish to continue to smoke, there is nothing to prevent you from doing so. You don't even have to cut down or stop smoking while you are reading the book, and remember, there is no shock treatment. On the contrary, I have only good news for you. Can you imagine how the Count of Monte Cristo felt when he finally escaped from that prison? That's how I felt when I escaped from the nicotine trap. That's how the millions of ex-smokers who have used my method feel. By the end of the book: **THAT'S HOW YOU WILL FEEL!**

GO FOR IT!

If you are a smoker all you have to do is read on.

If you are a non-smoker purchasing for loved ones, all you have to do is persuade them to read the book. If you cannot persuade them, then read the book yourself, and the last chapter will advise you how to get the message across—also how to prevent your children from starting. Do not be fooled by the fact that they hate it now. All children do before they become hooked.

Introduction

'I'M GOING TO CURE THE WORLD OF SMOKING.'

I was talking to my wife. She thought that I had flipped. Understandable if you consider that she had watched me fail on numerous attempts to quit. The most recent had been two years previously. I'd actually survived six months of sheer purgatory before I finally succumbed and lit a cigarette. I'm not ashamed to admit that I cried like a baby. I was crying because I knew that I was condemned to be a smoker for life. I'd put so much effort into that attempt and suffered so much misery that I knew I would never have the strength to go through that ordeal again. I'm not a violent man, but if some patronizing non-smoker had been stupid enough at that moment to suggest to me that all smokers can find it easy to quit, immediately and permanently, I would not have been responsible for my actions. However, I'm convinced that any jury in the world, comprised of smokers only, would have pardoned me on the grounds of justifiable homicide.

Perhaps you too find it impossible to believe that any smoker can find it easy to quit. If so, I beg you not to cast this book into the rubbish bin. Please trust me. I assure you that even you can find it easy to quit.

Anyway, there I was two years later, having just extinguished what I knew would be my final cigarette, not only telling my wife that I was already a non-smoker, but that I was going to cure the rest of the world. I must admit that at the time I found her scepticism somewhat irritating. However, in no way did it diminish my feeling of exaltation. I suppose that my exhilaration in knowing that I was already a happy non-smoker distorted my perspective somewhat. With the benefit of hindsight, I can sympathize with her attitude, I now understand why Joyce and my close friends and relatives thought I was a candidate for the funny farm.

As I look back on my life, it seems that my whole existence has been a preparation for solving the smoking problem. Even those hateful years of training and practising as a chartered accountant were invaluable in helping me to unravel the mysteries of the smoking trap. They say you can't fool all the people all of the time, but I believe the tobacco companies have done just that for years. I also believe that I am the first to really understand the smoking trap. If I appear to be arrogant, let me hasten to add that it was no credit to me, just the circumstances of my life.

The momentous day was 15 July 1983. I didn't escape from Colditz, but I imagine those who did felt the same sense of relief and exhilaration as I did when I extinguished that final cigarette. I realized I had discovered something that every smoker was praying for: an easy way to stop smoking.

After testing out the method on smoking friends and relatives, I gave up accountancy and became a full-time consultant, helping other smokers to get free.

I wrote the first edition of this book in 1985. One of my failures, the man I describe in chapter 25, was the inspiration. He visited me twice, and we were both reduced to tears on each occasion. He was so agitated that I couldn't get him to relax enough to absorb what I was saying. I hoped that if I wrote it all down, he could read it in his own good time, as many times as he wanted to, and this would help him to absorb the message.

I was in no doubt that EASYWAY would work just as effectively for other smokers as it had for me. However, when I contemplated putting the method into book form, I was apprehensive. I did my own market research. The comments were not very encouraging:

'How can a book help me to quit? What I need is willpower!'

'How can a book avoid the terrible withdrawal pangs?'

In addition to these pessimistic comments, I had my own doubts. Often at the clinics it became obvious that a client had misunderstood an important point that I was making. I was able to correct the situation. But how would a book be able to do that? I remembered well the times when I studied to qualify as an accountant, when I didn't understand or agree with a particular point in a book, the frustration because you couldn't ask the book to explain. I was also well aware, particularly in these days of television and videos, that many people are not accustomed to reading.

Added to all these factors, I had one doubt that overrode all the rest. I wasn't a writer and was very conscious of my limitations in this respect. I was confident that I could sit down face to face with a smoker and convince that smoker how much more enjoyable social occasions would be, how he or she would be better able to concentrate and handle stress as a non-smoker and just how easy and enjoyable the process of quitting could be. But could I transfer that facility to a book? I even doubted whether I had the right to put EASYWAY into book form and whether I should not have employed a professional writer. No way was I certain that it would be a success.

Thankfully the gods were kind to me. I've received thousands of complimentary letters containing comments such as:

'It's the greatest book ever written.'

'You are my guru.'

'You are a genius.'

'You should be knighted.'

'You should be Prime Minister.'

'You are a saint.'

I hope that I have not allowed such comments to go to my head. I'm fully aware that those comments were made, not to compliment me on my literary skills, but in spite of my lack of them. They were made because whether your preference is to read a book or to attend a clinic: The EASYWAY System Works!

Not only do we now have a worldwide network of EASYWAY clinics, but this book has been translated into over twenty different languages, and as I write, it is the number-one non-fiction bestseller in Germany.

After approximately a year of running smoking clinics, I thought I had learned everything that it was possible to learn about helping smokers to quit. Amazingly, fourteen years after discovering the method, I learn something new practically every day. This fact caused me some concern when I was asked to review the first edition after six years of publication. I had a horror that practically everything that I had written I would have to amend or retract.

I needn't have worried. The basic principles of EASYWAY are as sound today as when I first discovered the method. The beautiful truth is: **IT IS EASY TO STOP!**

That is a fact. My only difficulty is to convince every smoker of that fact. All of the later knowledge that I have accumulated over fourteen years has helped to enable every smoker to see the light. At the clinics we try to achieve perfection. Every failure hurts us deeply because we know every smoker can find it easy to quit. When smokers fail, they tend to regard it as their failure. We regard it as our failure—we failed to convince those smokers just how easy and enjoyable it is to quit.

I dedicated the first edition to the smokers that I had failed to cure. That failure rate was based on the money-back guarantee that we give at our clinics. The average current failure rate of our clinics worldwide is under 5 per cent. That means a success rate of over 95 per cent.

Although I was aware that I had discovered something marvellous, I never in my wildest dreams expected to achieve such rates. You might well argue that if I genuinely believed that I would cure the world of smoking, I must have expected to achieve 100 per cent.

No, I never ever expected to achieve 100 per cent. Snuff-taking was the previous most popular form of nicotine addiction until it became antisocial and died. However, there are still a few weirdos that continue to take snuff, and probably there always will be. Amazingly, the Houses of Parliament are one of the last bastions of snuff-taking. I suppose this is not so surprising when you think about it; politicians are generally about a hundred years behind the times. So there will always be a few weirdos that will continue to smoke. I certainly never expected to have to cure every smoker personally.

What I thought would happen was that once I had explained the mysteries of the smoking trap and dispelled such illusions as:

- Smokers enjoy smoking
- Smokers choose to smoke
- Smoking relieves boredom & stress
- Smoking aids concentration and relaxation
- Smoking is a habit
- It takes willpower to quit
- Once a smoker always a smoker
- Telling smokers that it kills them helps them to quit
- Substitutes, particularly nicotine replacement, help smokers to quit,

and that smokers have to go through a transitional period of misery in order to quit, I naïvely thought that the rest of the world would also see the light and adopt my method.

I thought my chief antagonist would be the tobacco industry. Amazingly, my chief stumbling blocks were the very institutions that I thought would be my greatest allies: the media, the Government, organizations like the Association on Smoking and Health, QUIT and the established medical profession.

You've probably seen the film *Sister Kenny*. In case you haven't, it was about the time when infantile paralysis, or polio, was the scourge of our children. I vividly remember that the words engendered the same fear in me as the word 'cancer' does today. The effect of polio was not only to paralyse the legs and arms but to distort the limbs. The established medical treatment was to put those limbs in irons and thus prevent the distortion. The result was paralysis for life.

Sister Kenny believed the irons inhibited recovery and proved a thousand times over that the muscles could be re-educated so that the child could walk again. However, Sister Kenny wasn't a doctor, she was merely a nurse. How dare she dabble in a province that was confined to qualified doctors? It didn't seem to matter that Sister Kenny had found the solution to the problem and had proved her solution to be effective. The children that were treated by Sister Kenny knew she was right, so did their parents, yet the established medical profession not only refused to adopt her methods but actually prevented her from practising. It took Sister Kenny twenty years before the medical profession would accept the obvious.

I first saw that film years before I discovered EASYWAY. The film was very interesting and no doubt there was an element of truth in it. However, it seemed equally obvious that Hollywood had used a large portion of poetic licence. Sister Kenny couldn't possibly have discovered something that the combined knowledge of medical science had failed to discover. Surely the established medical specialists weren't the dinosaurs they were being portrayed as? How could it possibly have taken them twenty years to accept the facts that were staring them in the face?

They say that fact is stranger than fiction. I apologize for accusing the makers of *Sister Kenny* of using poetic licence. Even in this so-called enlightened age of modern communications, after fourteen years, I've failed to get my message across. Oh, I've proved my point; the only reason that you are reading this book is that another ex-smoker has recommended it to you. Remember, I don't have the massive financial power of institutions like the British Medical Association or the Association on Smoking and Health. Like Sister Kenny, I'm a lone individual. Like her, I'm only famous because my system works. I'm already regarded as the number-one guru on helping smokers to quit. Like Sister Kenny, I've proved my point. But what good did it do that Sister Kenny proved her point, if the rest of the world was still adopting procedures which were the direct opposite to what they should be?

The last sentence of this book is identical to that in the original manuscript:

There is a wind of change in society. A snowball has started that I hope this book will help turn into an avalanche.

From my remarks above, you might have drawn the conclusion that I am no respecter of the medical profession. Nothing could be further from the truth. One of my sons is a doctor and I know of no finer profession. Indeed we receive more recommendations to our clinics from doctors than from any other source, and surprisingly, more of our clients come from the medical profession than any other single profession.

In the early years, I was generally regarded by the doctors as being somewhere between a charlatan and a quack. In August 1997, I had the great honour to be invited to lecture to the 10th World Conference on Tobacco and Health held in Beijing. I believe that I am the first non–qualified doctor to receive such an honour. The invitation itself is a measure of the progress that I have made.

However, I might just as well have been lecturing to a brick wall. Since the nicotine chewing gum and the patch have failed to cure the problem, smokers themselves appear to have accepted that you don't get cured from addiction to a drug by prescribing the same drug. It's equivalent to saying to a heroin addict: don't smoke heroin, smoking is dangerous, try injecting it into your vein (don't try this with nicotine, it will kill you instantly). Because the medical profession and the media haven't a clue about helping smokers to quit, they concentrate on telling smokers what they already know: smoking is unhealthy, it's filthy and disgusting, it's antisocial and expensive. It never seems to occur to them that smokers do not smoke because they don't understand the reasons that they shouldn't smoke. The real solution is to remove the reasons that they do smoke.

On national no-smoking days, the medical experts say something like: 'This is the day that every smoker tries to quit!' Every smoker knows that it is the one day in the year that most smokers will smoke twice as many as they usually do and twice as blatantly, because smokers don't like being told what to do, particularly by people who dismiss smokers as mere idiots and don't understand why they smoke.

Because they don't completely understand smokers themselves or how to make it easy for smokers to quit, their attitude is 'Try this method. If it doesn't work try another.' Can you imagine if there were ten different ways of treating appendicitis? Nine of them cured 10 per cent of the patients, which means they killed 90 per cent of them, and the tenth way cured 95 per cent. Imagine that knowledge of the tenth method had been available for over fourteen years, but the vast majority of the medical profession was still recommending the other nine.

One of the doctors at the conference raised a very pertinent point that hadn't occurred to me. He pointed out that doctors might well find themselves liable to a legal action for malpractice, by not advising their patients of the best way to quit smoking. Ironically he was a great advocate of nicotine replacement therapy (nicotine gums, patches, etc.). I try hard not to be vindictive, but I hope he becomes the first victim of his suggestion.

As I write, the British government has just wasted £2.5 million on a shock TV campaign trying to persuade youngsters not to get hooked. They might just as well have wasted it on trying to persuade them that motorbikes can kill you. Do they not realize that youngsters know that one cigarette won't kill them and that no youngster ever expects to get hooked? The link between smoking and lung cancer has been established for over forty years. Yet more youngsters are becoming hooked nowadays than ever before. Youngsters don't need to watch smoking horrors on TV. Smokers tend to avoid such programmes anyway. Practically every youngster in the country has witnessed the actual devastation that smoking causes within his or her own family. I watched my father and my sister destroyed by the weed; that didn't prevent me from falling into the trap.

I appeared on a national TV programme with a doctor from ASH who had never smoked in her life and had never cured a single smoker, categorically informing the nation how this campaign would prevent youngsters from becoming hooked. If only the government had had the common sense to give that £2.5 million to me. I could have financed a campaign that would have guaranteed the death of nicotine addiction within a few years.

I truly believe that the snowball has become a football. But after fourteen years that is still a spit in the ocean. I'm grateful to the thousands of ex-smokers who have visited my clinics, read my books, watched my videos and recommended EASYWAY to their friends, relatives and anyone who will listen to them, and I pray that you continue to do so. However, the snowball won't become an avalanche until the medical profession and the media stop recommending methods that make it harder to quit and accept that EASYWAY is not just another method: **BUT THE ONLY SENSIBLE METHOD TO USE!**

I don't expect you to believe me at this stage, but by the time you have finished the book, you will understand. Even the comparatively few failures that we have say something like: 'I haven't succeeded yet, but your way is better than any I know.'

If when you finish the book, you feel that you owe me a debt of gratitude, you can more than repay that debt. Not just by recommending EASYWAY to your friends, but whenever you see a TV or radio programme, or read a newspaper article advocating some other method, write to them or phone them asking why they aren't advocating EASYWAY. That will start the avalanche, and if I live to witness it, I will die a happy man.

This third edition of EASYWAY is to give you the state-of-the-art technology on just how easy and enjoyable it is to quit smoking. Do you have a feeling of doom and gloom? Forget it. I've achieved some marvellous things in my life. By far the greatest was to escape from the slavery of nicotine addiction. I escaped over fourteen years ago and still cannot get over the joy of being free. There is no need to feel depressed, nothing bad is happening; on the contrary, you are about to achieve something that every smoker on the planet would love to achieve: **TO BE FREE!**

The Worst Nicotine Addict
I Have Yet to Meet

Perhaps I should begin by describing my competence for writing this book. No, I am not a doctor or a psychiatrist; my qualifications are far more appropriate. I spent thirty-three years of my life as a confirmed smoker. In the later years I smoked a hundred a day on a bad day, and never less than sixty.

During my life I had made dozens of attempts to stop. I once stopped for six months, and I was still climbing up the wall, still standing near smokers trying to get a whiff of the tobacco, still travelling in the smokers' compartments on trains.

With most smokers, on the health side, it's a question of 'I'll stop before it happens to me.' I had reached the stage where I knew it was killing me. I had a permanent headache with the pressure of the constant coughing. I could feel the continuous throbbing in the vein that runs vertically down the centre of my forehead, and I honestly believed that any moment there would be an explosion in my head and I would die from a brain haemorrhage. It bothered me, but it still didn't stop me.

I had reached the stage where I gave up even trying to stop. It was not so much that I enjoyed smoking. Some time in their lives most smokers have suffered from the illusion that they enjoy the odd cigarette, but I never suffered from that illusion. I have always detested the taste and smell, but I thought a cigarette helped me to relax. It gave me courage and confidence, and I was always miserable when I tried to stop, never being able to visualize an enjoyable life without a cigarette.

Eventually my wife sent me to a hypnotherapist. I must confess that I was completely sceptical, knowing nothing about hypnosis in those days and having visions of a Svengali-type figure with piercing eyes and a waving pendulum. I had all the normal illusions that smokers have about smoking except one—I knew that I wasn't a weak willed person. I was in control of all other aspects of my life but cigarettes controlled me, I thought that hypnosis involved the forcing of wills, and although I was not obstructive (like most smokers, I dearly wanted to stop), I thought no one was going to kid me that I didn't need to smoke.

The whole session appeared to be a waste of time. The hypnotherapist tried to make me lift my arms and do various other things. Nothing appeared to be working properly. I didn't lose consciousness. I didn't go into a trance, or at least I didn't think I did, and yet after that session not only did I stop smoking but I actually enjoyed the process even during the withdrawal period.

Now, before you go rushing off to see a hypnotherapist, let me make something quite clear. Hypnotherapy is a means of communication. If the wrong message is communicated, you won't stop smoking. I'm loath to criticize the man whom I consulted because I would be dead by now if I hadn't seen him. But it was in spite of him, not because of him. Neither do I wish to appear to be knocking hypnotherapy; on the contrary, I use it as part of my own consultations. It is the power of suggestion and a powerful force that can be used for good or evil. Don't ever consult a hypnotherapist unless he or she has been personally recommended by someone you respect and trust.

During those awful years as a smoker I thought that my life depended on cigarettes, and I was prepared to die rather than be without them. Today people ask me whether I ever have the odd pang. The answer is, 'Never, never, never'—just the reverse. I've had a marvellous life. If I had died through smoking, I couldn't have complained. I have been a very lucky man, but the most marvellous thing that has ever happened to me is being freed from that nightmare, that slavery of having to go through life systematically destroying my own body and paying through the nose for the privilege.

Let me make it quite clear from the beginning: I am not a mystical figure. I do not believe in magicians or fairies. I have a scientific brain, and I couldn't understand what appeared to me like magic. I started reading up on hypnosis and on smoking. Nothing I read seemed to explain the miracle that had happened. Why had it been so ridiculously easy to stop, whereas previously it had been weeks of black depression?

It took me a long time to work it all out, basically because I was going about it back to front. I was trying to work out why it had been so easy to stop, whereas the real problem is trying to explain why smokers find it *difficult* to stop. Smokers talk about the terrible withdrawal pangs, but when I looked back and tried to remember those awful pangs, they didn't exist for me. There was no physical pain. It was all in the mind.

My full-time profession is now helping other people to kick the habit.

I'm very, very successful. I have helped to cure thousands of smokers. Let me emphasize from the start: there is no such thing as a confirmed smoker. I have still not met anybody who was as badly hooked (or, rather, *thought* he was as badly hooked) as myself. Anybody can not only stop smoking but find it easy to stop. It is basically fear that keeps us smoking: the fear that life will never be quite as enjoyable without cigarettes and the fear of feeling deprived. In fact, nothing could be further from the truth. Not only is life just as enjoyable without them but it is infinitely more so in many ways, and extra health, energy and wealth are the least of the advantages.

All smokers can find it easy to stop smoking—even you! All you have to do is read the rest of the book with an open mind. The more you can understand, the easier you will find it. Even if you do not understand a word, provided you follow the instructions, you will find it easy. Most important of all, you will not go through life moping for cigarettes or feeling deprived. The only mystery will be why you did it for so long.

Let me issue a warning. There are only two reasons for failure with my method:

1. **FAILURE TO CARRY OUT INSTRUCTIONS** Some people find it annoying that I am so dogmatic about certain recommendations. For example, I will tell you not to try cutting down or using substitutes like sweets, chewing gum, etc. (particularly anything containing nicotine). The reason why I am so dogmatic is that I know my subject. I do not deny that there are many people who have succeeded in stopping using such ruses, but they have succeeded in spite of, not because of them. There are people who can make love standing on a hammock, but it is not the easiest way. Everything I tell you has a purpose: to make it easy to stop and thereby ensure success.

2. **FAILURE TO UNDERSTAND** Do not take anything for granted. Question not only what I tell you but also your own views and what society has taught you about smoking. For example, those of you who think it is just a habit, ask yourselves why other habits, some of them enjoyable ones, are easy to break, yet a habit that tastes awful, costs us a fortune and kills us is so difficult to break.

   Those of you who think you enjoy a cigarette, ask yourselves why other things in life, which are infinitely more enjoyable, you can take or leave. Why do you *have* to have the cigarette and panic sets in if you don't?

The Easy Method

The object of this book is to get you into the frame of mind in which, instead of the normal method of stopping whereby you start off with the feeling that you are climbing Mount Everest and spend the next few weeks craving a cigarette and envying other smokers, you start right away with a feeling of elation, as if you had been cured of a terrible disease. From then on, the further you go through life the more you will look at cigarettes and wonder how you ever smoked them in the first place. You will look at smokers with pity as opposed to envy.

Provided that you are not a non-smoker or an ex-smoker, it is essential to keep smoking until you have finished the book completely. This may appear to be a contradiction. Later I shall be explaining that cigarettes do absolutely nothing for you at all. In fact, one of the many conundrums about smoking is that when we are actually smoking a cigarette, we look at it and wonder why we are doing it. It is only when we have been deprived that the cigarette becomes precious. However, let us accept that, whether you like it or not, you believe you are hooked. When you believe you are hooked, you can never be completely relaxed or concentrate properly unless you are smoking. So do not attempt to stop smoking before you have finished the whole book. As you read further your desire to smoke will gradually be reduced. Do not go off half-cocked; this could be fatal. Remember, all you have to do is to follow the instructions.

With the benefit of twelve years' feedback since the book's original publication, apart from chapter 28, 'Timing', this instruction to continue to smoke until you have completed the book has caused me more frustration than any other. When I first stopped smoking, many of my relatives and friends stopped, purely because I had done it. They thought, 'If he can do it, anybody can.' Over the years, by dropping little hints I managed to persuade the ones that hadn't stopped to realize just how nice it is to be free! When the book was first printed I gave copies to the hard core who were still puffing away. I worked on the basis that, even if it were the most boring book ever written, they would still read it, if only because it had been written by a friend. I was surprised and hurt to learn that, months later, they hadn't bothered to finish the book. I even discovered that the original copy I had signed and given to someone who was then my closest friend had not only been ignored but actually given away. I was hurt at the time, but I had overlooked the dreadful fear that slavery to the weed instils in the smoker. It can transcend friendship. I nearly provoked a divorce because of it. My mother once said to my wife, 'Why don't you threaten to leave him if he doesn't stop smoking?' My wife said, 'Because he'd leave me if I did.' I'm ashamed to admit it, but I believe she was right; such is the fear that smoking creates. I now realize that many smokers don't finish the book because they feel they have got to stop smoking when they do. Some deliberately read only one line a day in order to postpone the evil day. Now I am fully aware that many readers are having their arms twisted, by people that love them, to read the book. Look at it this way: what have you got to lose? If you don't stop at the end of the book, you are no worse off than you are now. **YOU HAVE ABSOLUTELY NOTHING TO LOSE AND SO MUCH TO GAIN!** Incidentally, if you have not smoked for a few days or weeks but are not sure whether you are a smoker, an ex-smoker or a non-smoker, then don't smoke while you read. In fact, you are already a non-smoker. All we've now got to do is to let your brain catch up with your body. By the end of the book you'll be a happy non-smoker.

Basically my method is the complete opposite of the normal method of trying to stop. The *normal* method is to list the considerable disadvantages of smoking and say, 'If only I can go long enough without a cigarette, eventually the desire to smoke will go. I can then enjoy life again, free of slavery to the weed.'

This is the logical way to go about it, and thousands of smokers are stopping every day using variations of this method. However, it is very difficult to succeed using this method for the following reasons:

1. Stopping smoking is not the real problem. Every time you put a cigarette out you stop smoking. You may have powerful reasons on day one to say, 'I do not want to smoke any more'—all smokers have, every day of their lives, and the reasons are more powerful than you can possibly imagine. The real problem is day two, **day** ten or day ten thousand, when in a weak moment, an inebriated

moment or even a strong moment, you have one cigarette, and because it is partly drug addiction you then want another, and suddenly you are a smoker again.

2. The health scares should stop us. Our rational minds say, 'Stop doing it. You are a fool,' but in fact they make it harder. We smoke, for example, when we are nervous. Tell smokers that it is killing them, and the first thing they will do is to light a cigarette. There are more cigarette butts outside the Royal Marsden Hospital, England's foremost cancer treatment establishment, than any other hospital in the country.

3. All reasons for stopping actually make it harder for two other reasons. *First*, they create a sense of sacrifice. We are always being forced to give up our little friend or prop or vice or pleasure, whichever way the smoker sees it. *Secondly*, they create a 'blind'. We do not smoke because we don't understand the reasons we should stop. The real question is 'Why do we want or need to do it?'

The Easy Method is basically this: initially to forget the reasons we'd like to stop, to face the cigarette problem and to ask ourselves the following questions:

1. What is it doing for me?

2. Do I actually enjoy it?

3. Do I really need to go through life paying through the nose just to stick these things in my mouth and suffocate myself?

The beautiful truth is that it does absolutely nothing for you at all. Let me make it quite clear, I do not mean that the disadvantages of being a smoker outweigh the advantages; all smokers know that all their lives. I mean there are not *any* advantages from smoking. The only advantage it ever had was the social 'plus'; nowadays even smokers themselves regard it as an antisocial habit.

Most smokers find it necessary to rationalize why they smoke, but the reasons are all fallacies and illusions.

The first thing we are going to do is to remove these fallacies and illusions. In fact, you will realize that there is nothing to give up. Not only is there nothing to give up but there are marvellous, positive gains from being a non-smoker, and health and money are only two of these gains. Once the illusion that life will never be quite as enjoyable without the cigarette is removed, once you realize that not only is life just as enjoyable without it but infinitely more so, once the feeling of being deprived or of missing out is eradicated, then we can go back to reconsider the health and money—and the dozens of other reasons for stopping smoking. These realizations will become positive additional aids to help you achieve what you really desire—to enjoy the whole of your life free from the slavery of the weed.

Why Is It Difficult
to Stop?

As I explained earlier, I got interested in this subject because of my own addiction. When I finally stopped it was like magic. When I had previously tried to stop there were weeks of black depression. There would be odd days when I was comparatively cheerful but the next day back with the depression. It was like clawing your way out of a slippery pit: you feel you are near the top, you see the sunshine and then find yourself sliding down again. Eventually you light that cigarette, it tastes awful and you try to work out why you have to do it.

One of the questions I always ask smokers prior to my consultations is 'Do you want to stop smoking?' In a way it is a stupid question. All smokers would love to stop smoking. If you say to the most confirmed smoker, 'If you could go back to the time before you became hooked, with the knowledge you have now, would you have started smoking?', **'NO WAY'** is the reply.

Say to the most confirmed smoker—someone who doesn't think that it injures his health, who is not worried about the social stigma and who can afford it (there are not many about these days)—'Do you encourage your children to smoke?', **'NO WAY'** is the reply.

All smokers feel that something evil has got possession of them. In the early days it is a question of 'I am going to stop, not today but tomorrow.' Eventually we get to the stage where we think either that we haven't got the willpower or that there is something inherent in the cigarette that we must have in order to enjoy life.

As I said previously, the problem is not explaining why it is easy to stop; *it is explaining why it is difficult.* In fact, the real problem is explaining why anybody does it in the first place or why, at one time, over 60 per cent of the population were smoking.

The whole business of smoking is an extraordinary enigma. The only reason we get on to it is because of the thousands of people already doing it. Yet every one of them wishes he or she had not started in the first place, telling us that it is a waste of time and money. We cannot quite believe they are not enjoying it. We associate it with being grown up and work hard to become hooked ourselves. We then spend the rest of our lives telling our own children not to do it and trying to kick the habit ourselves.

We also spend the rest of our lives paying through the nose. The average twenty-a-day smoker spends £50,000 in his or her lifetime on cigarettes. What do we do with that money? (It wouldn't be so bad if we threw it down the drain.) We actually use it systematically to congest our lungs with cancerous tars, progressively to clutter up and poison our blood vessels. Each day we are increasingly starving of oxygen every muscle and organ of our bodies, so that each day we become more lethargic. We sentence ourselves to a lifetime of filth, bad breath, stained teeth, burnt clothes, filthy ashtrays and the foul smell of stale tobacco. It is a lifetime of slavery. We spend half our lives in situations in which society forbids us to smoke (churches, hospitals, schools, tube trains, theatres, etc.) or, when we are trying to cut down or stop, feeling deprived. The rest of our smoking lives is spent in situations where we are allowed to smoke but wish we didn't have to. What sort of hobby is it that when you are doing it you wish you weren't, and when you are not doing it you crave a cigarette? It's a lifetime of being treated by half of society like some sort of leper and, worst of all, a lifetime of an otherwise intelligent, rational human being going through life in contempt. The smoker despises himself, every National Non-Smoking Day, every time he inadvertently reads the government health warning or there is a cancer scare or a bad-breath campaign, every time he gets congested or has a pain in the chest, every time he is the lone smoker in company with non-smokers. Having to go through life with these awful black shadows at the back of his mind, what does he get out of it? **ABSOLUTELY NOTHING!** Pleasure? Enjoyment? Relaxation? A prop? A boost? All illusions, unless you consider the wearing of tight shoes to enjoy the removal of them as some sort of pleasure!

As I have said, the real problem is trying to explain not only why smokers find it difficult to stop but why anybody does it at all.

You are probably saying, 'That's all very well. I know this, but once you are hooked on these things it is very difficult to stop.' But why is it so difficult, and why do we have to do it? Smokers search for the answer to these questions all of their lives.

Some say it is because of the powerful withdrawal symptoms. In fact, the actual withdrawal symptoms from nicotine are so mild (see chapter

6) that most smokers have lived and died without ever realizing they are drug addicts.

Some say cigarettes are very enjoyable. They aren't. They are filthy, disgusting objects. Ask any smoker who thinks he smokes only because he enjoys a cigarette if, when he hasn't got his own brand and can only obtain a brand he finds distasteful, he stops smoking. Smokers would rather smoke old rope than not smoke at all. Enjoyment has nothing to do with it. I enjoy lobster but I never got to the stage where I had to have twenty lobsters hanging round my neck. With other things in life we enjoy them whilst we are doing them but we don't sit feeling deprived when we are not.

Some search for deep psychological reasons, the 'Freudian syndrome', 'the child at the mother's breast'. Really it is just the reverse. The usual reason why we start smoking is to show we are grown up and mature. If we had to suck a pacifier in public, we would die of embarrassment.

Some think it is the reverse, the macho effect of breathing smoke or fire down your nostrils. Again this argument has no substance. A burning cigarette in the ear would appear ridiculous. How much more ridiculous to breathe cancer-triggering tars into your lungs.

Some say, 'It is something to do with my hands!' So, why light it?

'It is oral satisfaction.' So, why light it?

'It is the feeling of the smoke going into my lungs.' An awful feeling—it is called suffocation.

Many believe smoking relieves boredom. This is also a fallacy. Boredom is a frame of mind. There is nothing interesting about a cigarette.

For thirty-three years my reason was that it relaxed me, gave me confidence and courage. I also knew it was killing me and costing me a fortune. Why didn't I go to my doctor and ask him for an alternative to relax me and give me courage and confidence? I didn't go because I knew he would suggest an alternative. It wasn't my reason; it was my excuse.

Some say they only do it because their friends do it. Are you really that stupid? If so, just pray that your friends do not start cutting their heads off to cure a headache!

Most smokers who think about it eventually come to the conclusion that it is just a habit. This is not really an explanation but, having discounted all the usual rational explanations, it appears to be the only remaining excuse. Unfortunately, this explanation is equally illogical. Every day of our lives we change habits, and some of them are very enjoyable. We have been brainwashed to believe that smoking is a habit and that habits are difficult to break. Are habits difficult to break? In the UK we are in the habit of driving on the left side of the road. Yet when we drive on the Continent or in the States, we immediately break that habit with hardly any aggravation whatsoever. It is clearly a fallacy that habits are hard to break. The fact is that we make and break habits every day of our lives.

So why do we find it difficult to break a habit that tastes awful, that kills us, that costs us a fortune, that is filthy and disgusting and that we would love to break anyway, when all we have to do is to stop doing it? The answer is that smoking is not habit: **IT IS NICOTINE ADDICTION!** That is why it appears to be so difficult to 'give up'. Perhaps you feel this explanation explains why it *is* difficult to 'give up'? It does explain why most smokers find it difficult to 'give up'. That is because they do not understand drug addiction. The main reason is that smokers are convinced that they get some genuine pleasure and/or crutch from smoking and believe that they are making a genuine sacrifice if they quit.

The beautiful truth is that once you understand nicotine addiction and the true reasons why you smoke, you will stop doing it—just like that—and within three weeks the only mystery will be why you found it necessary to smoke as long as you have, and why you cannot persuade other smokers **HOW NICE IT IS TO BE A NON-SMOKER!**

The Sinister Trap

Smoking is the most subtle, sinister trap that man and nature have combined to devise. What gets us into it in the first place? The thousands of adults who are already doing it. They even warn us that it's a filthy, disgusting habit that will eventually destroy us and cost us a fortune, but we cannot believe that they are not enjoying it. One of the many pathetic aspects of smoking is how hard we have to work in order to become hooked.

It is the only trap in nature which has no lure, no piece of cheese. The thing that springs the trap is not that cigarettes taste so marvellous; it's that they taste so awful. If that first cigarette tasted marvellous, alarm bells would ring and, as intelligent human beings, we could then understand why half the adult population was systematically paying through the nose to poison itself. But because that first cigarette tastes awful, our young minds are reassured that we will never become hooked, and we think that because we are not enjoying cigarettes we can stop whenever we want to.

It is the only drug in nature that prevents you from achieving your aim. Boys usually start because they want to appear tough—it is the Humphrey Bogart/Clint Eastwood image. The last thing you feel with the first cigarette is tough. You dare not inhale, and if you have too many, you start to feel dizzy, then sick. All you want to do is get away from the other boys and throw the filthy things away.

With women, the aim is to be the sophisticated modern young lady. We have all seen them taking little puffs on a cigarette, looking absolutely ridiculous. By the time the boys have learnt to look tough and the girls have learnt to look sophisticated, they wish they had never started in the first place. I wonder whether women ever look sophisticated when they smoke, or whether this is a figment of our imaginations created by cigarette advertisements. It seems to me that there is no intermediary stage between the obvious learner and the veteran smoker.

We then spend the rest of our lives trying to explain to ourselves why we do it, telling our children not to get caught and, at odd times, trying to escape ourselves.

The trap is so designed that we try to stop only when we have stress in our lives, whether it be health, shortage of money or just plain being made to feel like a leper.

As soon as we stop, we have more stress (the fearful withdrawal pangs of nicotine) and the thing that we rely on to relieve stress (our old prop, the cigarette) we now must do without.

After a few days of torture we decide that we have picked the wrong time. We must wait for a period without stress, and as soon as that arrives the reason for stopping vanishes. Of course, that period will never arrive because, in the first place, we think that our lives tend to become more and more stressful. As we leave the protection of our parents, the natural process is setting up home, mortgages, babies, more responsible jobs, etc., etc. This is also an illusion. The truth is that the most stressful periods for any creature are early childhood and adolescence. We tend to confuse responsibility with stress. Smokers' lives automatically become more stressful because tobacco does not relax you or relieve stress, as society tries to make you believe. Just the reverse: it actually causes you to become more nervous and stressed.

Even those smokers who kick the habit (most do, one or more times during their lives) can lead perfectly happy lives yet suddenly become hooked again.

The whole business of smoking is like wandering into a giant maze. As soon as we enter the maze our minds become misted and clouded, and we spend the rest of our lives trying to escape. Many of us eventually do, only to find that we get trapped again at a later date.

I spent thirty-three years trying to escape from that maze. Like all smokers, I couldn't understand it. However, due to a combination of unusual circumstances, none of which reflect any credit on me, I wanted to know why previously it had been so desperately difficult to stop and yet, when I finally did, it was not only easy but enjoyable.

Since stopping smoking, my hobby and, later, my profession has been to resolve the many conundrums associated with smoking. It is a complex and fascinating puzzle and, like the Rubik's Cube, practically impossible to solve. However, like all complicated puzzles, if you know the solution, it is easy! I have the solution to stopping smoking easily. I will lead you out of the maze and ensure that you never wander into it again. All you have to do is *follow the instructions*. If you take a wrong turn, the rest of the instructions will be pointless.

Let me emphasize that anybody can find it easy to stop smoking, but first we need to establish the facts. No, I do not mean the scare facts. I know you are already aware of them. There is already enough information on the evils of smoking. If that was going to stop you, you would already have stopped. I mean, why do we find it difficult to stop? In order to answer this question we need to know the real reason why we are still smoking.

5

Why Do We Carry On Smoking?

We all start smoking for stupid reasons, usually social pressures or social occasions, but, once we feel we are becoming hooked, why do we carry on smoking?

No regular smoker knows why he or she smokes. If smokers knew the true reason, they would stop doing it. I have asked the question of thousands of smokers during my consultations. The true answer is the same for all smokers, but the variety of replies is infinite. I find this part of the consultation the most amusing and at the same time the most pathetic.

All smokers know in their heart of hearts that they are fools. They know that they had no need to smoke before they became hooked. Most of them can remember that their first cigarette tasted awful and that they had to work hard in order to become hooked. The most annoying part is that they sense that non-smokers are not missing anything and that they are laughing at them.

However, smokers are intelligent, rational human beings. They know that they are taking enormous health risks and that they spend a fortune on cigarettes in their lifetime. Therefore it is necessary for them to have a rational explanation to justify their habit.

The actual reason why smokers continue to smoke is a subtle combination of the factors that I will elaborate in the next two chapters. They are:

1. **NICOTINE ADDICTION**

2. **BRAINWASHING**

Nicotine Addiction

Nicotine, a colourless, oily compound, is the drug contained in tobacco that addicts the smoker. It is the fastest addictive drug known to mankind, and it can take just one cigarette to become hooked.

Every puff on a cigarette delivers, via the lungs to the brain, a small dose of nicotine that acts more rapidly than the dose of heroin the addict injects into his veins.

If there are twenty puffs for you in a cigarette, you receive twenty doses of the drug with just one cigarette.

Nicotine is a quick-acting drug, and levels in the bloodstream fall quickly to about half within thirty minutes of smoking a cigarette and to a quarter within an hour of finishing a cigarette. This explains why most smokers average about twenty per day.

As soon as the smoker extinguishes the cigarette, the nicotine rapidly starts to leave the body and the smoker begins to suffer withdrawal pangs.

I must at this point dispel a common illusion that smokers have about withdrawal pangs. Smokers think that withdrawal pangs are the terrible trauma they suffer when they try or are forced to stop smoking. These are, in fact, mainly mental; the smoker is feeling deprived of his pleasure or prop. I will explain more about this later.

The actual pangs of withdrawal from nicotine are so subtle that most smokers have lived and died without even realizing they are drug addicts. When we use the term 'nicotine addict' we think we just 'got into the habit'. Most smokers have a horror of drugs, yet that's exactly what they are—drug addicts. Fortunately it is an easy drug to kick, but you need first to accept that you are addicted.

There is no physical pain in the withdrawal from nicotine. It is merely an empty, restless feeling, the feeling of something missing, which is why many smokers think it is something to do with their hands. If it is prolonged, the smoker becomes nervous, insecure, agitated, lacking in confidence and irritable. It is like hunger—for a poison, **NICOTINE.**

Within seven seconds of lighting a cigarette fresh nicotine is supplied and the craving ends, resulting in the feeling of relaxation and confidence that the cigarette gives to the smoker.

In the early days, when we first start smoking, the withdrawal pangs and their relief are so slight that we are not even aware that they exist. When we begin to smoke regularly we think it is because we've either come to enjoy them or got into the 'habit'. The truth is we're already hooked; we do not realize it, but that little nicotine monster is already inside our stomach and every now and again we have to feed it.

All smokers start smoking for stupid reasons. Nobody has to. The only reason why anybody continues smoking, whether they be a casual or a heavy smoker, is to feed that little monster.

The whole business of smoking is a series of conundrums. All smokers know at heart that they are fools and have been trapped by something evil. However, I think the most pathetic aspect about smoking is that the enjoyment that the smoker gets from a cigarette is the pleasure of trying to get back to the state of peace, tranquillity and confidence that his body had before he became hooked in the first place.

You know that feeling when a neighbour's burglar alarm has been ringing all day, or there has been some other minor, persistent aggravation. Then the noise suddenly stops—that marvellous feeling of peace and tranquillity is experienced. It is not really peace but the ending of the aggravation.

Before we start the nicotine chain, our bodies are complete. We then force nicotine into the body, and when we put that cigarette out and the nicotine starts to leave, we suffer withdrawal pangs—not physical pain, just an empty feeling. We are not even aware that it exists, but it is like a dripping tap inside our bodies. Our rational minds do not understand it. They do not need to. All we know is that we want a cigarette, and when we light it the craving goes, and for the moment we are content and confident again just as we were before we became addicted. However, the satisfaction is only temporary because, in order to relieve the craving, you have to put more nicotine into the body. As soon as you extinguish that cigarette the craving starts again, and so the chain goes on. It is a chain for life—**UNLESS YOU BREAK IT**.

The whole business of smoking is like wearing tight shoes just to obtain the pleasure you feel when you take them off. There are three main reasons why smokers cannot see things that way.

1. From birth we have been subjected to massive brainwashing telling us that smokers receive immense pleasure and/or a crutch from smoking. Why should we not believe them? Why else would they waste all that money and take such horrendous risks?

2. Because the physical withdrawal from nicotine involves no actual pain but is merely an empty, insecure feeling, inseparable from hunger or normal stress, and because those are the very times that we tend to light up, we tend to regard the feeling as normal.

3. However, the main reason that smokers fail to see smoking in its true light is that it works back to front. It's when you are not smoking that you suffer that empty feeling, but because the process of getting hooked is very subtle and gradual in the early days, we regard that feeling as normal and don't blame it on the previous cigarette. The moment you light up, you get an almost immediate boost or buzz and do actually feel less nervous or more relaxed, and the cigarette gets the credit.

It is this reverse process that makes all drugs difficult to kick. Picture the panic state of a heroin addict who has no heroin. Now picture the utter joy when that addict can finally plunge a hypodermic needle into his vein. Can you visualize someone actually getting pleasure by injecting him- or herself, or does the mere thought fill you with horror? Non-heroin addicts don't suffer that panic feeling. The heroin doesn't relieve it. On the contrary, it causes it. Non-smokers don't suffer the empty feeling of needing a cigarette or start to panic when the supply runs out. Non-smokers cannot understand how smokers can possibly obtain pleasure from sticking those filthy things in their mouths, setting light to them and actually inhaling the filth into their lungs. And do you know something? Smokers cannot understand why they do it either.

We talk about smoking being relaxing or giving satisfaction. But how can you be satisfied unless you were dissatisfied in the first place? Why don't non-smokers suffer from this dissatisfied state and why, after a meal, when non-smokers are completely relaxed, are smokers completely unre-laxed until they have satisfied that little nicotine monster?

Forgive me if I dwell on this subject for a moment. The main reason that smokers find it difficult to quit is that they believe that they are giving up a genuine pleasure or crutch. It is absolutely essential to understand that you are giving up nothing whatsoever.

The best way to understand the subtleties of the nicotine trap is to compare it with eating. If we are in the habit of eating regular meals, we are not aware of being hungry between meals. Only if the meal is delayed are we aware of being hungry, and even then, there is no physical pain, just an empty, insecure feeling which we know as: 'I need to eat.' And the process of satisfying our hunger is a very pleasant pastime.

Smoking appears to be almost identical. The empty, insecure feeling which we know as 'wanting or needing a cigarette' is identical to a hunger for food, although one will not satisfy the other. Like hunger, there is no physical pain and the feeling is so imperceptible that we are not even aware of it between cigarettes. It's only if we want to light up and aren't allowed to do so that we become aware of any discomfort. But when we do light up we feel satisfied.

It is this similarity to eating which helps to fool smokers into believing that they receive some genuine pleasure. Some smokers find it very difficult to grasp that there is no pleasure or crutch whatsoever to smoking. Some argue: 'How can you say there is no crutch? You tell me when I light up that I'll feel less nervous than before.'

Although eating and smoking appear to be very similar. In fact they are exact opposites:

1. You eat to survive and to prolong your life, whereas smoking shortens your life.

2. Food does genuinely taste good, and eating is a genuinely pleasant experience that we can enjoy throughout our lives, whereas smoking involves breathing foul and poisonous fumes into your lungs.

3. Eating doesn't create hunger and genuinely relieves it, whereas the first cigarette starts the craving for nicotine and each subsequent one, far from relieving it, ensures that you suffer it for the rest of life.

This is an opportune moment to dispel another common myth about smoking—that smoking is a habit. Is eating a habit? If you think so, try breaking it completely. No, to describe eating as a habit would be the same as describing breathing as a habit. Both are essential for survival. It is true that different people are in the habit of satisfying their hunger at different times and with varying types of food. But eating itself is not a habit. Neither is smoking. The only reason any smoker lights a cigarette is to try to end the empty, insecure feeling that the previous cigarette created. It is true that different smokers are in the habit of trying to relieve their withdrawal pangs at different times, but smoking itself is not a habit.

Society frequently refers to the smoking habit and in this book, for convenience, I also refer to the 'habit'. However, be constantly aware that smoking is not habit; on the contrary it is no more nor less than **DRUG ADDICTION**!

When we start to smoke we have to force ourselves to learn to cope with it. Before we know it, we are not only buying cigarettes regularly but we *have* to have them. If we don't, panic sets in, and as we go through life we tend to smoke more and more.

This is because, as with any other drug, the body tends to become immune to the effects of nicotine and our intake tends to increase. After quite a short period of smoking the cigarette ceases to relieve completely the withdrawal pangs that it creates, so that when you light up a cigarette you feel better than you did a moment before, but you are in fact more nervous and less relaxed than you would be as a non-smoker, even when you are actually smoking the cigarette. The practice is even more ridiculous than wearing tight shoes because as you go through life an increasing amount of the discomfort remains even when the shoes are removed.

The position is even worse because, once the cigarette is extinguished, the nicotine rapidly begins to leave the body, which explains why, in stressful situations, the smoker tends to chain smoke.

As I said, the 'habit' doesn't exist. The real reason why every smoker goes on smoking is because of that little monster inside his stomach. Every now and again he has to feed it. The smoker himself will decide when he does that, and it tends to be on four types of occasion or a combination of them.

They are:

BOREDOM/CONCENTRATION two complete opposites!
STRESS/RELAXATION two complete opposites!

What magic drug can suddenly reverse the very effect it had twenty minutes before? If you think about it, what other types of occasion are there in our lives, apart from sleep? The truth is that smoking neither relieves boredom and stress nor promotes concentration and relaxation. It is all just illusion.

Apart from being a drug, nicotine is also a powerful poison and is used in insecticides (look it up in your dictionary). The nicotine content of just one cigarette, if injected directly into a vein, would kill you. In fact, tobacco contains many poisons, including carbon monoxide, and the tobacco plant is the same genus as 'deadly night-shade'.

In case you have visions of switching to a pipe or to cigars, I should make it quite clear that the content of this book applies to all tobacco and any substance that contains nicotine, including gum, patches, nasal sprays and inhalators.

The human body is the most sophisticated object on our planet. No species, even the lowest amoeba or worm, can survive without knowing the difference between food and poison.

Through a process of natural selection over thousands of years, our minds and bodies have developed techniques for distinguishing between food and poison and fail-safe methods for ejecting the latter.

All human beings are averse to the smell and taste of tobacco until they become hooked. If you blow diluted tobacco into the face of any animal or child before it becomes hooked, it will cough and splutter.

When we smoked that first cigarette, inhaling resulted in a coughing fit, or if we smoked too many the first time, we experienced a dizzy feeling or actual physical sickness. It was our body telling us, **'YOU ARE FEEDING ME POISON. STOP DOING IT.'** This is the stage that often decides whether we become smokers or not. It is a fallacy that physically weak and mentally weak-willed people become smokers. The lucky ones are those who find that first cigarette repulsive; physically their lungs cannot cope with it, and they are cured for life. Or, alternatively, they are not mentally prepared to go through the severe learning process of trying to inhale without coughing.

To me this is the most tragic part of this whole business. How hard we worked to become hooked, and this is why it is difficult to stop teenagers. Because they are still learning to smoke, because they still find cigarettes distasteful, they believe they can stop whenever they want to. Why do they not learn from us? Then again, why did we not learn from our parents?

Many smokers believe they enjoy the taste and smell of the tobacco. It is an illusion. What we are actually doing when we learn to smoke is teaching our bodies to become immune to the bad smell and taste in order to get our fix, like heroin addicts who think that they enjoy injecting themselves. The withdrawal pangs from heroin are relatively severe, and all they are really enjoying is the ritual of relieving those pangs.

The smoker teaches himself to shut his mind to the bad taste and smell to get his 'fix'. Ask a smoker who believes he smokes only because he enjoys the taste and smell of tobacco, 'If you cannot get your normal brand of cigarette and can only obtain a brand you find distasteful, do you stop smoking?' No way. A smoker will smoke old rope rather than abstain, and it doesn't matter if you switch to mentholated cigarettes, cigars or a pipe; to begin with they taste awful but if you persevere you will learn to like them. Smokers will even try to keep smoking during colds, flu, sore throats, bronchitis and emphysema.

Enjoyment has nothing to do with it. If it did, no one would smoke more than one cigarette. There are even thousands of ex-smokers hooked on that filthy nicotine chewing gum that doctors prescribe, and many of them are still smoking.

During my consultations some smokers find it alarming to realize they are drug addicts and think it will make it even more difficult to stop. In fact, it is all good news for two important reasons:

1. The reason why most of us carry on smoking is that, although we know the disadvantages outweigh the advantages, we believe that there is something in the cigarette that we actually enjoy or that it is some sort of prop. We feel that after we stop smoking there will be a void, that certain situations in our life will never be quite the same. This is an illusion. The fact is the cigarette gives nothing; it only takes away and then partially restores to create the illusion. I will explain this in more detail in a later chapter.

2. Although it is the world's most powerful drug because of the speed with which you become hooked, you are never badly hooked. Because it is a quick-acting drug it takes only three weeks for 99 per cent of the nicotine to leave your body, and the actual withdrawal pangs are so mild that most smokers have lived and died without ever realizing that they have suffered them.

You will quite rightly ask why it is that many smokers find it so difficult to stop, go through months of torture and spend the rest of their lives pining for a cigarette at odd times. The answer is the second reason why we smoke—the brainwashing. The chemical addiction is easy to cope with.

Most smokers go all night without a cigarette. The withdrawal pangs do not even wake them up.

Many smokers will actually leave the bedroom before they light that first cigarette; many will have breakfast first; many will wait until they arrive at work. They can suffer ten hours' withdrawal pangs, and it doesn't bother them, but if they went ten hours during the day without a cigarette, they'd be tearing their hair out.

Many smokers will buy a new car nowadays and refrain from smoking in it. Many will visit theatres, supermarkets, churches, etc., and not being able to smoke doesn't bother them. Even on the Tube trains there have been no riots. Smokers are almost pleased for someone or something to force them to stop smoking.

Nowadays many smokers will automatically refrain from smoking in the home of, or merely in the company of, non-smokers with little discomfort to themselves. In fact, most smokers have extended periods during which they abstain without effort. Even in my case I would quite happily relax all evening without a cigarette. In the later years as a smoker I actually used to look forward to the evenings when I could stop choking myself (what a ridiculous 'habit').

The chemical addiction is easy to cope with, even when you are still addicted, and there are thousands of smokers who remain casual smokers all their lives. They are just as heavily addicted as the heavy smoker. There are even heavy smokers who have kicked the 'habit' but will have an occasional cigar, and that keeps them addicted.

As I say, the actual nicotine addiction is not the main problem. It just acts like a catalyst to keep our minds confused over the real problem: the brainwashing.

It may be of consolation to lifelong and heavy smokers to know that it is just as easy for them to stop as casual smokers. In a peculiar way, it is easier. The further you go along with the 'habit', the more it drags you down and the greater the gain when you stop.

It may be of further consolation for you to know that the rumours that occasionally circulate (e.g., 'It takes seven years for the "gunk" to leave your body' or 'Every cigarette you smoke takes five minutes off your life') are untrue.

Do not think the bad effects of smoking are exaggerated. If anything, they are sadly understated, but the truth is the 'five minutes' rule is obviously an estimation and applies only if you contract one of the killer diseases or just 'gunk' yourself to a standstill.

In fact, the 'gunk' never leaves your body completely. If there are smokers about, it is in the atmosphere, and even non-smokers acquire a small percentage. However, these bodies of ours are incredible machines and have enormous powers of recovery, providing you haven't already triggered off one of the irreversible diseases. If you stop now, your body will recover within a matter of a few weeks, almost as if you had never been a smoker.

As I have said, it is never too late to stop. I have helped to cure many smokers in their fifties and sixties and even a few in their seventies and eighties. A 91-year-old woman attended my clinic with her 66-year-old son. When I asked her why she had decided to stop smoking, she replied,

'To set an example for him.' She contacted me six months later saying she felt like a young girl again.

The further it drags you down, the greater the relief. When I finally stopped I went straight from a hundred a day to **ZERO**, and didn't have one bad pang. In fact, it was actually enjoyable, even during the withdrawal period.

But we *must* remove the brainwashing.

7

Brainwashing and the Sleeping Partner

How or why do we start smoking in the first place? To understand this fully you need to examine the powerful effect of the subconscious mind or, as I call it, the 'sleeping partner'.

We all tend to think we are intelligent, dominant human beings determining our paths through life. In fact, 99 per cent of our make-up is moulded. We are a product of the society that we are brought up in—the sort of clothes we wear, the houses we live in, our basic life patterns, even those matters on which we tend to differ, e.g., Labour or Conservative governments. It is no coincidence that Labour supporters tend to come from the working classes and Conservatives from the middle and upper classes. The subconscious is an extremely powerful influence in our lives, and even in matters of fact rather than opinion millions of people can be deluded. Before Columbus sailed round the world the majority of people knew it to be flat. Today we know it is round. If I wrote a dozen books trying to persuade you that it was flat, I could not do it, yet how many of us have been into space to see the ball? Even if you have flown or sailed round the world, how do you know that you were not travelling in a circle above a flat surface?

Advertising men know well the power of suggestion over the subconscious mind, hence the large posters the smoker is hit with as he drives around, the advertisements in every magazine. You think they are a waste of money? That they do not persuade you to buy cigarettes? You are wrong! Try it out for yourself. Next time you go into a pub or restaurant on a cold day and your companion asks you what you are having to drink, instead of saying, 'A brandy' (or whatever), embellish it with 'Do you know what I would really enjoy today? That marvellous warm glow of a brandy.' You will find that even people who dislike brandy will join you.

From our earliest years our subconscious minds are bombarded daily

with information telling us that cigarettes relax us and give us confidence
and courage and that the most precious thing on this earth is a cigarette.
You think I exaggerate? Whenever you see a cartoon or film or play in
which people are about to be executed or shot, what is their last request?
That's right, a cigarette. The impact of this does not register on our conscious minds, but the sleeping partner has time to absorb it. What the
message is really saying is, 'The most precious thing on this earth, my
last thought and action, will be the smoking of a cigarette.' In every war
film the injured man is given a cigarette.

You think that things have changed recently? No, our children are
still being bombarded by large billboards and magazine advertisements.
Cigarette advertising is supposed to be banned on television nowadays,
yet during peak viewing hours the world's top snooker players and darts
players are seen constantly puffing away. The programmes are usually
sponsored by the tobacco giants, and this is the most sinister trend of all
in today's advertising: the link with sporting occasions and the jet set.
Grand Prix racing cars modelled and even named after cigarette brand
names—or is it the other way round? There are even plugs on television
nowadays depicting a naked couple sharing a cigarette in bed after having
sex. The implications are obvious. How my admiration goes out to the
advertisers of the small cigar, not for their motives but for the brilliance
of their campaign, whereby a man is about to face death or disaster—his
balloon is on fire and about to crash, or the sidecar of his motorbike is
about to crash into a river, or he is Columbus and his ship is about to
go over the edge of the world. Not a word is spoken. Soft music plays.
He lights up a cigar; a look of sheer bliss covers his face. The conscious
mind may not realize that the smoker is even watching the advertisement,
but the 'sleeping partner' is patiently digesting the obvious implications.

True, there is publicity the other way—the cancer scares, the legs
being amputated, the bad-breath campaigns—but these do not actually
stop people smoking. Logically they should, but the fact is they do not.
They do not even prevent youngsters from starting. All the years that I
remained a smoker I honestly believed that, had I known of the links
between lung cancer and cigarette smoking, I would never have become
a smoker. The truth is that it doesn't make the slightest bit of difference.
The trap is the same today as when Sir Walter Raleigh fell into it. All the
anti-smoking campaigns just help to add to the confusion. Even the products themselves, those lovely shining packets that lure you into trying
their contents, contain a deadly warning on their sides. What smoker
ever reads it, let alone brings himself to face the implications of it?

I believe that a leading cigarette manufacturer is actually using the

Government Health Warning to sell its products. Many of the scenes include frightening features such as spiders, dragonflies and the Venus flytrap. The health warning is now so large and bold that the smoker cannot avoid it, however hard he tries. The pang of fear that the smoker suffers prompts him or her to reach for the glossy gold packet.

Ironically, the most powerful force in this brainwashing is the smoker himself. It is a fallacy that smokers are weak-willed and physically weak specimens. You have to be physically strong in order to cope with the poison.

This is one of the reasons why smokers refuse to accept the overwhelming statistics that prove that smoking cripples your health. Everyone knows of an Uncle Fred who smoked forty a day, never had a day's illness in his life, and lived to eighty. Smokers refuse even to consider the hundreds of other smokers who are cut down in their prime or the fact that Uncle Fred might still be alive if he hadn't been a smoker.

If you do a small survey among your friends and colleagues, you will find that most smokers are, in fact, strong-willed people. They tend to be self-employed, business executives or in certain specialized professions, such as doctors, lawyers, policemen, teachers, salesmen, nurses, secretaries, housewives with children, etc.—in other words, anybody leading a stressful existence. The main delusion of smokers is that smoking relieves stress and tends to be associated with the dominant type, the type that takes on responsibility and stress, and, of course, that is the type that we admire and therefore tend to copy. Another group that tends to get hooked are people in monotonous jobs, because the other main reason for smoking is boredom. However, the idea that smoking relieves boredom is also an illusion, I am afraid.

The extent of the brainwashing is quite incredible. As a society we get all uptight about glue-sniffing, heroin addiction, etc. Actual deaths from glue-sniffing do not amount to ten per annum, and deaths from heroin are less than a hundred a year in England, for example.

There is another drug, nicotine, on which over 60 per cent of us become hooked at some time in our lives and the majority spend the rest of their lives paying for it through the nose. Most of their spare money goes toward cigarettes and hundreds of thousands of people have their lives ruined every year because they became hooked. It is the No. 1 killer in society, including road accidents, fires, etc.

Why is it that we regard glue-sniffing and heroin addiction as such great evils, while the drug that we spend most of our money on and is actually killing us we used to regard a few years ago as a perfectly acceptable social habit? In recent years it has been considered a slightly unsociable habit that may injure our health but is legal and on sale in glossy packets in every newsagent, pub, club, garage and restaurant. The biggest vested interest in Britain is our own government. It makes £8,000,000,000 per year out of smokers, and the tobacco companies spend over £100,000,000 per year in promotion alone.

You need to start building resistance to this brainwashing, just as if you were buying a car from a secondhand dealer. You would be nodding politely but you would not believe a word the man was saying.

Start looking behind these glossy packets at the filth and poison beneath. Do not be fooled by the cut-glass ashtrays or the gold lighter or the millions who have been conned. Start asking yourself:

Why am I doing it?

Do I really need to?

NO, OF COURSE YOU DON'T.

I find this brainwashing aspect the most difficult of all to explain. Why is it that an otherwise rational, intelligent human being becomes a complete imbecile about his own addiction? It pains me to confess that out of the thousands of people that I have assisted in kicking the habit, I was the biggest idiot of all.

Not only did I reach a hundred a day myself, but my father was a heavy smoker. He was a strong man, cut down in his prime due to smoking. I can remember watching him when I was a boy; he would be coughing and spluttering in the mornings. I could see he wasn't enjoying it and it was so obvious to me that something evil had got possession of him. I can remember saying to my mother, 'Don't ever let me become a smoker.'

At the age of fifteen I was a physical-fitness fanatic. Sport was my life and I was full of courage and confidence. If anybody had said to me in those days that I would end up smoking a hundred cigarettes a day, I would have gambled my lifetime's earnings that it would not happen, and I would have given any odds that had been asked.

At the age of forty I was a physical and mental cigarette junky. I had reached the stage where I couldn't carry out the most mundane physical or mental act without first lighting up. With most smokers the triggers are the normal stresses of life, like answering the telephone or socializing. I couldn't even change a television programme or a light bulb without lighting up.

I knew it was killing me. There was no way I could kid myself otherwise. But why I couldn't see what it was doing to me mentally I cannot understand. It was almost jumping up and biting me on the nose. The ridiculous thing is that most smokers suffer the delusion at some time in their life that they enjoy a cigarette. I never suffered that delusion. I smoked because I thought it helped me to concentrate and because it helped my nerves. Now I am a non-smoker, the most difficult part is trying to believe that those days actually happened. It's like awakening from a nightmare, and that is about the size of it. Nicotine is a drug, and your senses are drugged—your taste buds, your sense of smell. The worst aspect of smoking isn't the injury to your health or pocket, it is the warping of the mind. You search for any plausible excuse to go on smoking.

I remember at one stage switching to a pipe, after a failed attempt to kick cigarettes, in the belief that it was less harmful and would cut down my intake.

Some of those pipe tobaccos are absolutely foul. The aroma can be pleasant but, to start with, they are awful to smoke. I can remember that for about three months the tip of my tongue was as sore as a boil. A liquid brown goo collects in the bottom of the bowl of the pipe. Occasionally you unwittingly bring the bowl above the horizontal and before you realize it you have swallowed a mouthful of the filthy stuff. The result is usually to throw up immediately, no matter what company you are in.

It took me three months to learn to cope with the pipe, but what I cannot understand is why I didn't sit down sometime during that three months and ask myself why I was subjecting myself to the torture.

Of course, once they learn to cope with the pipe, no one appears more contented than pipe smokers. Most of them are convinced that they smoke because they enjoy the pipe. But why did they have to work so hard to learn to like it when they were perfectly happy without it?

The answer is that once you have become addicted to nicotine, the brainwashing is increased. Your subconscious mind knows that the little monster has to be fed, and you block everything else from your mind. As I have already stated, it is fear that keeps people smoking, the fear of that empty, insecure feeling that you get when you stop supplying the nicotine. Because you are not aware of it doesn't mean it isn't there. You don't have to understand it any more than a cat needs to understand where the under-floor hot-water pipes are. It just knows that if it sits in a certain place it gets the feeling of warmth.

It is the brainwashing that is the main difficulty in giving up smoking. The brainwashing of our upbringing in society reinforced with the brainwashing from our own addiction and, most powerful of all, the brainwashing of our friends, relatives and colleagues.

Did you notice that up to now I've frequently referred to 'giving up' smoking. I used the expression at the beginning of the previous paragraph. This is a classic example of the brainwashing. The expression implies a genuine sacrifice. The beautiful truth is that there is absolutely nothing to give up. On the contrary, you will be freeing yourself from a terrible disease and achieving marvellous positive gains. We are going to start removing this brainwashing now. From this point on, no longer will we refer to 'giving up', but to stopping, quitting or the true position: **ESCAPING!**

The only thing that persuades us to smoke in the first place is all the other people doing it. We feel we are missing out. We work so hard to become hooked, yet nobody ever finds out what he or she has been missing. But every time we see another smoker he reassures us that there must be something in it, otherwise he wouldn't be doing it. Even when he has kicked the habit, the ex-smoker feels he is being deprived when a smoker lights up at a party or other social function. He feels safe. He can have just one. And, before he knows it, he is hooked again.

This brainwashing is very powerful and you need to be aware of its effects. Many older smokers will remember the Paul Temple detective series that was a very popular radio programme after the war. One of the series was dealing with addiction to marijuana, commonly known as 'pot' or 'grass'. Unbeknown to the smoker, wicked men were selling cigarettes that contained 'pot'. There were no harmful effects. People merely became addicted and had to go on buying the cigarettes. (During my consultations literally hundreds of smokers have admitted to trying 'pot'. None of them said they became hooked on it.) I was about seven years old when I listened to the programme. It was my first knowledge of drug addiction. The concept of addiction, being compelled to go on taking the drug, filled me with horror, and even to this day, in spite of the fact that I am fairly convinced that 'pot' is not addictive, I would not dare take one puff of marijuana. How ironic that I should have ended up a junky on the world's No. 1 addictive drug. If only Paul Temple had warned me about the cigarette itself. How ironic too that over forty years later mankind spends thousands of pounds on cancer research, yet millions are spent persuading healthy teenagers to become hooked on the filthy weed, the British government having the largest vested interest.

We are about to remove the brainwashing. It is not the non-smoker who is being deprived but the poor smoker who is forfeiting a lifetime of:

- **HEALTH**
- **ENERGY**
- **WEALTH**
- **PEACE OF MIND**

- CONFIDENCE
- COURAGE
- SELF-RESPECT
- HAPPINESS
- FREEDOM.

And what does he gain from these considerable sacrifices?

ABSOLUTELY NOTHING—except the illusion of trying to get back to the state of peace, tranquillity and confidence that the non-smoker enjoys all the time.

Relieving
Withdrawal Pangs

As I explained earlier, smokers think they smoke for enjoyment, relaxation or some sort of boost. In fact, this an illusion. The actual reason is the relief of withdrawal pangs.

In the early days we use the cigarette as a social prop. We can take it or leave it. However, the subtle chain has started. Our subconscious mind begins to learn that a cigarette taken at certain times tends to be pleasurable.

The more you become hooked on the drug, the greater the need to relieve the withdrawal pangs and the further the cigarette drags you down, the more you are fooled into believing it is doing the opposite. It all happens so slowly, so gradually, you are not even aware of it. Each day you feel no different from the day before. Most smokers don't even realize they are hooked until they actually try to stop, and even then many won't admit to it. A few stalwarts just keep their heads in the sand all their lives, trying to convince themselves and other people that they enjoy it.

I have had the following conversation with hundreds of teenagers.

ME: You realize that nicotine is a drug and that the only reason why you are smoking is that you cannot stop.

T: Nonsense! I enjoy it. If I didn't, I would stop.

ME: Just stop for a week to prove to me you can if you want to.

T: No need. I enjoy it. If I wanted to stop, I would.

ME: Just stop for a week to prove to yourself you are not hooked.

T: What's the point? I enjoy it.

As already stated, smokers tend to relieve their withdrawal pangs at times of stress, boredom, concentration, relaxation or a combination of these. This point is explained in greater detail in the next few chapters.

9

Stress

I am referring not only to the great tragedies of life but also to the minor stresses, the socializing, the telephone call, the anxieties of the housewife with noisy young children and so on.

Let us use the telephone conversation as an example. For most people the telephone is slightly stressful, particularly for the businessman. Most calls aren't from satisfied customers or your boss congratulating you. There's usually some sort of aggravation—something going wrong or somebody making demands. At that time the smoker, if he isn't already doing so, will light up a cigarette. He doesn't know why he does this, but he does know that for some reason it appears to help.

What has actually happened is this. Without being conscious of it, he has already been suffering aggravation (i.e. the withdrawal pangs). By partially relieving that aggravation at the same time as normal stress, the total stress is reduced and the smoker gets a boost. At this point the boost is not, in fact, an illusion. The smoker will feel better than before he lit the cigarette. However, even when smoking that cigarette the smoker is more tense than if he were a non-smoker because the more you go into the drug, the more it knocks you down and the less it restores you when you smoke.

I promised no shock treatment. In the example I am about to give, I am not trying to shock you, I am merely emphasizing that cigarettes destroy your nerves rather than relax them.

Try to imagine getting to the stage where a doctor tells you that unless you stop smoking he is going to have to remove your legs. Just for a moment pause and try to visualize life without your legs. Try to imagine the frame of mind of a man who, issued with that warning, actually continues smoking and then has his legs removed.

I used to hear stories like that and dismissed them as crank. In fact, I used to wish a doctor would tell me that; then I would have stopped.

Yet I was already fully expecting any day to have a brain haemorrhage, and lose not only my legs but my life. I didn't think of myself as a crank, just a heavy smoker.

Such stories are not crank. That is what this awful drug does to you. As you go through life it systematically takes away your nerve and courage. The more it takes your courage away, the more you are deluded into believing the cigarette is doing the opposite. We have all heard of the panic that overtakes smokers when they are out late at night and in fear of running out of cigarettes. Non-smokers do not suffer from it. The cigarette causes that feeling. At the same time, as you go through life the cigarette not only destroys your nerves but is a powerful poison, progressively destroying your physical health. By the time the smoker reaches the stage at which it is killing him, he believes the cigarette is his courage and cannot face life without it.

Get it clear in your head that the cigarette is not relieving your nerves; it is slowly but steadily destroying them. One of the great gains of breaking the habit is the return of your confidence and self-assurance.

10

Boredom

I f you are already smoking at this moment, you had probably already forgotten about it until I reminded you.

Another fallacy about smoking is that cigarettes relieve boredom. Boredom is a frame of mind. When you smoke a cigarette your mind isn't saying, 'I'm smoking a cigarette. I'm smoking a cigarette.' The only time that happens is when you have been deprived for a long time or are trying to cut down, or during those first few cigarettes after a failed attempt to stop.

The true situation is this: when you are addicted to nicotine and are not smoking, there is something missing. If you have something to occupy your mind that isn't stressful, you can go for long periods without being bothered by the absence of the drug. However, when you are bored there's nothing to take your mind off it, so you feed the monster. When you are indulging yourself (i.e. not trying to stop or cut down), even lighting up becomes subconscious. Even pipe smokers and roll-your-own smokers can perform this ritual automatically. If any smoker tries to remember the cigarettes he has smoked during the day, he can only remember a small proportion of them—e.g. the first of the day or the one after a meal.

The truth is that cigarettes tend to increase boredom indirectly because they make you feel lethargic, and instead of undertaking some energetic activity smokers tend to lounge around, bored, relieving their withdrawal pangs.

This is why countering the brainwashing is so important. Because it's a fact that smokers tend to smoke when they are bored and that we've been told since birth that smoking relieves boredom, it doesn't occur to us to question the fact. We've also been brainwashed into believing that chewing gum aids relaxation. It is a fact that when under stress people tend to grind their teeth. All chewing gum does is to give you a logical

35

reason to grind your teeth. Next time you watch someone chewing gum, observe them closely and ask yourself whether they looked relaxed or tense. Observe smokers who are smoking because they are bored. They still looked bored. The cigarette doesn't relieve the boredom.

As an ex–chain-smoker I can assure you that there are no more boring activities in life than lighting up one filthy cigarette after another, day in day out, year in year out.

Concentration

Cigarettes do not help concentration. That is just another illusion. When you are trying to concentrate, you automatically try to avoid distractions like feeling cold or hot. The smoker is already suffering: that little monster wants his fix. So when he wants to concentrate he doesn't even have to think about it. He automatically lights up, partially ending the craving, gets on with the matter at hand and has already forgotten that he is smoking.

Cigarettes do not help concentration. They help to ruin it because after a while, even while smoking a cigarette, the smoker's withdrawal pangs cease to be completely relieved. The smoker then increases his intake, and the problem then increases.

Concentration is also affected adversely for another reason. The progressive blocking up of the arteries and veins with poisons starves the brain of oxygen. In fact, your concentration and inspiration will be greatly improved as this process is reversed.

It was the concentration aspect that prevented me from succeeding when using the willpower method. I could put up with the irritability and bad temper, but when I really needed to concentrate on something difficult, I had to have that cigarette. I can well remember the panic I felt when I discovered that I was not allowed to smoke during my accountancy exams. I was already a chain-smoker and convinced that I would not be able to concentrate for three hours without a cigarette. But I passed the exams, and I can't even remember thinking about smoking at the time, so, when it came to the crunch, it obviously didn't bother me.

The loss of concentration that smokers suffer when they try to stop smoking is not, in fact, due to the physical withdrawal from nicotine. When you are a smoker, you have mental blocks. When you have one, what do you do? If you are not already smoking one, you light a cigarette. That doesn't cure the mental block, so then what do you do? You do what you have to do: you get on with it, just as non-smokers do. When you are a smoker nothing gets blamed on the cigarette. Smokers never have smoking coughs; they just have permanent colds. The moment you stop smoking, everything that goes wrong in your life is blamed on the fact that you've stopped smoking. Now when you have a mental block, instead of just getting on with it you start to say, 'If only I could light up now, it would solve my problem.' You then start to question your decision to quit smoking.

If you believe that smoking is a genuine aid to concentration, then worrying about it will guarantee that you won't be able to concentrate. It's the doubting, not the physical withdrawal pangs, that causes the problem. Always remember: it is smokers who suffer withdrawal pangs and not non-smokers.

When I extinguished my last cigarette I went overnight from a hundred a day to zero without any apparent loss of concentration.

12

Relaxation

Most smokers think that a cigarette helps to relax them. The truth is that nicotine is a chemical stimulant. If you take your pulse and then smoke two consecutive cigarettes, there will be a marked increase in your pulse rate.

One of the favourite cigarettes for most smokers is the one after a meal. A meal is a time of day when we stop working; we sit down and relax, relieve our hunger and thirst and are then completely satisfied. However, the poor smoker cannot relax, as he has another hunger to satisfy. He thinks of the cigarette as the icing on the cake, but it is the little monster that needs feeding.

The truth is that the nicotine addict can never be completely relaxed, and as you go through life it gets worse.

The most unrelaxed people on this planet aren't non-smokers but fifty-year-old business executives who chain-smoke, are permanently coughing and spluttering, have high blood pressure and are constantly irritable. At this point cigarettes cease to relieve even partially the symptoms that they have created.

I can remember when I was a young accountant, bringing up a family. One of my children would do something wrong and I would lose my temper to an extent that was out of all proportion to what he had done. I really believed that I had an evil demon in my make-up. I now know that I had, however it wasn't some inherent flaw in my character, but the little nicotine monster that was creating the problem. During those times I thought I had all the problems in the world, but when I look back on my life I wonder where all the great stress was. In everything else in my life I was in control. The one thing that controlled me was the cigarette. The sad thing is that even today I can't convince my children that it was the smoking that caused me to be so irritable. Every time they hear a smoker trying to justify his addiction, the message is 'Oh, they calm me. They help me to relax.'

A couple of years ago, the adoption authorities in the UK threatened to prevent smokers from adopting children. A man rang up, irate. He said, 'You are completely wrong. I can remember when I was a child, if I had a contentious matter to raise with my mother, I would wait until she lit a cigarette because she was more relaxed then.' Why couldn't he talk to his mother when she wasn't smoking a cigarette? Why are smokers so unrelaxed when they are not smoking, even after a meal at a restaurant? Why are non-smokers completely relaxed then? Why are smokers not able to relax without a cigarette? The next time you are in a supermarket and you see a young housewife screaming at a child, just watch her leave. The first thing she will do is to light a cigarette. Start watching smokers, particularly when they are not allowed to smoke. You'll find that they have their hands near their mouths, or they are twiddling their thumbs, or tapping their feet, or fiddling with their hair, or clenching their jaw. Smokers aren't relaxed. They've forgotten what it feels like to be completely relaxed. That's one of the many joys you have to come.

The whole business of smoking can be likened to a fly being caught in a pitcher plant. To begin with, the fly is eating the nectar. At some imperceptible stage the plant begins to eat the fly.

Isn't it time you climbed out of that plant?

Combination Cigarettes

No, a combination cigarette is not when you are smoking two or more at the same time. When that happens, you begin to wonder why you were smoking the first one. I once burnt the back of my hand trying to put a cigarette in my mouth when there was already one there. Actually, it is not quite as stupid as you think. As I have already said, eventually the cigarette ceases to relieve the withdrawal pangs, and even when you are smoking the cigarette there is still something missing. This is the terrible frustration of the chain-smoker. Whenever you need the boost, you are already smoking, and this is why heavy smokers often turn to drink or other drugs. But I digress.

A combination cigarette is one occasioned by two or more of our usual reasons for smoking, e.g., social functions, parties, weddings, meals in restaurants. These are examples of occasions that are both stressful and relaxing. This might at first appear to be a contradiction, but it isn't. Any form of socializing can be stressful, even with friends, and at the same time you want to be enjoying yourself and be completely relaxed.

There are situations where all four reasons are present at one and the same time. Driving can be one of these. If you are leaving a tense situation, like a visit to the dentist or the doctor, you can now relax. At the same time driving always involves an element of stress. Your life is at stake. You are also having to concentrate. You may not be aware of the last two factors, but the fact that they are subconscious doesn't mean they aren't there. And if you are stuck in a traffic jam, or have a long motorway drive, you may also be bored.

Another classic example is a game of cards. If it's a game like bridge or poker, you have to concentrate. If you are losing more than you can afford, it is stressful. If you have long periods of not getting a decent hand, it can be boring. And, while all this is going on, you are at leisure; you are supposed to be relaxing. During a game of cards, no matter how slight the withdrawal pangs are, all smokers will be chain-smoking, even otherwise casual smokers. The ashtrays will fill and overflow in no time. There'll be a constant fall-out cloud above head height. If you were to tap any of the smokers on the shoulder and ask him if he was enjoying it, the answer would be 'You have got to be joking.' It is often after nights like these, when we wake up with a throat like a cess pit, that we decide to stop smoking.

These combination cigarettes are often special ones, the ones that we think we'll miss most when we are contemplating stopping smoking. We think that life will never be quite as enjoyable again. In fact, it is the same principle at work: these cigarettes simply provide relief from withdrawal pangs, and at certain times we have greater need to relieve them than at others.

Let us make it quite clear. It is not the cigarette that is special; it is the occasion. Once we have removed the need for the cigarette, such occasions will become more enjoyable and the stressful situations less stressful. This will be explained in greater detail in the next chapter.

What Am I Giving Up?

ABSOLUTELY NOTHING! The thing that makes it difficult for us to give up is fear. The fear that we are being deprived of our pleasure or prop. The fear that certain pleasant situations will never be quite the same again. The fear of being unable to cope with stressful situations.

In other words, the effect of brainwashing is to delude us into believing that there is a weakness in us, or something inherent in the cigarette that we need, and that when we stop smoking there will be a void.

Get it clear in your mind: **CIGARETTES DO NOT FILL A VOID. THEY CREATE IT!**

These bodies of ours are the most sophisticated objects on this planet. Whether you believe in a creator, a process of natural selection or a combination of both, whatever being or system devised these bodies of ours, it is a thousand times more effective than man! Man cannot create the smallest living cell, let alone the miracle of eyesight, reproduction, our circulatory system or our brains. If the creator or process had intended us to smoke, we would have been provided with some filter device to keep the poisons out of our bodies and some sort of chimney.

Our bodies are, in fact, provided with failsafe warning devices in the form of the cough, dizziness, sickness, etc., and we ignore these at our peril.

The beautiful truth is—there is nothing to give up. Once you purge that little monster from your body and the brainwashing from your mind, you will neither want cigarettes nor need them.

Cigarettes do not improve meals. They ruin them. They destroy your sense of taste and smell. Observe smokers in a restaurant, smoking between courses. It is not the meal that they are enjoying; they cannot wait for the meal to be over, as it is interfering with the cigarettes. Many of them do it in spite of the fact that they know it causes offence to non-smokers. It is not that smokers are generally inconsiderate people; it is just that they are miserable without the cigarette. They are between the devil and the deep blue sea. They either have to abstain and be miserable because they cannot smoke, or smoke and be miserable because they are offending other people, feel guilty and despise themselves for it.

Watch smokers at an official function where they have to wait for the loyal toast. Many of them develop weak bladders and have to sneak off for a quick smoke. That is when you see smoking for the true addiction that it is. Smokers do not smoke because they enjoy it. They do it because they are miserable without it.

Because many of us start smoking on social occasions when we are young and shy, we acquire the belief that we cannot enjoy social occasions without a cigarette. This is nonsense. Tobacco takes away your confidence. The greatest evidence of the fear that cigarettes instil in smokers is their effect on women. Practically all women are fastidious about their personal appearance. They wouldn't dream of appearing at a social function not immaculately turned out and smelling beautiful. Yet knowing that their breath smells like a stale ashtray does not seem to deter them in the least. I know that it *bothers* them greatly—many hate the smell of their own hair and clothes—yet it doesn't *deter* them. Such is the fear that this awful drug instils in the smoker.

Cigarettes do not help social occasions; they destroy them. Having to hold a drink in one hand and a cigarette in the other, trying to dispose of the ash and the continual chain of cigarette butts, trying not to breathe smoke and fumes into the face of the person you are conversing with, wondering whether they can smell your breath or see the stains on your teeth.

Not only is there nothing to give up, but there are marvellous positive gains. When smokers contemplate quitting smoking they tend to concentrate on health, money and social stigma. These are obviously valid and important issues, but I personally believe the greatest gains from stopping are psychological, and for varying reasons they include:

1. The return of your confidence and courage.

2. Freedom from the slavery.

3. Not to have to go through life suffering the awful black shadows at the back of your mind, knowing you are being despised by half of the population and, worst of all, despising yourself.

Not only is life better as a non-smoker but it is infinitely more enjoyable. I do not only mean you will be healthier and wealthier. I mean you will be happier and enjoy life far more.

The marvellous gains from being a non-smoker are discussed in the next few chapters.

Some smokers find it difficult to appreciate the concept of the 'void', and the following analogy may assist you.

Imagine having a cold sore on your face. I've got this marvellous ointment. I say to you, 'Try this stuff.' You rub the ointment on, and the sore disappears immediately. A week later it reappears. You ask, 'Do you have any more of that ointment?' I say, 'Keep the tube. You might need it again.' You apply the ointment. Hey presto, the sore disappears again. Every time the sore returns, it gets larger and more painful and the interval gets shorter and shorter. Eventually the sore covers your whole face and is excruciatingly painful. It is now returning every half hour. You know that the ointment will remove it temporarily, but you are very worried. Will the sore eventually spread over your whole body? Will the interval disappear completely? You go to your doctor. He can't cure it. You try other things, but nothing helps except this marvellous ointment.

By now you are completely dependent on the ointment. You never go out without ensuring that you have a tube of the ointment with you. If you go abroad, you make sure that you take several tubes with you. Now, in addition to your worries about your health, I'm charging you $100 per tube. You have no choice but to pay.

You then read in the medical column of your newspaper that this isn't happening just to you; many other people have been suffering from the same problem. In fact, pharmacists have discovered that the ointment doesn't actually cure the sore. All that it does is to take the sore beneath the surface of the skin. It is the ointment that has caused the sore to grow. All you have to do to get rid of the sore is to stop using the ointment. The sore will eventually disappear in due course.

Would you continue to use the ointment?

Would it take willpower not to use the ointment? If you didn't believe the article, there might be a few days of apprehension, but once you realized that the sore was beginning to get better, the need or desire to use the ointment would go.

Would you be miserable? Of course you wouldn't. You had an awful problem, which you thought was insoluble. Now you've found the solution. Even if it took a year for that sore to disappear completely, each day, as it improved, you'd think, 'Isn't it marvellous? I'm not going to die.'

This was the magic that happened to me when I extinguished that final cigarette. Let me make one point quite clear in the analogy of the sore and the ointment. The sore isn't lung cancer, or arterial sclerosis, or emphysema, or angina, or chronic asthma, or bronchitis, or coronary heart disease. They are all in addition to the sore. It isn't the thousands in cash that we burn, or the lifetime of bad breath and stained teeth, the lethargy, the wheezing and coughing, the years we spend choking ourselves and wishing we didn't, the times when we are being punished because we are not allowed to smoke. It isn't the lifetime of being despised by other people, or, worst of all, despising yourself. These are all in addition to the sore. The sore is what makes us close our minds to all these things. It's that panic feeling of 'I want a cigarette.' Non-smokers don't suffer from that feeling. The worst thing we ever suffer from is fear, and the greatest gain you will receive is to be rid of that fear.

It was as if a great mist had suddenly lifted from my mind. I could see so clearly that that panic feeling of wanting a cigarette wasn't some sort of weakness in me, or some magic quality in the cigarette. It was caused by the first cigarette; and each subsequent one, far from relieving the feeling, was causing it. At the same time I could see that all these other 'happy' smokers were going through the same nightmare that I was. Not as bad as mine, but all putting up phoney arguments to try to justify their stupidity.

IT'S SO NICE TO BE FREE!

15

Self-imposed Slavery

Usually when smokers try to stop the main reasons are health, money, and social stigma. Part of the brainwashing of this awful drug is the sheer slavery.

Man fought hard in the last century to abolish slavery, and yet the smoker spends his life suffering self-imposed slavery. He seems to be oblivious to the fact that, when he is allowed to smoke, he wishes that he were a non-smoker. With most of the cigarettes we smoke in our lives, not only do we not enjoy them but we aren't even aware that we are smoking them. It is only after a period of abstinence that we actually suffer the delusion of enjoying a cigarette (e.g., the first in the morning, the one after a meal, etc.).

The only time that the cigarette becomes precious is when we are trying to cut down or abstain, or when society tries to force us to (e.g., when attending churches, hospitals, supermarkets, theatres and so on).

The confirmed smoker should bear in mind that this trend will get worse and worse. Today it is Tube trains. Tomorrow it will be all public places.

Gone are the days when the smoker could enter a friend's or stranger's house and say, 'Do you mind if I smoke?' Nowadays the poor smoker, on entering a strange house, will search desperately for an ashtray and hope to find butts in it. If there is no ashtray, he will generally try to last out, and if he cannot, he will ask for permission to smoke and is likely to be told: 'Smoke if you have to,' or 'Well, we would rather you didn't. The smell seems to linger on.'

The poor smoker, who was already feeling wretched, wants the ground to open up and swallow him.

I remember during my smoking days, every time I went to church, it was an ordeal. Even during my own daughter's wedding, when I should have been standing there a proud father, what was I doing? I was thinking, 'Let's get on with it, so that we can get outside and have a drag.'

It will help you to observe smokers on these occasions. They huddle together. There is never just one packet. There are twenty packets being thrust about, and the conversation is always the same.

'Do you smoke?'

'Yes, but have one of mine.'

'I will have one of yours later.'

They light up and take a deep drag, thinking, 'Aren't we lucky? We have got our little reward. The poor non-smoker hasn't got a reward.'

The 'poor' non-smoker doesn't need a reward. We were not designed to go through life systematically poisoning our own bodies. The pathetic thing is that even when smoking a cigarette, the smoker doesn't achieve the feeling of peace, confidence and tranquillity that the non-smoker has experienced for the whole of his non-smoking life. The non-smoker isn't sitting in the church feeling agitated and wishing his life away. He can enjoy the whole of his life.

I can also remember playing indoor bowls in the winter and pretending to have a weak bladder in order to nip off for a puff. No, this wasn't a fourteen-year-old schoolboy but a forty-year-old chartered accountant. How pathetic. And even when I was back playing the game I wasn't enjoying it. I was looking forward to the finish so that I could smoke again, yet this was supposed to be my way of relaxing and enjoying my favourite hobby.

To me one of the tremendous joys of being a non-smoker is to be freed from that slavery, to be able to enjoy the whole of my life and not spend half of it craving for a cigarette and then, when I light up, wishing I didn't have to do it.

Smokers should bear in mind that when they are in the houses of non-smokers or even in the company of non-smokers, it is not the self-righteous non-smoker who is depriving them but the 'little monster'.

16

I'll Save £x a Week

cannot repeat too often that it is brainwashing that makes it difficult to stop smoking, and the more brainwashing we can dispel before we start, the easier you will find it to achieve your goal.

Occasionally I get into arguments with people whom I call confirmed smokers. By my definition a confirmed smoker is somebody who can afford it, doesn't believe it injures his health and isn't worried about the social stigma. (There are not many about nowadays.)

If he is a young man, I say to him, 'I cannot believe you are not worried about the money you are spending.'

Usually his eyes light up. If I had attacked him on health grounds or on the social stigma, he would feel at a disadvantage, but on money— 'Oh, I can afford it. It is only £x per week and I think it is worth it. It is my only vice or pleasure,' etc.

If he is a twenty-per-day smoker I say to him, 'I still cannot believe you are not worried about the money. You are going to spend over £40,000 in your lifetime. What are you doing with that money? You are not even setting light to it or throwing it away. You are actually using that money to ruin your physical health, to destroy your nerves and confidence, to suffer a lifetime of slavery, a lifetime of bad breath and stained teeth. Surely that must worry you?'

It is apparent at this point, particularly with young smokers, that they have never considered it a lifetime expense. For most smokers the price of a packet is bad enough. Occasionally we work out what we spend in a week, and that is alarming. Very occasionally (and only when we think about stopping) we estimate what we spend in a year and that is frightening, but over a lifetime—it is unthinkable.

However, because it is an argument the confirmed smoker will say, 'I can afford it. It is only so much a week.' He does an 'encyclopedia salesman' on himself.

I then say, 'I will make you an offer you cannot refuse. You pay me £1,000 now, and I will provide you with free cigarettes for the rest of your life.'

If I were offering to take over a £40,000 mortgage for £1,000, the smoker would have my signature on a piece of paper before I could move, and yet not one confirmed smoker (and please bear in mind I am not now talking to someone like yourself who plans to stop, I am talking to someone who has no intention of stopping) has ever taken me up on that offer. Why not?

Often at this point in my consultation, a smoker will say, 'Look, I am not really worried about the money aspect.' If you are thinking along these lines, ask yourself why you are not worried. Why in other aspects of life will you go to a great deal of trouble to save a few pounds here and there and yet spend thousands of pounds poisoning yourself and hang the expense?

The answer to these questions is this. Every other decision that you make in your life will be the result of an analytical process of weighing the pros and cons and arriving at a rational answer. It may be the wrong answer, but at least it will be the result of rational deduction. Whenever any smoker weighs the pros and cons of smoking, the answer is a dozen times over: **'STOP SMOKING! YOU ARE A FOOL!'** Therefore all smokers are smoking not because they want to or because they decided to but because they think they cannot stop. They have to brainwash themselves. They have to keep their heads in the sand.

The strange thing is smokers will arrange pacts among themselves, such as 'First one to give in pays the other £50', yet the thousands of pounds that they would save by stopping don't seem to affect them. This is because they are still thinking with the brainwashed mind of the smoker.

Just take the sand out of your eyes for a moment. Smoking is a chain reaction and a chain for life. If you do not break that chain, you will remain a smoker for the rest of your life. Now estimate how much you think you will spend on smoking for the rest of your life. The amount will obviously vary with each individual, but for the purpose of this exercise let us assume it is £10,000.

You will shortly be making the decision to smoke your final cigarette (not yet, please—remember the initial instructions). All you have to do to remain a non-smoker is not to fall for the trap again. That is, do not smoke that first cigarette. If you do, that one cigarette will cost you £10,000.

If you think this is a trick way of looking at it, you are still kidding yourself. Just work out how much money you would have saved if you hadn't smoked your first cigarette.

If you see the argument as factual, ask yourself how you would feel if there were a check from Publisher's Clearinghouse for $15,000.00 on your carpet tomorrow. You'd be dancing with delight! So start dancing! You are about to start receiving that bonus, and that's just one of the several marvellous gains you are about to receive.

During the withdrawal period you may be tempted to have just one final cigarette. It will help you to resist the temptation if you remind yourself it will cost you $15,000 (or whatever your estimate is)!

I've been making that offer on television and radio programmes for years. I still find it incredible that not one confirmed smoker has ever taken my offer up. There are members of my golf club whom I taunt every time I hear them complain about an increase in tobacco prices. In fact, I'm frightened that if I goad them too much, one of them will take me up on it. I'd lose a fortune if he did.

If you are in the company of happy, cheerful smokers who tell you how much they enjoy it, just tell them that you know an idiot who, if they pay him a year's smoking money in advance, will provide them with free cigarettes for the rest of their lives. Perhaps you can find me someone who will take up the offer?

17

Health

This is the area where the brainwashing is the greatest. Smokers think they are aware of the health risks. They are not.

Even in my case, when I was expecting my head to explode any moment and honestly believed I was prepared to accept the consequences, I was still kidding myself.

If in those days I had taken a cigarette out of the packet and a red bleeper started to sound, followed by a warning voice saying, 'OK, Allen, this is the one! Fortunately you do get a warning, and this is it. Up to now you have got away with it, but if you smoke another cigarette your head will explode,' do you think I would have lit that cigarette?

If you are in doubt about the answer, just try walking up to a main road with busy traffic, stand on the curb with your eyes closed and try to imagine you have the choice of either stopping smoking or walking blindfolded across the road before taking your next cigarette.

There is no doubt what your choice would be. I had been doing what every smoker does all his smoking life: closing my mind and keeping my head in the sand, hoping that I would wake up one morning and just not want to smoke any more. Smokers cannot allow themselves to think of the health risks. If they do, even the illusion of enjoying the 'habit' goes.

This explains why the shock treatment used by the media on National No-Smoking Days is so ineffective. It is only non-smokers who can bring themselves to watch. It also explains why smokers, recalling Uncle Fred who smoked forty a day and lived until he was eighty, will ignore the thousands of people who are brought down in their prime because of this poisonous weed.

About six times a week I have the following conversation with smokers (usually the younger ones):

ME: Why do you want to stop?

SMOKER: I can't afford it.

ME: Aren't you worried about the health risks?

SMOKER: No. I could step under a bus tomorrow.

ME: Would you deliberately step under a bus?

SMOKER: Of course not.

ME: Do you not bother to look left and right
    when you cross the road?

SMOKER: Of course I do.

Exactly. The smoker goes to a lot of trouble not to step under a bus, and the odds are hundreds of thousands to one against it happening. Yet the smoker risks the near certainty of being crippled by the weed and appears to be completely oblivious to the risks. Such is the power of the brainwashing.

I remember one famous British golfer who wouldn't go on the American circuit because he was afraid of flying. Yet he would chain-smoke round the golf course. Isn't it strange that, if we felt there was the slightest fault in an aeroplane, we wouldn't go up in it, even though the risks are hundreds of thousands to one against death, yet we take a one-in-four certainty with the cigarette and are apparently oblivious to it. And what does the smoker get out of it?

ABSOLUTELY NOTHING!

Another common myth about smoking is the smoker's cough. Many of the younger people who come to see me are not worried about their health because they do not cough. The true facts are just the reverse. A cough is one of nature's fail-safe methods of dispelling foreign matter from the lungs. The cough itself is not a disease; it is just a symptom. When smokers cough it is because their lungs are trying to dispel cancer-triggering tars and poisons. When they do not cough those tars and poisons remain in their lungs, and that is when they cause cancer. Smokers tend to avoid exercise and get into the habit of shallow breathing in order not to cough. I used to believe that my permanent smokers' cough would kill me. By expelling much of the filth from my lungs, it possibly saved my life.

Just think of it this way. If you had a nice car and allowed it to rust without doing anything about it, that would be pretty stupid, as it would soon be a heap of rust and would not carry you about. However, that would not be the end of the world; it is only a question of money and you could always buy a new one. Your body is the vehicle that carries you through life. We all say that our health is our most valued asset. How true that is, as sick millionaires will tell you. Most of us can look back at some illness or accident in our lives when we prayed to get better. (**HOW SOON WE FORGET**.) By being a smoker you are not only letting rust get in and doing nothing about it; you are systematically destroying the vehicle you need to go through life, and you only get one.

Wise up. You don't have to do it, and remember: it is doing **ABSOLUTELY NOTHING FOR YOU.**

Just for a moment take your head out of the sand and ask yourself, if you knew for certain that the next cigarette would be the one to trigger off cancer in your body, whether you would actually smoke it. Forget the disease (it is difficult to imagine it), but imagine you have to go to the Royal Marsden Hospital to suffer those awful tests—radium treatment, etc. Now you are not planning the rest of your life. You are planning your death. What is going to happen to your family and loved ones, your plans and dreams?

I often see the people that it happens to. They didn't think it would happen to them either, and the worst thing about it isn't the disease itself but the knowledge they have brought it on themselves. All our lives as smokers we are saying, 'I'll stop tomorrow.' Try to imagine how those people feel who 'hit the button'. For them the brainwashing is ended. They then see the 'habit' as it really is and spend the remainder of their lives thinking, 'Why did I kid myself I needed to smoke? If only I had the chance to go back!'

Stop kidding yourself. You have the chance. It's a chain reaction. If you smoke the next cigarette, it will lead to the next one and the next. It's already happening to you.

At the beginning of the book I promised you no shock treatment. If you have already decided you are going to stop smoking, this isn't shock treatment for you. If you are still in doubt, skip the remainder of this chapter and come back to it when you have read the rest of the book.

Volumes of statistics have already been written about the damage that cigarettes can cause to the smoker's health. The trouble is that until the smoker decides to stop he doesn't want to know. Even the government health warning is a waste of time because the smoker puts blinders on, and if he inadvertently reads it, the first thing he does is light up a cigarette.

Smokers tend to think of the health hazard as a hit-and-miss affair, like stepping on a mine. Get it into your head: it is already happening. Every time you puff on a cigarette you are breathing cancer-triggering tars into your lungs, and cancer is by no means the worst of the killer diseases that cigarettes cause or contribute to. They are also a powerful contributory cause of heart disease, arteriosclerosis, emphysema, angina, thrombosis, chronic bronchitis and asthma.

While I was still smoking, I'd never heard of arteriosclerosis or emphysema. I knew the permanent wheezing and coughing and the ever-increasing asthma and bronchitis attacks were a direct result of my smoking. But though they caused me discomfort there was no real pain and I could handle the discomfort.

I confess that the thought of contracting lung cancer terrified me, which is probably why I just blocked it from my mind. It's amazing how the fear of the horrendous health risks attached to smoking is overshadowed by the fear of stopping. It's not so much that the latter is a greater fear, but that if we quit today the fear is immediate, whereas the fear of contracting lung cancer is a fear of the future. Why look on the black side? Perhaps it won't happen. I'm bound to have quit by then anyway.

We tend to think of smoking as a tug-of-war. On one side fear: it's unhealthy, expensive, filthy and enslaving. On the other side the pluses: it's my pleasure, my friend, my crutch. It never seems to occur to us that this side is also fear. It's not so much that we enjoy cigarettes, but that we tend to be miserable without them.

Think of heroin addicts deprived of their heroin: the abject misery they go through. Now picture their utter joy when they are allowed to plunge a needle into their veins and end that terrible craving. Try to imagine how anyone could actually believe they get pleasure from sticking a hypodermic syringe into a vein.

Non–heroin addicts don't suffer that panic feeling. Heroin doesn't relieve the feeling; on the contrary, it causes it. Non-smokers don't feel miserable if they are not allowed to smoke after a meal. It's only smokers that suffer that feeling. Nicotine doesn't relieve it; on the contrary it causes it.

The fear of contracting lung cancer didn't make me quit because I believed it was rather like walking through a minefield. If you got away with it—fine. If you were unlucky you stepped on a mine. You knew the risks you were taking and if you were prepared to take the risk, what had it to do with anyone else?

So if a non-smoker ever tried to make me aware of those risks, I would use the typical evasive tactics that all addicts invariably adopt.

'You have to die of something.'

Of course you do, but is that a logical reason for deliberately shortening your life?

'Quality of life is more important than longevity.'

Exactly, but you are surely not suggesting that the quality of life of an alcoholic or a heroin addict is greater than that of someone that isn't addicted to alcohol or heroin? Do you really believe that the quality of a smoker's life is better than a non-smoker's? Surely the smoker loses on both counts—his life is both shorter and more miserable.

'My lungs probably suffer more damage from car exhausts than from smoking.'

Even if that were true, is that a logical reason for punishing your lungs further? Can you possibly conceive of anyone being stupid enough to actually put his or her mouth over an exhaust pipe and deliberately inhale those fumes into his or her lungs?

THAT'S WHAT SMOKERS EFFECTIVELY DO!

Think of that next time you watch a poor smoker inhale deeply on one of those 'precious' cigarettes!

I can understand why the congestion and the risks of contracting lung cancer didn't help me to quit. I could cope with the former and block my mind to the latter. As you are already aware, my method is not to frighten you into quitting, but the complete opposite—to make you realize just how more enjoyable your life will be when you have escaped.

However, I do believe that if I could have seen what was happening inside my body, this would have helped me to quit. Now I'm not referring to the shock technique of showing a smoker the colour of a smoker's lungs. It was obvious to me from my nicotine-stained teeth and fingers that my lungs weren't a pretty sight. Provided they kept functioning, they were less embarrassment than my teeth and fingers—at least nobody could see my lungs.

What I am referring to is the progressive gunking-up of our arteries and veins and the gradual starving of every muscle and organ of our bodies of oxygen and nutrients and replacing them with poisons and carbon monoxide (not just from car exhausts but also from smoking).

Like the majority of motorists, I don't like the thought of dirty oil or a dirty filter in my car engine. Could you imagine buying a brand-new Rolls Royce and never changing the oil or the oil filter? That's what we effectively do to our bodies when we become smokers.

Many doctors are now relating all sorts of diseases to smoking, including diabetes, cervical cancer and breast cancer. This is no surprise to me. The tobacco industry has belaboured the fact that the medical profession has never scientifically proved that smoking is the direct cause of lung cancer.

The statistical evidence is so overwhelming as not to need proof. No one ever scientifically proved to me exactly why when I bang my thumb with a hammer, it hurts. I soon got the message.

I must emphasize that I am not a doctor, but just like the hammer and the thumb, it soon became obvious to me that my congestion, my permanent cough, my frequent asthma and bronchial attacks were directly related to my smoking. However, I truly believe that the greatest hazard that smoking causes to our health is the gradual and progressive deterioration of our immune system caused by this gunking-up process.

All plants and animals on this planet are subjected to a lifetime of attack from germs, viruses, parasites, etc. The most powerful defence we have against disease is our immune system. We all suffer infections and diseases throughout our lives. I believe we all suffer from some form of cancer during our lives. However, I do not believe that the human body was designed to be diseased, and if you are strong and healthy, your immune system will fight and defeat these attacks. How can your immune system work effectively when you are starving every muscle and organ of oxygen and nutrients and replacing them with carbon monoxide and poisons? It's not so much that smoking causes these other diseases, it works rather like AIDS, it gradually destroys your immune system.

Several of the adverse effects that smoking had on my health, some of which I had been suffering from for years, did not become apparent to me until many years after I had stopped smoking.

While I was busy despising those idiots and cranks who would rather lose their legs than quit smoking, it didn't even occur to me that I was already suffering from arteriosclerosis myself. My almost permanently grey complexion I attributed to my natural colouring or to lack of exercise. It never occurred to me that it was really due to the blocking up of my capillaries. I had varicose veins in my thirties, which have miraculously disappeared since I stopped smoking. I reached the stage about five years before I stopped when every night I would have this weird sensation in my legs. It wasn't a sharp pain or like pins and needles, just a sort of restless feeling. I would get my wife Joyce to massage my legs every night. It didn't occur to me until at least a year after I had stopped that I no longer needed the massage.

About two years before I quit, I would occasionally get violent pains in my chest, which I feared must be lung cancer but now assume to have been angina. I haven't had a single attack since I quit.

When I was a child I would bleed profusely from cuts. This frightened me. No one explained to me that bleeding was in fact a natural and essential healing process and that the blood would clot when its healing purpose was completed. I suspected that I was a haemophiliac and feared that I might bleed to death. Later in life I would sustain quite deep cuts yet hardly bleed at all. This browny-red gunk would ooze from the cut.

The colour worried me. I knew that blood was meant to be bright red and I assumed that I had some sort of blood disease. However I was pleased about the consistency, which meant that I no longer bled profusely. Not until after I had stopped smoking did I learn that smoking coagulated the blood and that the brownish colour was due to lack of oxygen. I was ignorant of the effect at the time, but in hindsight, it was this effect that smoking was having on my health that most fills me with horror. When I think of my poor heart trying to pump that gunk around restricted blood vessels, day in and day out, without missing a single beat, I find it a miracle that I didn't suffer a stroke or a heart attack. It made me realize, not how fragile our bodies are, but how strong and ingenious that incredible machine is!

I had liver spots on my hands in my forties. In case you don't know, liver spots are those brown or white spots that very old people have on their face and hands. I tried to ignore them, assuming that they were due to early senility caused by the hectic lifestyle that I had led. It was five years after I had quit that a smoker at the Raynes Park clinic remarked that when he had stopped previously, his liver spots disappeared. I had forgotten about mine, and to my amazement, they too had disappeared.

As long as I can remember, I had spots flashing in front of my eyes if ever I stood up too quickly, particularly if I were in a bath. I would feel dizzy, as if I were about to black out. I never related this to smoking. In fact I was convinced that it was quite normal and that everyone else had a similar reaction. Not until only five years ago, when an ex-smoker told me that he no longer had that sensation did it occur to me that I no longer had it either.

You might conclude that I am somewhat of a hypochondriac. I believe that I was when I was a smoker. One of the great evils about smoking is that it fools us into believing that nicotine gives us courage, when in fact it gradually and imperceptibly dissipates it. I was shocked when I heard my father say that he had no wish to live to be fifty. Little did I realize that twenty years later I would have exactly the same lack of *joie de vivre*. You might conclude that this chapter has been one of necessary, or unnecessary, doom and gloom. I promise you it is the complete opposite. I used to fear death when I was a child. I used to believe that smoking removed that fear. Perhaps it did. If so, it replaced it with something infinitely worse: **A FEAR OF LIVING!**

Now my fear of dying has returned. It does not bother me. I realize that it only exists because I now enjoy life so much. I don't brood over my fear of dying any more than I did when I was a child. I'm far too busy living my life to the full. The odds are against my living to a hundred, but I'll try to. I'll also try to enjoy every precious moment!

There were two other advantages on the health side that never occurred to me until I had stopped smoking. One was that I used to have repetitive nightmares every night. I would dream that I was being chased. I can only assume that these nightmares were the result of the body being deprived of nicotine throughout the night and the insecure feeling that would result. Now the only nightmare that I have is that I occasionally dream that I am smoking again. This is quite a common dream among ex-smokers. Some worry that it means that they are still subconsciously pining for a cigarette. Don't worry about it. The fact that it was a nightmare means that you are very pleased not to be a smoker. There is that twilight zone after any nightmare when you wake up and are not sure whether it is a genuine catastrophe, but isn't it marvellous when you realize that it was only a dream?

When I described being chased every night in a dream, I originally typed 'chaste'. Perhaps this was just a 'Freudian slip', but it does give me a convenient lead into the second advantage. At clinics, when covering the effect that smoking has on concentration, I would sometimes say: 'Which organ in your body has the greatest need of a good supply of blood?' The stupid grins, usually on the faces of the men, would indicate that they had missed the point. However, they were absolutely right. Being a somewhat shy Englishman, I find the subject rather embarrassing, and I have no intention of doing a miniature 'Kinsey' report by going into detail about the adverse effect that smoking had on my own sexual activity and enjoyment, or that of other ex-smokers with whom I have discussed the subject. Again, I was not aware of this effect until some time after I had stopped smoking and had attributed my sexual prowess and activity, or rather lack of it, to advancing years.

However, if you watch natural-science films, you will be aware that the first rule of nature is survival, and that the second rule is survival of the species, or reproduction. Nature ensures that reproduction does not take place unless the partners feel physically healthy and know that they have secured a safe home, territory, supply of food and a suitable mate. Man's ingenuity has enabled him to bend these rules somewhat, however, I know for a fact that smoking can lead to impotency. I can also assure you, that when you feel fit and healthy, you'll enjoy sex much more and more often.

Smokers also suffer the illusion that the ill-effects of smoking are overstated. The reverse is the case. There is no doubt that cigarettes are the No. 1 cause of death in society. The trouble is that in many cases where cigarettes cause the death or are a contributory factor, it is not blamed on cigarettes in the statistics.

It has been estimated that 44 per cent of household fires are caused by cigarettes, and I wonder how many road accidents have been caused by cigarettes during that split second when you take your eye off the road to light up.

I am normally a careful driver, but the nearest I came to death (except from smoking itself) was when trying to roll a cigarette while driving, and I hate to think of the number of times I coughed a cigarette out of my mouth while driving—it always seemed to end up between the seats. I am sure many other smoking drivers have had the experience of trying to locate the burning cigarette with one hand while trying to drive with the other.

The effect of the brainwashing is that we tend to think like the man who, having fallen off a 100-storey building, is heard to say, as he passes the fiftieth floor, 'So far, so good!' We think that as we have got away with it so far, one more cigarette won't make the difference.

Try to see it another way: the 'habit' is a continuous chain for life, each cigarette creating the need for the next. When you start the habit you light a fuse. The trouble is, **YOU DON'T KNOW HOW LONG THE FUSE IS.** Every time that you light a cigarette you are one step nearer to the bomb exploding. **HOW WILL YOU KNOW IF IT'S THE NEXT ONE?**

Energy

Most smokers are aware of the effect that this progressive process of gunking-up and starvation of oxygen and nutrients has on their lungs. However, they are not so aware of the effect it has on their energy level.

One of the subtleties of the smoking trap is that the effects it has on us, both physical and mental, happen so gradually and imperceptibly that we are not aware of them and regard them as normal.

It is very similar to the effects of bad eating habits. The pot-belly appears so gradually that it causes us no alarm. We look at people who are grossly overweight and wonder how they could possibly have allowed themselves to reach that state.

But supposing it happened overnight. You went to bed weighing 140 pounds, trim, rippling with muscles and not an ounce of fat on your body. You awoke weighing 182 pounds, fat, bloated and pot-bellied. Instead of waking up feeling fully rested and full of energy, you wake up feeling miserable, lethargic and you can hardly open your eyes. You would be panic-stricken, wondering what awful disease you had contracted overnight. Yet the disease is exactly the same. The fact that it took you twenty years to reach that state is irrelevant.

So it is with smoking. If I could immediately transfer you into your mind and body to give you a direct comparison on how you would feel having stopped smoking for just three weeks, that is all I would need to do to persuade you to quit. You would think: 'Will I really feel this good?' Or what it really amounts to: 'Have I really sunk that low?' I emphasize that I don't just mean how you would feel healthier and have more energy, but how you would feel more confident and relaxed and better able to concentrate.

As a teenager, I can remember rushing around just for the hell of it. For thirty-odd years, I was permanently tired and lethargic. I used to struggle to wake up at nine o'clock in the morning. After my evening meal I would lie on a couch watching television and nod off after five minutes. Because my father used to be the same, I thought this behaviour was normal. I believed that energy was the exclusive prerogative of children and teenagers, and that old age began in the early twenties.

Shortly after I extinguished my final cigarette, I was relieved that the congestion and the coughing disappeared, and I haven't had an asthma or bronchitis attack since. However something truly marvellous and unexpected also happened. I started waking at seven o'clock in the morning feeling completely rested and full of energy, actually wanting to exercise, jog and swim. At forty-eight I couldn't run a step or swim a stroke. My sporting activities were confined to such dynamic pursuits as green bowling, affectionately referred to as the old man's game, and golf, for which I had to use a motorized buggy. At the age of sixty-four I jog two to three miles daily, exercise for half an hour and swim twenty lengths. It's great to have energy, and when you feel physically and mentally strong, it feels great to be alive.

The problem is that when you quit smoking, the return of your physical and mental health is also gradual. True it's nothing like as slow as the slide into the pit, and if you are going through the trauma of the willpower method of quitting, any health or financial gains will be obliterated by the depression you will be going through.

Unfortunately, I cannot immediately transfer you into your mind and body in three weeks' time. But you can! You know instinctively that what I am telling you is correct. All you need to do is: **USE YOUR IMAGINATION!**

19

It Relaxes Me and Gives Me Confidence

This is the worst fallacy of all about smoking, and for me it ranks with the ending of the slavery, the greatest benefit from quitting—not to have to go through life with the permanent feeling of insecurity that smokers suffer from.

Smokers find it very difficult to believe that the cigarette actually causes that insecure feeling you get when you are out late at night and running out of cigarettes. Non-smokers do not suffer from that feeling. It is the tobacco that causes it.

I only became aware of many of the advantages of stopping months afterwards, as a result of my consultations with other smokers.

For twenty-five years I refused to have a medical. If I wanted life insurance, I insisted on 'no medical' and paid higher premiums as a result. I hated visiting hospitals, doctors or dentists. I couldn't face the thought of getting old, pensions and so on.

None of these things did I relate to my smoking 'habit', but getting off it has been like awakening from a bad dream. Nowadays I look forward to each day. Of course, bad things happen in my life, and I am subject to the normal stresses and strains, but it is wonderful to have the confidence to cope with them, and extra health, energy and confidence make the good times more enjoyable too.

Those Sinister
Black Shadows

Another of the great joys of quitting the weed is to be free of those sinister black shadows at the back of our minds.

All smokers know they are fools and close their minds to the ill-effects of smoking. For most of our lives smoking is automatic, but the black shadows are always lurking in our subconscious minds, just beneath the surface.

There are several marvellous advantages to achieve from quitting smoking. Some of them I was consciously aware of throughout my smoking life, such as the health risks, the waste of money and the sheer stupidity of being a smoker. However, such was my fear of quitting, so obsessed was I in resisting all the attempts of do-gooders and anyone else who tried to persuade me to quit, that all my imagination and energy were directed to finding any flimsy excuse that would allow me to continue to smoke.

Amazingly, my most ingenious thoughts occurred when I was actually trying to quit. They were of course inspired by the fear and misery I suffered when attempting to quit by using willpower. No way could I block my mind from the health and financial aspects. But now that I am free it amazes me how I successfully blocked my mind from even more important advantages to be gained from quitting. I've already mentioned the sheer slavery—spending half our lives being allowed to smoke, doing it automatically and wishing we had never started, the other half feeling miserable and deprived because society won't allow us to smoke. In the last chapter I've referred to the incredible joy of having energy again. But for me the greatest joy of being free was not the health, the money, the energy, or the ending of the slavery, it was the removal of those sinister black shadows, the removal of feeling despised by and feeling apologetic to non-smokers, and most of all the ability to respect myself.

Most smokers aren't the weak-willed, spineless jellyfish that both society and they tend to believe. In every other aspect of my life I was in control. I loathed myself for being dependent on an evil weed that I knew was ruining my life. I cannot tell you of the utter joy of being free of those sinister black shadows, the dependency and the self-despising. I can't tell you how nice it is to be able to look at all other smokers, whether they be young, old, casual or heavy, not with a feeling of envy, but with a feeling of pity for them and elation for you that you are no longer the slave of that insidious weed.

The last two chapters have dealt with the considerable advantages of being a non-smoker. I feel it necessary to give a balanced account, so the next chapter lists the advantages of being a smoker.

The Advantages of
Being a Smoker

The Willpower Method
of Stopping

I t is an accepted fact in our society that it is very difficult to stop smoking. Even books advising you how to do so usually start off by telling you how difficult it is. The truth is that it is ridiculously easy. Yes, I can understand your questioning that statement, but just consider it.

If your aim is to run a mile in under four minutes, that's difficult. You may have to undergo years of hard training, and even then you may be physically incapable of doing it. (Much of our achievement lies in the mind. Isn't it strange how difficult it was until Roger Bannister actually did it but nowadays it is commonplace?)

However, in order to stop smoking all you have to do is not smoke any more. No one forces you to smoke (apart from yourself) and, unlike food or drink, you don't need it to survive. So if you want to stop doing it, why should it be difficult? In fact, it isn't. It is smokers who make it difficult by using the Willpower Method. I define the Willpower Method as any method that forces the smoker to feel he is making some sort of sacrifice. Let us just consider the Willpower Method.

We do not decide to become smokers. We merely experiment with the first few cigarettes and because they taste awful we are convinced that we can stop whenever we want to. In the main, we smoke those first few cigarettes only when we want to, and that is usually in the company of other smokers on social occasions.

Before we realize it, we are not only buying them regularly and smoking when we want to, we are smoking every day. Smoking has become a part of our lives. We ensure that we always have cigarettes on our person. We believe that social occasions and meals are improved by them and that they help to relieve stress. It doesn't seem to occur to us that the same cigarette out of the same packet will taste exactly the same after a meal as it does first thing in the morning. In fact smoking neither improves meals and social occasions nor does it relieve stress, it's just that smokers believe they can't enjoy a meal or handle stress without a cigarette.

It usually takes us a long time to realize that we are hooked because we suffer from the illusion that smokers smoke because they enjoy a cigarette, not because they have to have a cigarette. While we are not enjoying cigarettes (which we never do), we suffer from the illusion that we can stop whenever we want to.

Usually it is not until we actually try to stop that we realize a problem exists. The first attempts to stop are more often than not in the early days and are usually triggered off by shortage of money (boy meets girl and they are saving to set up home and do not want to waste money on cigarettes) or health (the teenager is still active in sport and finds he is short of breath). Whatever the reason, the smoker always waits for a stressful situation, whether it be health or money. As soon as he stops, the little monster needs feeding. The smoker then wants a cigarette, and because he cannot have one this makes him more distressed. The thing he usually takes to relieve stress is now not available, so he suffers a triple blow. The probable result after a period of torture is the compromise 'I'll cut down' or 'I've picked the wrong time' or 'I'll wait until the stress has gone from my life.' However, once the stress has gone, he has no need to stop and doesn't decide to do so again until the next stressful time. Of course, the time is never right because life for most people doesn't become less stressful; it becomes more so. We leave the protection of our parents and enter the world of setting up home, taking on mortgages, having children, more responsible jobs, etc. Of course, the smoker's life can never become less stressful because it is the cigarette that actually causes stress. As the smoker's rate of nicotine intake rises, the more distressed he becomes and the greater the illusion of his dependency becomes.

In fact, it is an illusion that life becomes more stressful, and it's the smoking itself, or a similar crutch, that creates the illusion. This will be discussed in greater detail in chapter 28.

After the initial failures the smoker usually relies on the possibility that one day he will wake up and just not want to smoke any more. This hope is usually kindled by the stories that he has heard about other ex-smokers (e.g., 'I had a bout of flu and afterwards I didn't want to smoke any more').

Don't kid yourself. I have probed all of these rumours, and they are never quite as simple as they appear. Usually the smoker has already been preparing himself to stop and merely used the flu as a springboard. I spent thirty-odd years waiting to wake up one morning wanting never to smoke again. Whenever I had a bad cold I would look forward to its ending because it was interfering with my smoking.

More often in the case of people who stop 'just like that' they have suffered a shock. Perhaps a close relative has died from a cigarette-related disease or they have had a scare themselves. It is so much easier to say, 'I just decided to stop one day. That's the sort of chap I am.' Stop kidding yourself! It won't happen unless you make it happen.

Let's consider in greater detail why the Willpower Method is so difficult. For most of our lives we adopt the head-in-the-sand, 'I'll stop tomorrow' approach.

At odd times something will trigger off an attempt to stop. It may be concern about health, money, social stigma or we may have been going through a particularly heavy bout of choking and realize that we don't actually enjoy it.

Whatever the reason, we take our head out of the sand and start weighing up the pros and cons of smoking. We then find out what we have known all our lives: on a rational assessment the conclusion is, a dozen times over, **STOP SMOKING**.

If you were to sit down and give points out of ten to all the advantages of stopping and do a similar exercise with the advantages of smoking, the total point count for stopping would far outweigh the disadvantages.

However, although the smoker knows that he will be better off as a non-smoker, he does believe that he is making a sacrifice. Although it is an illusion, it is a *powerful* illusion. The smoker doesn't know why, but he believes that during the good times and the bad times of life the cigarette does appear to help.

Before he starts the attempt he has the brainwashing of our society, reinforced by the brainwashing of his own addiction. To these must be added the even more powerful brainwashing of 'how difficult it is to give up'.

He has heard stories of smokers who have stopped for many months and are still desperately craving a cigarette. There are all the disgruntled stoppers (people who stop and then spend the rest of their lives bemoaning the fact that they'd love a cigarette). He has heard of smokers who have stopped for many years, apparently leading happy lives, but have one cigarette and are suddenly hooked again. Probably he also knows several smokers in the advanced stages of the disease who are visibly destroying themselves and are clearly not enjoying cigarettes—yet they continue to smoke. Added to all this, he has probably already suffered one or more of these experiences himself.

So, instead of starting with the feeling 'Great! Have you heard the news? I haven't got to smoke any more,' he starts with a feeling of doom and gloom, as if he were trying to climb Everest, and he firmly believes that once the little monster has got his hooks into you, you are hooked for life. Many smokers even start the attempt by apologizing to their friends and relatives: 'Look, I am trying to give up smoking. I will probably be irritable during the next few weeks. Try to bear with me.' Most attempts are doomed before they start.

Let's assume that the smoker survives a few days without a cigarette. The congestion is rapidly disappearing from his lungs. He hasn't bought cigarettes and consequently has more money in his pocket. So the reasons why he decided to stop in the first place are rapidly disappearing from his thoughts. It is like seeing a bad road accident when you are driving. It slows you down for a while, but the next time you are late for an appointment you have forgotten all about it and your foot stamps on the throttle.

On the other side of the tug-of-war, that little monster inside your stomach hasn't had his fix. There is no physical pain; if you had the same feeling because of a cold, you wouldn't stop working or get depressed. You would laugh it off. All the smoker knows is that he wants a cigarette. Quite why it is so important to him he doesn't know. The little monster in the stomach then starts off the big monster in the mind, and now the person who a few hours or days earlier was listing all the reasons to stop is desperately searching for any excuse to start again. Now he is saying things like:

1. Life is too short. The bomb could go off. I could step under a bus tomorrow. I have left it too late. They tell you everything gives you cancer these days.

2. I have picked the wrong time. I should have waited until after Christmas/after my holidays/after this stressful event in my life.

3. I cannot concentrate. I am getting irritable and bad tempered. I cannot do my job properly. My family and friends won't love me. Let's face it, for everybody's sake I have got to start smoking again. I am a confirmed smoker and there is no way I will ever be happy again without a cigarette. (This one kept me smoking for thirty-three years.)

At this stage the smoker usually gives in. He lights a cigarette and the schizophrenia increases. On the one hand there is the tremendous relief of ending the craving, when the little monster finally gets his fix; on the other hand, if he has survived a long time, the cigarette tastes awful and the smoker cannot understand why he is smoking it. This is why the smoker thinks he lacks willpower. In fact, it is not lack of will-power; all he has done is to change his mind and make a perfectly rational decision in the light of the latest information. What's the point of being healthy if you are miserable? What is the point of being rich if you are miserable? Absolutely none. Far better to have a shorter enjoyable life than a lengthy miserable life.

Fortunately, that is not true—just the reverse. Life as a non-smoker is infinitely more enjoyable, but it was this delusion that kept me smoking for thirty-three years, and I must confess, if that were the true situation, I would still be smoking (correction—I wouldn't be here).

The misery that the smoker is suffering has nothing to do with with-drawal pangs. True, they trigger the misery off, but the actual agony is in the mind and it is caused by doubt and uncertainty. Because the smoker starts by feeling he is making a sacrifice, he begins to feel de-prived—this is a form of stress. One of the times when his brain tells him, 'Have a cigarette,' is a time of stress. Therefore as soon as he stops, he wants a cigarette. But now he can't have one because he has stopped smoking. This makes him more depressed, which sets the trigger off again.

Another thing that makes it so difficult is the waiting for something to happen. If your object is to pass a driving test, as soon as you have passed the test it is certain you have achieved your object. Under the Willpower Method you say, 'If I can go long enough without a cigarette, the urge to smoke will eventually go.'

How do you know when you have achieved it? The answer is that you never do because you are waiting for something to happen and noth-ing else is going to happen. You stopped when you smoked that last cigarette, and what you are really doing now is waiting to see how long it will be before you give in.

As I said above, the agony that the smoker undergoes is mental, caused by the uncertainty. Although there is no physical pain, it still has a powerful effect. The smoker is miserable and feeling insecure. Far from forgetting about smoking, his mind becomes obsessed with it.

There can be days or even weeks of black depression. His mind is obsessed with doubts and fears.

'How long will the craving last?'

'Will I ever be happy again?'

'Will I ever want to get up in the morning?'

'Will I ever enjoy a meal again?'

'How will I ever cope with stress in future?'

'Will I ever enjoy a social function again?'

The smoker is waiting for things to improve, but of course while he is still moping, the cigarette is becoming more precious.

In fact, something does happen, but the smoker isn't conscious of it. If he can survive three weeks without inhaling any nicotine at all, the physical craving for nicotine disappears. However, as stated before, the pangs of withdrawal from nicotine are so mild that the smoker isn't aware of them. But after about three weeks many smokers sense that they have 'kicked it'. They then light a cigarette to prove it, and it does just that. It tastes awful, but the ex-smoker has now supplied nicotine to the body, and as soon as he extinguishes that cigarette the nicotine starts to leave the body. There is now a little voice at the back of his mind saying, 'You want another one.' In fact, he had kicked it but now he has hooked himself again.

The smoker will not usually light another cigarette immediately. He thinks, 'I don't want to get hooked again.' So he allows a safe period to pass. It might be hours, days, even weeks. The ex-smoker can now say, 'Well, I didn't get hooked, so I can safely have another.' He has fallen into the same trap as he did in the first place and is already on the slippery slope.

Smokers who succeed under the Willpower Method tend to find it long and difficult because the main problem is the brainwashing, and long after the physical addiction has died the smoker is still moping about cigarettes. Eventually, if he can survive long enough, it begins to dawn on him that he is not going to give in. He stops moping and accepts that life goes on and is enjoyable without the cigarette.

Many smokers are succeeding with this method, but it is difficult and arduous, and there are many more failures than successes. Even those who do succeed go through the rest of their lives in a vulnerable state. They are left with a certain amount of the brainwashing and believe that during good and bad times the cigarette can give you a boost. (Most non-smokers also suffer from that illusion. They are subjected to the brain-washing also but either find they cannot learn to 'enjoy' smoking or don't want the bad side, thank you very much.) This explains why many smok-ers who have stopped for long periods start smoking again.

Many ex-smokers will have the occasional cigar or cigarette either as a 'special treat' or to convince themselves how awful they are. It does exactly that, but as soon as they put it out the nicotine starts to leave and a little voice at the back of their mind is saying, 'You want another one.' If they light another one, it still tastes awful and they say, 'Marvellous! While I am not enjoying them I won't get hooked. After Christmas/ the holiday/this trauma, I will stop.'

Too late. They are already hooked. The trap that they fell into in the first place has claimed its victim again.

As I keep saying, enjoyment doesn't come into it. It never did! If we smoked because we enjoyed it, nobody would ever smoke more than one cigarette. We assume we enjoy them only because we cannot believe we would be so stupid as to smoke if we didn't enjoy them. This is why so much of our smoking is subconscious. If, while smoking every cigarette, you were aware of the foul fumes going into your lungs and you had to say to yourself, 'This is going to cost £50,000 in my lifetime, and this cigarette might just be the one to trigger off cancer in my lungs,' even the illusion of enjoyment would go. When we try to block our minds to the bad side, we feel stupid. If we had to face up to it, that would be intolerable! If you watch smokers, particularly at social functions, you will see that they are happy only when they are not aware that they are smoking. Once they become aware of it, they tend to be uncomfortable and apologetic. We smoke to feed that little monster . . . and once you have purged the little monster from your body and the big monster from your brain, you will have neither need nor desire to smoke.

Beware of Cutting Down

any smokers resort to cutting down either as a stepping-stone towards stopping or as an attempt to control the little monster, and many doctors and advisers recommend cutting down as an aid.

Obviously, the less you smoke the better off you are, but, as a stepping-stone to stopping, cutting down is fatal. It is our attempts to cut down that keep us trapped all our lives.

Usually cutting down follows failed attempts to stop. After a few hours or days of abstinence the smoker says to himself something like, 'I cannot face the thought of being without a cigarette, so from now on I will just smoke the special ones or I will cut down to ten a day. If I can get in the habit of smoking ten a day, I can either hold it there or cut down further.'

Certain terrible things now happen.

1. He has the worst of all worlds. He is still addicted to nicotine and is keeping the monster alive not only in his body but also in his mind.

2. He is now wishing his life away waiting for the next cigarette.

3. Prior to cutting down, whenever he wanted a cigarette he lit one up and at least partially relieved his withdrawal pangs. Now, in addition to the normal stresses and strains of life, he is actually causing himself to suffer the withdrawal pangs from nicotine most of his life. So he is causing himself to be miserable and bad tempered.

4. While he was indulging himself, he didn't enjoy most of the cigarettes and he didn't realize he was smoking them. It was automatic. The only cigarettes that he imagined he enjoyed were after a period

of abstinence (e.g., the first in the morning, the one after a meal, etc.).

Now that he waits an extra hour for each cigarette, he 'enjoys' every one. The longer he waits, the more enjoyable each cigarette appears to become because the 'enjoyment' in a cigarette isn't the cigarette itself; it's the ending of the agitation caused by the craving, whether it be the slight physical craving for nicotine or the mental moping. The longer you suffer, the more 'enjoyable' each cigarette becomes.

The main difficulty of stopping smoking is not the chemical addiction. That's easy. Smokers will go all night without a cigarette; the craving doesn't even wake them up. Many smokers will actually leave the bedroom before they light up. Many will actually have breakfast. Some will even wait until they arrive at work.

They will go ten hours without a cigarette and it doesn't bother them. If they went ten hours during the day without one, they would be tearing their hair out.

Many smokers will buy a new car and abstain from smoking in it. Smokers will visit supermarkets, theatres, doctors, hospitals, dentists and so on without undue inconvenience. Many smokers will abstain in the company of non-smokers. Even on the Tube trains there have been no riots. Smokers are almost pleased for someone to say they cannot smoke. In fact, smokers get a secret pleasure out of going long periods without a cigarette. It gives them the hope that maybe one day they will never want another one.

The real problem when stopping smoking is the brainwashing, the illusion that the cigarette is some sort of prop or reward and life will never be quite the same without it. Far from turning you off smoking, all cutting down does is to leave you feeling insecure and miserable and to convince you that the most precious thing on this earth is the next cigarette, that there is no way that you will ever be happy again without one.

There is nothing more pathetic than the smoker who is trying to cut down. He suffers from the delusion that the less he smokes, the less he will want to smoke. In fact, the reverse is true. The less he smokes, the longer he suffers the withdrawal pangs; the more he enjoys the cigarette, the more distasteful they become. But that won't stop him smoking. Taste never, ever came into it. If smokers smoked because they enjoyed the taste, nobody would ever smoke more than one cigarette. You find that difficult to believe? OK, let's talk it out. Which is the worst-tasting ciga rette? That's right, the first in the morning, the one that in winter sets us coughing and spluttering. Which is one of the most precious cigarettes for most smokers? That's right, the first cigarette in the morning! Now do you really believe you are smoking it to enjoy the taste and smell, or do you think a more rational explanation is that you are relieving nine hours' withdrawal pangs?

It is essential that we remove all the illusions about smoking before you extinguish that final cigarette. Unless you've removed the illusion that you enjoy the taste of certain cigarettes before you extinguish the final one, there is no way you can prove it afterwards without getting hooked again. So, unless you are already smoking one, light one up now. Inhale six deep lungfuls of that glorious tobacco and ask yourself what is so glorious about the taste. Perhaps you believe that it is only certain cigarettes that taste good, like the one after a meal. If so, why do you bother to smoke the others? Because you got into the habit of doing it? Now why would anyone get into the habit of smoking cigarettes that he or she finds distasteful? And why should the same cigarette out of the same packet taste different after a meal than it tastes first thing in the morning? Food doesn't taste different after a cigarette, so why should a cigarette taste different after food?

Don't just rely on me, check it out, smoke a cigarette consciously after a meal to prove that it tastes no different. The reason smokers believe that cigarettes taste better after a meal or at social occasions with alcohol, is that those are the times when both non-smokers and smokers are really happy, but a nicotine addict can never be really happy if that little nicotine monster remains unsatisfied. It's not so much that smokers enjoy the taste of tobacco after a meal; after all, we don't eat tobacco, where does taste come into it? It's just that they are miserable if they aren't allowed to relieve their withdrawal symptoms at those times. So the difference between smoking and not smoking is the difference between being happy and miserable. That's why the cigarette appears to taste better. Whereas smokers who light up first thing in the morning are miserable whether they are smoking or not.

Cutting down not only doesn't work but it is the worst form of torture. It doesn't work because initially the smoker hopes that by getting into the habit of smoking less and less, he will reduce his desire to smoke a cigarette. It is not a habit. It is an addiction, and the nature of any addiction is to want more and more, not less and less. Therefore in order to cut down, the smoker has to exercise willpower and discipline for the rest of his life.

The main problem of stopping smoking is not the chemical addiction to nicotine. That's easy to cope with. It is the mistaken belief that the cigarette gives you some pleasure. This mistaken belief is brought about initially by the brainwashing we receive before we start smoking, which is then reinforced by the actual addiction. All cutting down does is reinforce the fallacy further to the extent that smoking dominates the smoker's life completely and convinces him that the most precious thing on this earth is the next cigarette.

As I have already said, cutting down never works anyway because you have to exercise willpower and discipline for the rest of your life. If you had not enough willpower to stop, then you certainly have not got enough to cut down. Stopping is far easier and less painful.

I have heard of literally thousands of cases in which cutting down has failed. The handful of successes I have known have been achieved after a relatively short period of cutting down, followed by the 'cold turkey'. The smokers really stopped in spite of cutting down, not because of it. All it did was prolong the agony. A failed attempt to cut down leaves the smoker a nervous wreck, even more convinced that he is hooked for life. This is usually enough to keep him puffing away for another five years before the next attempt.

However, cutting down helps to illustrate the whole futility of smoking because it clearly illustrates that a cigarette is enjoyable only after a period of abstinence. You have to bang your head against a brick wall (i.e., suffer withdrawal pangs) to make it nice when you stop.

So the choice is:

1. Cut down for life. This will be self-imposed torture, and you will not be able to do it anyway.

2. Increasingly choke yourself for life. What is the point?

3. Be nice to yourself. Stop doing it.

The other important point that cutting down demonstrates is that there is no such thing as the odd or occasional cigarette. Smoking is a chain reaction that will last the rest of your life unless you make a positive effort to break it.

REMEMBER: CUTTING DOWN WILL DRAG YOU DOWN.

Just One Cigarette

Just one cigarette' is a myth you must get out of your mind.

It is just one cigarette that gets us started in the first place.

It is just one cigarette to tide us over a difficult patch or on a special occasion that defeats most of our attempts to stop.

It is just one cigarette that, when smokers have succeeded in breaking the addiction, sends them back into the trap. Sometimes it is just to confirm that they do not need them any more, and that one cigarette does just that. It tastes horrible and convinces the smoker he will never become hooked again, but he already is.

It is the thought of that one special cigarette that often prevents smokers from stopping. The first one in the morning or the one after a meal.

Get it firmly in your mind there is no such thing as just one cigarette. It is a chain reaction that will last the rest of your life unless you break it.

It is the myth about the odd, special cigarette that keeps smokers moping about it when they stop. Get into the habit of never seeing the odd cigarette or packet—it is a fantasy. Whenever you think about smoking, see a whole filthy lifetime of spending a small fortune just for the privilege of destroying yourself mentally and physically, a lifetime of slavery, a lifetime of bad breath.

It is a pity that there isn't something like a cigarette that, during good and bad times, we can use for an occasional boost or pleasure. But get it clearly into your mind: the cigarette isn't it. You are stuck with either a lifetime of misery or none at all. You wouldn't dream of taking cyanide because you liked the taste of almonds, so stop punishing yourself with the thought of the occasional cigarette or cigar.

Ask a smoker, 'If you had the opportunity to go back to the time before you became hooked, would you have become a smoker?' The answer is inevitably 'You have got to be joking', yet every smoker has that choice every day of his life. Why doesn't he opt for it? The answer is fear. The fear that he cannot stop or that life won't be the same without it.

Stop kidding yourself. You can do it. Anybody can. It's ridiculously easy.

In order to make it easy to stop smoking there are certain fundamentals to get clear in your mind. We have already dealt with three of them up to now:

1. There is nothing to give up. There are only marvellous positive gains to achieve.

2. Never see the odd cigarette. It doesn't exist. There is only a lifetime of filth and disease.

3. There is nothing different about you. Any smoker can find it easy to stop.

Many smokers believe that they are confirmed smokers or have addictive personalities. I promise you there is no such thing. No one needs to smoke before he or she becomes hooked on the drug. It is the drug that hooks you and not the nature of your character or personality. That is the effect of these drugs, they make you believe that you have an addictive personality. However, it is essential that you remove this belief, because if you believe that you are dependent on nicotine, you will be, even after the little nicotine monster inside your body is dead. It is essential to remove all of the brainwashing.

Casual Smokers, Teenagers, Non-smokers

Heavy smokers tend to envy casual smokers. We've all met these characters: 'Oh, I can go all week without a cigarette, it really doesn't bother me.' We think: 'I wish I were like that.' I know this is hard to believe, but no smoker enjoys being a smoker. Never forget:

- No smoker ever decided to become a smoker casual or otherwise, therefore:
- All smokers feel stupid, therefore:
- All smokers have to lie to themselves and other people in a vain attempt to justify their stupidity.

I used to be a golf fanatic. But I would brag about how often I played and I wanted to play more. Why do smokers brag about how little they smoke? If that's the true criterion, then surely the true accolade is not to smoke at all.

If I said to you, 'Do you know, I can go all week without carrots and it doesn't bother me in the slightest.' You would think I was some sort of nutcase. If I enjoy carrots, why would I want go all week without them? If I didn't enjoy them, why would I make such a statement? So when a smoker makes a statement like 'I can go all week without a cigarette, it really doesn't bother me,' he's trying to convince both himself and you that he has no problem. But there would be no need to make the statement if he had no problem. What he is really saying is: 'I managed to survive a whole week without smoking.' Like every smoker, he was probably hoping that after this he could survive the rest of his life. But he could only survive a week, and can you imagine how precious that cigarette must have been, having felt deprived for a whole week?

This is why casual smokers are effectively more hooked than heavy smokers. Not only is the illusion of pleasure greater, but they have less incentive to quit because they spend less money and are less vulnerable to the health risks.

Remember, the only pleasure smokers get is to relieve withdrawal pangs and as I have already explained, even that pleasure is an illusion. Imagine the little nicotine monster inside your body as a permanent itch so imperceptible that most of the time we aren't even aware of it.

Now if you have a permanent itch, the natural tendency is to scratch it. As our bodies become more and more immune to nicotine the natural tendency is to chain-smoke.

There are three main factors that prevent smokers from chain-smoking:

1. **MONEY.** Most cannot afford to.

2. **HEALTH.** In order to relieve our withdrawal pangs, we have to take a poison. Capacity to cope with that poison varies with each individual and at different times and situations in his or her life. This acts as an automatic restraint.

3. **DISCIPLINE.** This is imposed by society, or the smoker's job, or friends and relatives, or by the smoker himself as a result of the natural tug-of-war that goes on in every smoker's mind.

I used to think of my chain-smoking as a weakness. I couldn't understand why my friends could limit their intake to ten or twenty a day. I knew I was a very strong-willed person. It never occurred to me that most smokers are incapable of chain-smoking; you need very strong lungs in order to do it. Some of these five-a-day smokers that heavy smokers tend to envy smoke five a day because physically their constitution cannot smoke more, or because they cannot afford to smoke more, or because their job, or society, or their own hatred of being hooked won't allow them to smoke more.

It may be of advantage at this stage to provide a few definitions.

THE NON-SMOKER. Someone who has never fallen for the trap but should not be complacent. He is a non-smoker only by the grace of God. All smokers were convinced that they would never become hooked, and some non-smokers keep trying an occasional cigarette.

THE CASUAL SMOKER. There are two basic classifications of casual smokers:

1. The smoker who has fallen for the trap but doesn't realize it. Do not envy such smokers. They are merely sampling the nectar at

the mouth of the pitcher plant and in all probability will soon be heavy smokers. Remember, just as all alcoholics started off as casual drinkers, so all smokers started off as casual smokers.

2. The smoker who was previously a heavy smoker and thinks he cannot stop. These smokers are the most pathetic of all. They fall into various categories, each of which needs separate comment.

THE FIVE-A-DAY SMOKER. If he enjoys a cigarette, why does he smoke only five a day? If he can take it or leave it, why does he bother to smoke at all? Remember, the 'habit' is really banging your head against the brick wall to make it relaxing when you stop. The five-a-day smoker is relieving his withdrawal pangs for less than one hour each day. The rest of the day, although he doesn't realize it, he is banging his head against the wall and does so for most of his life. He is smoking only five a day because either he cannot afford to smoke more or he is worried about the health risk. It is easy to convince the heavy smoker that he doesn't enjoy it, but you try convincing a casual smoker. Anybody who has gone through an attempt to cut down will know it is the worst torture of all and almost guaranteed to keep you hooked for the rest of your life.

THE MORNING- OR EVENING-ONLY SMOKER. He punishes himself by suffering withdrawal pangs for half the day in order to relieve them the other half. Again, ask him why, if he enjoys a cigarette, he doesn't smoke the whole day or, if he doesn't enjoy a cigarette, he bothers at all.

THE SIX-MONTHS-ON, SIX-MONTHS-OFF SMOKER. (Or 'I can stop whenever I want to. I have done it thousands of times.') If he enjoys smoking, why does he stop for six months? If he does not enjoy it, why does he start again? The truth is he is still hooked. Although he gets rid of the physical addiction, he is left with the main problem—the brainwashing. He hopes each time that he will stop for good and soon falls for the trap again. Many smokers envy these stoppers and starters. They think, 'How lucky to be able to control it like that, to smoke when you want to and stop when you want to.' What they always overlook is that these stoppers and starters aren't controlling it. When they are smokers, they wish they weren't. They go through the hassle of stopping, then begin to feel deprived and fall for the trap again, then wish they hadn't. They get the worst of all worlds. When they are smokers they wish they weren't; when they are non-smokers they wish they could smoke. If you think about it, this is true all our smoking lives. When we are allowed to smoke we either take it for granted or wish we didn't. It's only when we can't have cigarettes that they appear so precious. This is the awful dilemma of smokers. They can never win because they are moping for a myth, an illusion. There is one way they can win and that is to stop smoking *and* stop moping!

THE 'I ONLY SMOKE ON SPECIAL OCCASIONS' SMOKER. Yes, we all do to start with, but isn't it amazing how the number of occasions seem rapidly to increase and before we know it we seem to be smoking on all occasions?

THE 'I HAVE STOPPED BUT I HAVE AN OCCASIONAL CIGAR/CIGARETTE' SMOKER. In a way such smokers are the most pathetic of all. Either they go through their lives believing they are being deprived or, more often, the occasional cigar becomes two. They remain on the slippery slope and it goes only one way—**DOWNWARDS**. Sooner or later they are back to being heavy smokers. They have fallen again for the very trap that they fell into in the first place.

There are two other categories of casual smoker. The first is the type who smokes just the occasional cigarette or cigar at social occasions. These people are really non-smokers. They don't enjoy smoking. It's just that they feel they are missing out. They want to be part of the action. We all start off like this. Next time the cigars go round, watch how, after a while, the smokers stop lighting those cigars. Even heavy cigarette smokers can't wait to finish them. They would much rather be smoking their own brand. The more expensive and the larger the cigar, the more frustrating it is—the damn thing seems to last all night.

The second category is very rare indeed. In fact, of all the thousands who have sought my assistance, I can think of only about a dozen examples. The type can best be described by outlining a recent case.

A woman phoned me, seeking a private session. She is a solicitor, had been smoking for about twelve years and had never smoked more or less than two cigarettes a day in her smoking life. She was, incidentally, a very strong-willed lady. I explained that the success rate in group sessions was just as high as in individual sessions, and in any event I was able to give individual therapy only if the face were so famous that it would disrupt the group. She began to cry, and I was not able to resist the tears.

The session was expensive; indeed, most smokers would wonder why she wanted to stop in the first place. They would gladly pay what I charged that lady to be able to smoke only two cigarettes a day. They make the mistake of assuming that casual smokers are happier and more in control. In control they may be, but happy they are not. In this case, both the woman's parents had died from lung cancer before she became hooked. Like me, she had a great fear of smoking before she smoked the first cigarette. Like me, she eventually fell victim to the massive pressures and tried that first cigarette. Like me, she can remember the foul taste. Unlike me, who capitulated and became a chain-smoker very quickly, she resisted the slide.

All you ever enjoy in a cigarette is the ending of the craving for it, whether it be the almost imperceptible physical craving for nicotine or the mental torture caused by not being allowed to scratch the itch. Cigarettes themselves are filth and poison. This is why you only suffer the illusion of enjoying them after a period of abstinence. Just like a hunger or thirst, the longer you suffer it, the greater the pleasure when you finally relieve it. Smokers make the mistake of believing smoking is just a habit. They think, 'If I can only keep it down to a certain level or smoke only on special occasions, my brain and body will accept it. I can then keep my smoking at that level or cut down further should I wish to.' Get it clear in your mind: the 'habit' doesn't exist. Smoking is drug addiction. The natural tendency is to relieve withdrawal pangs, not to endure them. Even to hold it at the level you are already at, you would have to exercise willpower and discipline for the rest of your life because, as your body becomes immune to the drug, it wants more and more, not less and less. As the drug begins to destroy you physically and mentally, as it gradually breaks down your nervous system, your courage and confidence, so you are increasingly unable to resist reducing the interval between each cigarette. That is why, in the early days, we can take it or leave it. If we get a cold, we just stop. It also explains why someone like me, who never even suffered the illusion of enjoying them, had to go on chain-smoking even though every cigarette had become physical torture.

Don't envy that woman. When you smoke only one cigarette every twelve hours it appears to be the most precious thing on earth. For twelve years that poor woman had been at the centre of a tug-of-war. She had been unable to stop smoking, yet was frightened to increase the intake in case she got lung cancer like her parents. But for twenty-three hours and ten minutes of every one of those days she had to fight the temptation. It took tremendous willpower to do what she did, and, as I have said, such cases are rare. But it reduced her to tears in the end. Just look at it logically: either there is a genuine crutch or pleasure in smoking or there isn't. If there is, who wants to wait an hour, or a day, or a week? Why should you be denied the crutch or pleasure in the meantime? If there is no genuine crutch or pleasure, why bother to smoke at all?

I remember another case, that of a five-a-day man. He started the telephone conversation in a croaky voice: 'Mr Carr, I just want to stop smoking before I die.' This is how that man described his life.

'I am sixty-one years old. I have got cancer of the throat through smoking. Now I can only physically cope with five roll-ups a day.

'I used to sleep soundly through the night. Now I wake up every hour of the night and all I can think about is cigarettes. Even when I am sleeping, I dream about smoking.

'I cannot smoke my first cigarette until 10 o'clock. I get up at 5 o'clock and make endless cups of tea. My wife gets up at about 8 o'clock and, because I am so bad-tempered, she will not have me in the house. I go down to the greenhouse and try to putter about, but my mind is obsessed with smoking. At 9 o'clock I begin to roll my first cigarette and I do so until it is perfect. It is not that I need it to be perfect, but it gives me something to do. I then wait for 10 o'clock. When it arrives my hands are shaking uncontrollably. I do not light the cigarette then. If I do, I have to wait three hours for the next one. Eventually I light the cigarette, take one puff and extinguish it immediately. By continuing this process I can make the cigarette last one hour. I smoke it down to about a quarter of an inch and then wait for the next one.'

In addition to his other troubles, this poor man had burns all over his lips caused by smoking the cigarette too low. You probably have visions of a pathetic imbecile. Not so. This man was over six feet tall and an ex-sergeant in the Marines. He was a former athlete and didn't want to become a smoker. However, in World War II, society believed that cigarettes gave courage, and servicemen were issued free rations of them. This man was virtually ordered to become a smoker. He has spent the rest of his life paying through the nose, subsidizing other people's taxes, and it has ruined him physically and mentally. If he were an animal, our society would have put him out of his misery, yet we still allow mentally and physically healthy young teenagers to become hooked.

You may think the above case is exaggerated. It is extreme but not unique. There are literally thousands of similar stories. That man poured his heart out to me, but you can be sure that many of his friends and acquaintances envied him for being a five-a-day man. If you think this couldn't happen to you, **STOP KIDDING YOURSELF**.

IT IS ALREADY HAPPENING.

In any event smokers are notorious liars, even to themselves. They have to be. Most casual smokers smoke far more cigarettes, and on far more occasions, than they will admit to. I have had many conversations with so-called five-a-day smokers during which they have smoked more than five cigarettes in my presence. Observe casual smokers at social events such as weddings and parties. They will be chain-smoking like the best of them.

You do not need to envy casual smokers. You do not need to smoke. Life is infinitely sweeter without cigarettes.

Teenagers are generally more difficult to cure, not because they find it difficult to stop but because either they do not believe they are hooked or they are at the primary stage of the disease and suffer from the delusion that they will automatically have stopped before the secondary stage.

I would like particularly to warn parents of children who loathe smoking not to have a false sense of security. All children loathe the smell and taste of tobacco until they become hooked. You did too at one time. Also do not be fooled by government scare campaigns. The trap is the same as it always was. Children know that cigarettes kill, but they also know that one cigarette will not do it. At some stage they may be influenced by a girlfriend or boyfriend, schoolfriend or work colleague. You may think that all they need is to try one, which will taste horrible and convince them they could never become hooked.

I find society's failure to prevent our children from becoming addicted to nicotine and other drugs to be the most disturbing of all of the many disturbing facets of drug addiction. I have given much thought to this problem and have written a book designed specifically to address the problem of how to prevent your children from becoming hooked and how to help them escape if they have already done so. It is a fact that the vast majority of youngsters that become dependent on heavier drugs are introduced to the concept of chemical dependency by first falling for the nicotine trap. If you can help them avoid the nicotine trap you will greatly reduce the risk of them becoming dependent on heavier drugs. I beg you not to be complacent in this matter. It is necessary to protect youngsters at the earliest possible age, and if you have a child, I strongly urge you to read that book. Even if you suspect your child might already be hooked on a drug, the book will provide excellent guidance to assist your child to escape.

The Secret Smoker

The secret smoker should be grouped with casual smokers, but the effects of secret smoking are so insidious that it merits a separate chapter. It can lead to the breakdown of personal relationships. In my case it nearly caused a divorce.

I was three weeks into one of my failed attempts to stop. The attempt had been triggered off by my wife's worry about my constant wheezing and coughing. I had told her I was not worried about my health. She said, 'I know you are not, but how would you feel if you had to watch someone you love systematically destroying themselves?' It was an argument that I found irresistible, hence the attempt to stop. The attempt ended after three weeks, following a heated argument with an old friend. It did not register until years afterwards that my devious mind had deliberately triggered off the argument. I felt justly aggrieved at the time, but I do not believe that it was coincidence, as I had never argued with this particular friend before, nor have I since. It was clearly the little monster at work. Anyway, I had my excuse. I desperately needed a cigarette and started smoking again.

I could not bear to think of the disappointment this would cause my wife, so I did not tell her. I just smoked when alone. Then gradually I smoked in the company of friends until it got to the point where everybody knew I was smoking except my wife. I remember being quite pleased at the time. I thought, 'Well, at least it is cutting my consumption down.' Eventually she accused me of continuing to smoke. I had not realized it, but she described the times I had caused an argument and stormed out of the house. At other times I had taken two hours to purchase some minor item, and on occasions when I would normally have invited her to accompany me, I had made feeble excuses to go alone.

As the antisocial split between smokers and non-smokers widens, there are literally thousands of cases where the company of friends or relatives is restricted or avoided because of this awful weed. The worst thing about secret smoking is that it supports the fallacy in the smoker's mind that he is being deprived. At the same time, it causes a major loss of self-respect; an otherwise honest person may force himself to deceive his family and friends.

It has probably happened or is still happening to you in some form.

It happened to me several times. Have you ever watched the TV detective series *Columbo*? The theme of each episode is similar. The villain, usually a wealthy and respected businessman, has committed what he is convinced is the perfect murder, and his confidence in his crime remaining undetected receives a boost when he discovers that the rather shabby and unimpressive-looking Columbo is in charge of the case.

Columbo has this frustrating practice of closing the door after finishing his interrogation, having assured the suspect that he is in the clear, and before the satisfied look has disappeared from the murderer's face, Columbo reappears with: 'Just one small point, sir, which I'm sure you can explain . . .' The suspect stammers, and from that point on we know and he knows that Columbo will gradually wear him down.

No matter how heinous the crime, from that point on my sympathies were with the murderer. It was almost as if I were the criminal and that's exactly how those bouts of secret smoking made me feel. The hours of not being allowed to smoke, then sneaking into the garage for a quick smoke, the ten minutes of shivering in the cold, wondering where the pleasure was. The fear of being caught red-handed. Would she discover where I'd hidden the cigarettes, lighter and cigarette butts? The relief of returning to the house undiscovered, immediately followed by the fear that she would smell the nicotine on my breath and clothes. As I took longer and more frequent risks, the certain knowledge that sooner or later I was bound to be discovered. The final humiliation and shame when that certainty became a fact, followed by the immediate return to chain-smoking.

OH, THE JOYS OF BEING A SMOKER!

27

A Social Habit?

The main reason why there are over 15 million ex-smokers in Britain since the 1960s is the social revolution that is taking place.

Yes, I know: health followed by money are the main reasons why we should want to stop, but then they always have been. We do not actually need cancer scares to tell us that cigarettes shatter our lives. These bodies of ours are the most sophisticated objects on the planet, and any smoker knows instantly, from the first puff, that cigarettes are poisonous.

The only reason why we ever get involved with smoking is the social pressure of our friends. The only valid 'plus' smoking ever had was that it was at one time considered a perfectly acceptable social habit.

Today it is generally considered, even by smokers themselves, to be an antisocial habit.

In the old days the strong man smoked. If you didn't smoke, you were considered a sissy, and we all worked very hard to become hooked. In every pub or club bar the majority of men would be proudly inhaling and exhaling tobacco smoke. There would be the permanent fall-out cloud, and all the ceilings that were not regularly decorated soon became yellow or brown.

Today the position is completely reversed. Today's strong man doesn't need to smoke. Today's strong man is not dependent on a drug.

With the social revolution all smokers nowadays are giving serious thought to stopping, and today's smokers are considered to be generally weak people.

The most significant trend that I have noticed since writing the first edition of this book in 1985 is the increasing emphasis on the antisocial aspect of smoking. The days when the cigarette was the proud badge of the sophisticated woman or the tough guy have gone forever. Everyone now knows that the only reason why people continue to smoke is that they have failed to stop or are too frightened to try. Every day as the smoker is pilloried by office bans, extended bans in public places and attacks from holier-than-thou ex-smokers, so the mannerisms of smokers are changing. I've recently seen situations that I remember as a boy but I haven't seen for years—like smokers flicking ash into their hands or pockets because they are too embarrassed to ask for an ashtray.

I was in a restaurant some years ago. It was midnight. Everyone had stopped eating. At a time when the cigarettes and cigars are normally rife, not one person was smoking. I conceitedly thought, 'Ah! I'm beginning to make an impression.' I said to the waiter, 'Is this now a non-smoking restaurant?' The reply was negative. I thought, 'That's strange. I know that a lot of people are stopping, but there must be one smoker here.' Eventually someone lit up in a corner, and the result was like a series of beacons going through the restaurant. All those other smokers had been sitting there thinking, 'Surely I can't be the only smoker here.'

Many smokers won't smoke between courses now because they feel so self-conscious. Many not only apologize to people on the same table but also look around to see if they'll get flak from elsewhere. As every day more and more smokers leave the sinking ship, so those left on it become terrified they'll be the last.

DON'T LET IT BE YOU!

28

Timing

Apart from the obvious point that as it is doing you no good, now is the right time to stop, I believe timing is important. Our society treats smoking flippantly as a slightly distasteful habit that can injure your health. It is not. It is drug addiction, a disease and the No. 1 killer in society. The worst thing that happens in most smokers' lives is getting hooked on that awful weed. If they stay hooked, horrendous things happen. Timing is important to give yourself the right to a proper cure.

First of all, identify the times or occasions when smoking appears to be important to you. If you are a businessman and smoke for the illusion of relief of stress, pick a relatively slack period; a good idea is to choose your annual holiday. If you smoke mainly during boring or relaxing periods, do the opposite. In any event take the matter seriously and make the attempt the most important thing in your life.

Look ahead for a period of about three weeks and try to anticipate any event that might lead to failure. Occasions like a wedding or Christmas need not deter you, providing you anticipate them in advance and do not feel you will be deprived. Do not attempt to cut down in the meantime, as this will only create the illusion that the cigarette is enjoyable. In fact, it helps to force as many of the filthy things down your throat as possible. While you are smoking that last cigarette, be conscious of the bad smell and taste and think how marvellous it will be when you allow yourself to stop doing it.

WHATEVER YOU DO, DON'T FALL INTO THE TRAP OF JUST SAYING, 'NOT NOW. LATER,' AND PUTTING IT OUT OF YOUR MIND. WORK OUT YOUR TIMETABLE NOW AND LOOK FORWARD TO IT. Remember you aren't giving anything up. On the contrary: you are about to receive marvellous positive gains.

For years I've been saying I know more about the mysteries of smoking than anyone on this planet. The problem is this: although every smoker smokes purely to relieve the chemical craving for nicotine, it is not the nicotine addiction itself that hooks the smoker but the brainwashing that results from that addiction. An intelligent person will fall for a confidence trick. But only a fool will go on falling for it once he realizes that it's a confidence trick. Fortunately, most smokers aren't fools; they only think they are. Each individual smoker has his own private brainwashing. That is why there appears to be such a wide range of different types of smoker, which only serves to compound the mysteries.

With the benefit of the years of feedback that I have had since the original publication of this book, and bearing in mind that each day I learn something new about smoking, I was agreeably surprised to realize that the philosophy I propounded in the first edition was still sound. The accumulated knowledge that I have acquired over the years is how to communicate that knowledge to each individual smoker. The fact that I know every smoker can not only find it easy to stop but can actually enjoy the process is not only pointless but exceedingly frustrating unless I can make the smoker realize it.

Many people have said to me, 'You say, "Continue to smoke until you have finished the book." This tends to make the smoker take ages to read the book or just not finish it, period. Therefore you should change that instruction.' This sounds logical, but I know that if the instruction were 'Stop Immediately', some smokers wouldn't even start reading the book.

I had a smoker consult me in the early days. He said, 'I really resent having to seek your help. I know I'm strong-willed. In every other area of my life I'm in control. Why is it that all these other smokers are stopping by using their own willpower, yet I have to come to you?' He continued, 'I think I could do it on my own, if I could smoke while I was doing it.'

This may sound like a contradiction, but I know what the man meant. We think of stopping smoking as something that is very difficult to do. What do we need when we have something difficult to do? We need our little friend. So stopping smoking appears to be a double blow. Not only do we have a difficult task to perform, which is hard enough, but the crutch on which we normally rely on such occasions is no longer available.

It didn't occur to me until long after the man had left that my instruction to keep smoking is the real beauty of my method. You can continue to smoke while you go through the process of stopping. You get rid of all your doubts and fears first, and when you extinguish that final cigarette you are already a non-smoker and enjoying being one.

The only chapter that has caused me to question my original advice seriously is this chapter on the matter of the right timing. Above I advise that if your special cigarette occasions are stress situations at the office, then pick a holiday to make an attempt to give up, and vice versa. In fact, that isn't the easiest way to do it. The easiest way is to pick what you consider to be the most *difficult* time to do it, whether it be stress, social, concentration or boredom. Once you've proved that you can cope with, and enjoy, life in the worst possible situation, every other situation becomes easy. But if I gave that as a definite instruction, would you even make the attempt to stop?

Let me use an analogy. My wife and I intend to swim together. We arrive at the pool at the same time, but we rarely swim together. The reason is that she immerses one toe, and half an hour later she's actually swimming. I cannot stand that slow torture. I know in advance that at some stage, no matter how cold the water is, eventually I'm going to have to brave it. So I've learned to do it the easy way: I dive straight in. Now, assuming that I were in a position to insist that if she didn't dive straight in, she couldn't swim at all, I know that she wouldn't swim at all. You see the problem.

From feedback I know that many smokers have used the original advice I gave on timing to delay what they think will be the evil day. My next thoughts were to use the technique that I used for the chapter on the advantages of smoking, something like: 'timing is very important, and in the next chapter I will advise you about the best time for you to make the attempt.' You turn the page over, and there is just a huge **NOW**. That is, in fact, the best advice, but would you take it?

This is the most subtle aspect of the smoking trap. When we have genuine stress in our lives, it's not the time to stop, and if we have no stress in our lives, we have no desire to stop.

Ask yourself these following questions.

When you smoked that very first cigarette, did you really decide then that you would continue to smoke the rest of your life, all day, every day, without ever being able to stop?

OF COURSE YOU DIDN'T!

Are you going to continue the rest of your life all day, every day, without ever being able to stop?

OF COURSE YOU AREN'T!

So when will you stop? Tomorrow? Next year? The year after?

Isn't this what you've been asking yourself since you first realized you were hooked? Are you hoping that one morning you will wake up and just not want to smoke any more? Stop kidding yourself. I waited thirty-three years for it to happen to me. With drug addiction you get progressively more hooked, not less. You think it will be easier tomorrow? You're still kidding yourself. If you can't do it today, what makes you think it will be easier tomorrow? Are you going to wait until you've actually contracted one of the killer diseases? That would be a bit pointless.

The real trap is the belief that now isn't the right time—it will always be easier tomorrow.

We believe that we live stressful lives. In fact, we don't. We've taken most genuine stress out of our lives. When you leave your home you don't live in fear of being attacked by wild animals. Most of us don't have to worry where our next meal is coming from, or whether we'll have a roof over our head tonight. But just think of the life of a wild animal. Every time a rabbit comes out of its burrow, it is facing Vietnam the whole of its life. But the rabbit can handle it. It's got adrenalin and other hormones—and so have we. The truth is, the most stressful periods for any creature are early childhood and adolescence. But 3 billion years of natural selection have equipped us to cope with stress. I was five years old when the war started. We were bombed out, and I was separated from my parents for two years. I was billeted with people who treated me unkindly. It was an unpleasant period in my life, but I was able to cope with it. I don't believe it has left me with any permanent scars; on the contrary, I believe it has made me a stronger person. When I look back on my life there has only been one thing that I couldn't handle and that was my slavery to that damned weed.

A few years ago I thought I had all the worries in the world. I was suicidal—not in the sense that I would have jumped off a roof but in the sense that I knew that smoking would soon kill me. I argued that if this was life with my crutch, life just wouldn't be worth living without it. What I didn't realize was that when you are physically and mentally depressed everything gets you down. Now I feel like a young boy again. Only one thing made the change in my life: I'm now out of the smoking pit.

I know it's a cliché to say, 'If you haven't got your health, you've got nothing,' but it's absolutely true. I used to think that physical-fitness fanatics like Gary Player were a pain. I used to claim there's more to life than feeling fit; there's booze and tobacco. That's nonsense. When you feel physically and mentally strong you can enjoy the highs and handle the lows. We confuse responsibility with stress. Responsibility becomes stressful only when you don't feel strong enough to handle it. The Richard Burtons of this world are physically and mentally strong. What destroys them is not the stresses of life, or their jobs, or old age but the so-called crutches they turn to, which are just illusions. Sadly, in his case and for millions like him, the crutches kill.

Look at it this way. You've already decided that you are not going to stay in the trap the rest of your life. Therefore at some time in your life, whether you find it easy or difficult, you will have to go through the process of getting free. Smoking is not a habit or pleasure. It is drug addiction and a disease. We've already established that, far from being easier to stop tomorrow, it will get progressively harder. With a disease that's going to get progressively worse, the time to get rid of it is **NOW**— or as near to now as you can manage. Just think how quickly each week of our lives comes and goes. That's all it takes. Just think how nice it will be to enjoy the rest of your life without that ever-increasing black shadow hanging over you. And if you follow all my instructions, you won't even have to wait five days. You won't only find it easy after extinguishing the final cigarette: **YOU'LL ENJOY IT!**

Will I Miss the Cigarette?

No! Once that little nicotine monster is dead and your body stops craving nicotine, any remaining brainwashing will vanish and you will find that you will be both physically and mentally better equipped not only to cope with the stresses and strains of life but to enjoy the good times to the full.

There is only one danger and that is the influence of people who are still smoking. 'The other man's grass is always greener' is commonplace in many aspects of our lives and is easily understandable. Why is it in the case of smoking, where the disadvantages are so enormous as compared with even the illusory 'advantages', that ex-smokers tend to envy the smoker?

With all the brainwashing of our childhood it is quite understandable that we fall into the trap. Why is it that, once we realize what a fool's game it is and many of us manage to kick the habit, we walk straight back into the same trap? It is the influence of smokers.

It usually happens on social occasions, particularly after a meal. The smoker lights up and the ex-smoker has a pang. This is indeed a curious anomaly, particularly if you consider this piece of market research: not only is every non-smoker in the world happy to be a non-smoker but every smoker in the world, even with his warped, addicted, brainwashed mind suffering the delusion that he enjoys it or it relaxes him, wishes he had never become hooked in the first place. So why do some ex-smokers envy the smoker on these occasions? There are two reasons:

1. 'Just one cigarette.' Remember: it doesn't exist. Stop seeing that isolated occasion and start looking at it from the point of view of the smoker. You may be envying him, but he doesn't approve of himself: He envies you. Start observing other smokers. They can be the most powerful boost of all to help you quit. Notice how

quickly the cigarette burns, how quickly the smoker has to light up another. Notice particularly that not only is he not aware that he is smoking the cigarette but even the lighting up appears to be automatic. Remember, he is not enjoying it; it's just that he cannot enjoy himself without it. Particularly remember that when he leaves your company he is going to have to go on smoking. The next morning, when he wakes up with a chest like a cesspit, he is going to have to carry on choking himself. The next time he has a pain in the chest, the next National No-Smoking Day, the next time he inadvertently sees the government health warning, the next time there is a cancer scare, the next time he is in church, on a Tube train, visiting a hospital, library, dentist, doctor, super-market, etc., the next time he is in the company of a non-smoker, he has to continue this lifetime chain of paying through the nose just for the privilege of destroying himself physically and mentally. He is facing a lifetime of filth, bad breath, stained teeth, a lifetime of slavery, a lifetime of destroying himself, a lifetime of black shad-ows at the back of his mind. And all of this is to achieve what purpose? The illusion of trying to get back to the state he was in before he became hooked in the first place.

2. The second reason why some ex-smokers have pangs on these oc-casions is that the smoker is doing something, i.e., smoking a ciga-rette, and the non-smoker is not, so he tends to feel deprived. Get it clear in your mind before you start: it is not the non-smoker who is being deprived. It is the poor smoker who is being deprived of

- **HEALTH**
- **ENERGY**
- **MONEY**
- **CONFIDENCE**
- **PEACE OF MIND**
- **COURAGE**
- **TRANQUILLITY**
- **FREEDOM**
- **SELF-RESPECT.**

Get out of the habit of envying smokers and start seeing them as the miserable, pathetic creatures they really are. I know: I was the world's worst. That is why you are reading this book, and the ones who cannot face up to it, who have to go on kidding themselves, are the most pathetic of all.

You wouldn't envy a heroin addict. Heroin kills around 100 people a year in England. Nicotine kills over 120,000 a year and 2.5 million a year worldwide. It's already killed more people on this planet than all the wars of history combined. Like all drug addiction, yours won't get better. Each year it will get worse and worse. If you don't enjoy being a smoker today, you'll enjoy it even less tomorrow. Don't envy other smokers. Pity them. Believe me: **THEY NEED YOUR PITY.**

Will I Put on Weight?

This is another myth about smoking, spread mainly by smokers who, when attempting to stop on the Willpower Method, substitute sweets, etc., to help relieve withdrawal pangs. The withdrawal pangs of nicotine are very similar to hunger pangs, and the two are easily confused. However, whereas the pangs of hunger can be satisfied by food, the withdrawal pangs of nicotine are never completely satisfied.

As with any drug, after a while the body becomes immune and the drug ceases to relieve the withdrawal pangs completely. As soon as we extinguish a cigarette, the nicotine rapidly leaves our body, so that the nicotine addict has a permanent hunger. The natural inclination is eventually to chain-smoke. However, most smokers are prevented from doing this for one, or both, of two reasons.

1. Money—they cannot afford to increase their intake.

2. Health—in order to relieve the withdrawal pangs we have to intake a poison, which acts as an automatic check on the number of cigarettes we can smoke.

The smoker is therefore left with a permanent hunger that he can never satisfy. This is why many smokers turn to over-eating, heavy drinking or even harder drugs in order to satisfy the void. **(MOST ALCOHOLICS ARE HEAVY SMOKERS. I WONDER IF IT IS REALLY A SMOKING PROBLEM?)**

For the smoker the normal tendency is to start by substituting nicotine for food. During my own nightmare years I got to the stage where I cut out breakfast and lunch completely. I would chain-smoke during the day. In the later years I would actually look forward to the evenings only because then I could stop smoking. However, I would be picking at food all evening. I thought it was hunger, but it was really the withdrawal pangs from nicotine. In other words, during the day I would substitute nicotine for food and during the evenings I would substitute food for nicotine.

In those days I was twenty-eight pounds heavier than I am now and there was nothing I could do about it.

Once that little monster leaves your body, the awful feeling of insecurity ends. Your confidence returns, together with a marvellous feeling of self-respect. You obtain the assurance to take control of your life, not only in your eating habits but also in all other ways. This is one of the many great advantages of being free from the weed.

As I have said, the weight myth is due to using substitutes during the withdrawal period. In fact, they do not make it easier to stop. They make it harder. This is explained in greater detail in a later chapter dealing with substitutes.

Provided you follow all the instructions, weight gain should not be a problem to you.

31

Avoid False Incentives

Many smokers, while trying to stop on the Willpower Method, try to increase the motivation to stop by building up false incentives.

There are many examples of this. A typical one is 'My family and I can have a marvellous holiday on the money I will save.' This appears to be a logical and sensible approach, but in fact it is false because any self-respecting smoker would rather smoke fifty-two weeks in the year and not have a holiday. In any case there is a doubt in the smoker's mind because not only will he have to abstain for fifty weeks but will he even enjoy that holiday without a cigarette? All this does is to increase the sacrifice that the smoker feels he is making, which makes the cigarette even more precious in his mind. Instead concentrate on the other side: 'What am I getting out of it? Why do I need to smoke?' Another example: 'I'll be able to afford a better car.' That's true, and the incentive may make you abstain until you get that car, but once the novelty has gone you will feel deprived, and sooner or later you will fall for the trap again.

Another typical example is office or family pacts. These have the advantage of eliminating temptation for certain periods of the day. However, they generally fail for the following reasons:

1. The incentive is false. Why should you want to stop smoking just because other people are doing so? All this does is to create an additional pressure, which increases the feeling of sacrifice. It is fine if all smokers genuinely want to stop at one particular time. However, you cannot force smokers to stop, and although all smokers secretly want to, until they are ready to do so a pact just creates additional pressure, which increases their desire to smoke. This

turns them into secret smokers, which further increases the feeling of dependency.

2. The 'Rotten apple' theory, or dependency on each other. Under the Willpower Method of stopping, the smoker is undergoing a period of penance during which he waits for the urge to smoke to go. If he gives in, there is a sense of failure. Under the Willpower Method one of the participants is bound to give in sooner or later. The other participants now have the excuse they have been waiting for. It's not their fault. They would have held out. It is just that Fred has let them down. The truth is that most of them have already been cheating.

3. 'Sharing the credit' is the reverse of the 'Rotten apple' theory. Here the loss of face due to failure is not so bad when shared. There is a marvellous sense of achievement in stopping smoking. When you are doing it alone the acclaim you receive from your friends, relatives and colleagues can be a tremendous boost to help you over the first few days. When everybody is doing it at the same time the credit has to be shared and the boost is consequently reduced.

Another classic example of false incentives is the bribe (e.g., the parent offering the teenager a sum of money to abstain or the bet, 'I will give you £100 if I fail'). There was once an example in a TV programme. A policeman trying to give up smoking put a £20 note in his cigarette packet. He had a pact with himself. He could smoke again, but he had to set light first to the £20 note. This stopped him for a few days, but eventually he burnt the note.

Stop kidding yourself. If the £50,000 that the average smoker spends in his life won't stop him, or the one-in-two risk of horrendous diseases, or the lifetime of bad breath, mental and physical torture and slavery or being despised by most of the population and despising yourself, a few phoney incentives will not make the slightest bit of difference. They will only make the sacrifice appear worse. Keep looking at the other side of the tug-of-war.

What is smoking doing for me? **ABSOLUTELY NOTHING.**

Why do I need to do it? **YOU DON'T! YOU ARE ONLY PUNISHING YOURSELF.**

The Easy Way to Stop

This chapter contains instructions about the easy way to stop smoking. Providing you follow the instructions, you will find that stopping ranges from relatively easy to enjoyable! But remember the definition of a brunette: 'a girl who didn't read the instructions on the bottle'.

It is ridiculously easy to stop smoking. All you have to do is two things:

1. Make the decision that you are never going to smoke again.

2. Don't mope about it. Rejoice.

You are probably asking, 'Why the need for the rest of the book? Why couldn't you have said that in the first place?' The answer is that you would at some time have moped about it, and consequently, sooner or later, you would have changed your decision. You have probably already done it many times before.

As I have already said, the whole business of smoking is a subtle, sinister trap. The main problem of stopping isn't the chemical addiction but the brainwashing, and it was necessary first to explode the myths and delusions. Understand your enemy. Know his tactics, and you will easily defeat him.

I've spent most of my life trying to stop smoking and I've suffered weeks of black depression. When I finally stopped I went from a hundred a day to zero without one bad moment. It was enjoyable even during the withdrawal period, and I have never had the slightest pang since. On the contrary, it is the most wonderful thing that has happened in my life.

I couldn't understand why it had been so easy and it took me a long time to find out the reason. It was this. I knew for certain that I was never going to smoke again. During previous attempts, no matter how determined I was, I was basically *trying* to stop smoking, hoping that if I could survive long enough without a cigarette, the urge would eventually go. Of course it didn't go because I was waiting for something to happen, and the more I moped about it, the more I wanted a cigarette, so the craving never went.

My final attempt was different. Like all smokers nowadays, I had been giving the problem serious thought. Up to then, whenever I failed, I had consoled myself with the thought that it would be easier next time. It had never occurred to me that I would have to go on smoking the rest of my life. This latter thought filled me with horror and started me thinking very deeply about the subject.

Instead of lighting up cigarettes subconsciously, I began to analyse my feelings as I was smoking them. This confirmed what I already knew. I wasn't enjoying them, and they were filthy and disgusting.

I started looking at non-smokers. Until then I had always regarded non-smokers as wishy-washy, unsociable, finicky people. However, when I examined them they appeared, if anything, stronger and more relaxed. They appeared to be able to cope with the stresses and strains of life, and they seemed to enjoy social functions more than the smokers. They certainly had more sparkle and zest than smokers.

I started talking to ex-smokers. Up to this point I had regarded ex-smokers as people who had been forced to give up smoking for health and money reasons and who were always secretly longing for a cigarette. A few did say, 'You get the odd pangs, but they are so few and far between they aren't worth bothering about.' But most said, 'Miss it? You must be joking. I have never felt better in my life.'

Talking to ex-smokers exploded another myth that I had always had in my mind. I had thought that there was an inherent weakness in me, and it suddenly dawned on me that all smokers go through this private nightmare. Basically I said to myself, 'Millions of people are stopping now and leading perfectly happy lives. I didn't need to do it before I started, and I can remember having to work hard to get used to the filthy things. So why do I need to do it now?' In any event I didn't enjoy smoking. I hated the whole filthy ritual and I didn't want to spend the rest of my life being the slave of this disgusting weed.

I then said to myself: 'Allen, **WHETHER YOU LIKE IT OR NOT, YOU HAVE SMOKED YOUR LAST CIGARETTE**.'

I knew, right from that point, that I would never smoke again. I wasn't expecting it to be easy; in fact, just the reverse. I fully believed that I was in for months of black depression and that I would spend the rest of my life having the occasional pang. Instead it has been absolute bliss right from the start.

It took me a long time to work out why it had been so easy and why this time I hadn't suffered those terrifying withdrawal pangs. The reason is that they do not exist. It is the doubt and uncertainty that causes the pangs. The beautiful truth is: **IT IS EASY TO STOP SMOKING.** It is only the indecision and moping about it that makes it difficult. Even while they are addicted to nicotine, smokers can go for relatively long periods at certain times in their lives without bothering about it. It is only when you want a cigarette but can't have one that you suffer.

Therefore the key to making it easy is to make stopping certain and final. Not to *hope* but to *know* you have kicked it, having made the decision. Never to doubt or question it. In fact, just the reverse—always to rejoice about it.

If you can be certain from the start, it will be easy. But how can you be certain from the start unless you know it is going to be easy? This is why the rest of the book is necessary. There are certain essential points and it is necessary to get them clear in your mind before you start:

1. Realize that you can achieve it. There is nothing different about you, and the only person who can make you smoke that next cigarette is you.

2. There is absolutely nothing to give up. On the contrary, there are enormous positive gains to be made. I do not only mean you will be healthier and richer. I mean you will enjoy the good times more and be less miserable during the bad times.

3. Get it clear in your head that there is no such thing as one cigarette. Smoking is a drug addiction and a chain reaction. By moaning about the odd cigarette you will only be punishing yourself needlessly.

4. See the whole business of smoking not as a sociable habit that might injure you, but as drug addiction. Face up to the fact that, whether you like it or not, **YOU HAVE GOT THE DISEASE.** It will not go away because you bury your head in the sand. Remember: like all crippling diseases, it not only lasts for life but gets worse and worse. The easiest time to cure it is *now*.

5. Separate the disease (i.e. the chemical addiction) from the frame of mind of being a smoker or a non-smoker. All smokers, if given

the opportunity to go back to the time before they became hooked, would jump at that opportunity. You have that opportunity today! Don't even think about it as 'giving up' smoking. When you have made the final decision that you have smoked your last cigarette you will already be a non-smoker. A smoker is one of those poor wretches who have to go through life destroying themselves with cigarettes. A non-smoker is someone who doesn't. Once you have made that final decision, you have already achieved your object. Rejoice in the fact. Do not sit moping waiting for the chemical addiction to go. Get out and enjoy life immediately. Life is marvellous even when you are addicted to nicotine, and each day it will get better when you aren't.

The key to making it easy to quit smoking is to be certain that you will succeed in abstaining completely during the withdrawal period (maximum three weeks). If you are in the correct frame of mind, you will find it ridiculously easy.

By this stage, if you have opened your mind as I requested at the beginning, you will already have decided you are going to stop. You should now have a feeling of excitement, like a dog straining at the leash, unable to wait to get the poison out of your system.

If you have a feeling of doom and gloom, it will be for one of the following reasons:

1. Something has not gelled in your mind. Re-read the above five points, and ask yourself if you believe them to be true. If you doubt any point, re-read the appropriate sections in the book.

2. You fear failure itself. Do not worry. Just read on. You will succeed. The whole business of smoking is like a confidence trick on a gigantic scale. Intelligent people fall for confidence tricks, but it is only a fool who, having once found out about the trick, goes on kidding himself.

3. You agree with everything, but you are still miserable. Don't be! Open your eyes. Something marvellous is happening. You are about to escape from the prison.

It is essential to start with the correct frame of mind: isn't it marvellous that I am a non-smoker!

All we have to do now is to keep you in that frame of mind during the withdrawal period, and the next few chapters deal with specific points to enable you to stay in that frame of mind during that time. After the withdrawal period you won't have to think that way. You will think that way automatically, and the only mystery in your life will be 'It is so obvious, why couldn't I see it before?' However, two important warnings:

1. Delay your plan to extinguish your last cigarette until you have finished the book.

2. I have mentioned several times a withdrawal period of up to three weeks. This can cause misunderstanding. First, you may subconsciously feel that you have to suffer for three weeks. You don't. Secondly, avoid the trap of thinking, 'Somehow I have just got to abstain for three weeks and then I will be free.' Nothing will actually happen after three weeks. You won't suddenly feel like a non-smoker. Non-smokers do not feel any different from smokers. If you are moping about stopping during the three weeks, in all probability you will still be moping about it after the three weeks. What I am saying is, if you can start right now by saying, 'I am never going to smoke again. Isn't it marvellous?' after three weeks all temptation will go. Whereas if you say, 'If only I can survive three weeks without a cigarette,' you will be dying for a cigarette after the three weeks are up.

The Withdrawal Period

For up to three weeks after your last cigarette you may be subjected to withdrawal pangs. These consist of two quite separate factors.

1. The withdrawal pangs of nicotine, that empty, insecure feeling, like a hunger, which smokers identify as a craving or something to do with their hands.

2. The psychological trigger of certain events such as a telephone conversation.

It is the failure to understand and to differentiate between these two distinct factors that makes it so difficult for smokers to achieve success on the Willpower Method, and it's also the reason why many smokers who do achieve it fall into the trap again.

Although the withdrawal pangs of nicotine cause no physical pain, do not underestimate their power. We talk of 'hunger pains' if we go without food for a day; there may be 'tummy rumblings', but there is no physical pain. Even so, hunger is a powerful force, and we are likely to become very irritable when deprived of food. It is similar when our body is craving nicotine. The difference is that our body needs food but it doesn't need poison and with the right frame of mind the withdrawal pangs are easily overcome and disappear very quickly.

If smokers can abstain for a few days on the Willpower Method, the craving for nicotine soon disappears. It is the second factor that causes the difficulty. The smoker has got into the habit of relieving his withdrawal pangs at certain times or occasions, which causes an association of ideas (e.g., 'I cannot enjoy a drink without a cigarette'). It may be easier to understand the effect with the help of an example.

You have a car for a few years, and let's say the turn indicator is on the left of the steering column. On your next car it is on the right. You know it is on the right, but for a couple of weeks you put the windshield wipers on whenever you want to turn.

Stopping smoking is similar. During the early days of the withdrawal period the trigger mechanism will operate at certain times. You will think, 'I want a cigarette.' It is essential to counter the brainwashing right from square one, then these automatic triggers will quickly disappear. Under the Willpower Method, because the smoker believes he is making a sacrifice, is moping about it and is waiting for the urge to smoke to go, far from removing these trigger mechanisms he is actually increasing them.

A common trigger is a meal, particularly one at a restaurant with friends. The ex-smoker is already miserable because he is being deprived of his cigarette. His friends light up and he feels even more deprived. Now he is not enjoying the meal or what should be a pleasant social occasion. Because of his association of the cigarette with the meal and the social occasion he is now suffering a triple blow, and the brainwashing is actually being increased. If he is resolute and can hold out long enough, he eventually accepts his lot and gets on with his life. However, part of the brainwashing remains, and I think the second most pathetic thing about smoking is the smoker who has given up for health or money reasons, yet even after several years still craves a cigarette on certain occasions. He is pining for an illusion that exists only in his mind and is needlessly torturing himself.

Even under my method responding to triggers is the most common failing. The ex-smoker tends to regard the cigarette as a sort of placebo or sugar pill. He thinks: 'I know the cigarette does nothing for me, but if I think it does, on certain occasions it will be a help to me.'

A sugar pill, although giving no actual physical help, can be a powerful psychological aid to relieve genuine symptoms and is therefore a benefit. The cigarette, however, is not a sugar pill. It creates the symptoms that it relieves and after a while ceases even to relieve these symptoms completely; the 'pill' is causing the disease, and quite apart from that it also happens to be the No. 1 killer poison in society.

You may find it easier to understand the effect when related to non-smokers or a smoker who has quit for several years. Take the case of a wife who loses her husband. It is quite common at such times for a smoker, with the best intentions, to say, 'Have a cigarette. It will help calm you down.'

If the cigarette is accepted, it will not have a calming effect because the woman is not addicted to nicotine and there are no withdrawal pangs to relieve. At best all it will do is to give her a momentary psychological boost. As soon as the cigarette is extinguished, the original tragedy is still there. In fact, it will be increased because the woman is now suffering withdrawal pangs, and her choice is now either to endure them or to relieve them by smoking another cigarette and start the chain of misery. All the cigarette will have done is to give a momentary psychological boost. The same effect could have been achieved by offering a word of comfort or a drink. Many non-smokers and ex-smokers have become addicted to the weed as a result of such occasions.

It is essential to counter the brainwashing right from the start. Get it quite clear in your head: you don't need the cigarette, and you are only torturing yourself by continuing to regard it as some sort of prop or boost. There is no need to be miserable. Cigarettes do not make meals or social occasions; they ruin them. Remember too that the smokers at that meal are not smoking because they are enjoying the cigarette. They are smoking because they have got to. They are drug addicts. They cannot enjoy the meal or life without it.

Abandon the concept of the smoking habit as pleasurable in itself. Many smokers think, 'If only there were a clean cigarette.' There *are* clean cigarettes. Any smoker who tries herbal cigarettes soon finds out they are a waste of time. Get it clear in your mind that the only reason you have been smoking is to get the nicotine. Once you have got rid of the craving for nicotine you will have no more need to stick a cigarette in your mouth than in your ear.

Whether the pang is due to actual withdrawal symptoms (the empty feeling) or a trigger mechanism, accept it. The physical pain is non-existent and with the right frame of mind cigarettes become no problem. Do not worry about withdrawal. The feeling itself isn't bad. It is the association with wanting a cigarette and then feeling denied that is the problem.

Instead of moping about it, say to yourself, 'I know what it is. It's the withdrawal pang from nicotine. That's what smokers suffer all their lives and that's what keeps them smoking. Non-smokers do not suffer these pangs. It is another of the many evils of this drug. Isn't it marvellous I am purging this evil from my body!'

In other words, for the next three weeks you will have a slight trauma inside your body, but during those weeks, and for the rest of your life, something marvellous will be happening. You will be ridding yourself of an awful disease. That bonus will more than outweigh the slight trauma, and you will actually enjoy the withdrawal pangs. They will become moments of pleasure.

Think of the whole business of stopping as an exciting game. Think of the nicotine monster as a sort of tape worm inside your stomach. You have got to starve him for three weeks, and he is going to try to trick you into lighting a cigarette to keep him alive.

At times he will try to make you miserable. At times you will be off guard. Someone may offer you a cigarette and you may forget that you have stopped. There is a slight feeling of deprivation when you remember. Be prepared for these traps in advance. Whatever the temptation, get it into your mind that it is only there because of the monster inside your body, and every time you resist the temptation you have dealt another mortal blow in the battle.

Whatever you do, don't try to forget about smoking. This is one of the things that causes smokers using the Willpower Method hours of depression. They try to get through each day hoping that eventually they'll just forget about it.

It is like not being able to sleep. The more you worry about it, the harder it becomes.

In any event you won't be able to forget about it. For the first few days the 'little monster' will keep reminding you, and you won't be able to avoid it; while there are still smokers and extensive cigarette promotions about, you will have constant reminders.

The point is, you have no need to forget. Nothing bad is happening. Something marvellous is taking place. Even if you are thinking about it a thousand times a day, **SAVOUR EACH MOMENT. REMIND YOURSELF HOW MARVEL-LOUS IT IS TO BE FREE AGAIN. REMIND YOURSELF OF THE SHEER JOY OF NOT HAVING TO CHOKE YOURSELF ANY MORE.**

As I have said, you will find that the pangs become moments of pleasure, and you will be surprised how quickly you will then forget about smoking.

Whatever you do—**DO NOT DOUBT YOUR DECISION.** Once you start to doubt, you will start to mope, and it will get worse. Instead use the moment as a boost. If the cause is depression, remind yourself that's what cigarettes were doing to you. If you are offered one by a friend, take pride in saying, 'I'm happy to say I do not need them any more.' That will hurt him, but when he sees that it isn't bothering you he will be halfway to joining you.

Remember that you had very powerful reasons for stopping in the first place. Remind yourself of all the money that one cigarette will cost you, and ask yourself whether you really want to risk those fearful diseases. Above all, remember that the feeling is only temporary and each moment is a moment nearer to your goal.

Some smokers fear that they will have to spend the rest of their lives reversing the 'automatic triggers'. In other words, they believe that they will have to go through life kidding themselves that they don't really need a cigarette by the use of psychology. This is not so. Remember that the optimist sees the bottle as half full and the pessimist sees it as half empty. In the case of smoking, the bottle is empty and the smoker sees it as full. It is the smoker who has been brainwashed. Once you start telling yourself that you don't need to smoke, in a very short time you won't even need to say it because the beautiful truth is . . . you do not need to smoke. It's the last thing you need to do; make sure it's not the last thing you do.

Just One Puff

This is the undoing of many smokers who try to stop on the Willpower Method. They will go through three or four days and then have the odd cigarette or a puff or two to tide them over. They do not realize the devastating effect this has on their morale.

For most smokers that first puff doesn't taste good, and this gives their conscious minds a boost. They think, 'Good. That wasn't enjoyable. I am losing the urge to smoke.' In fact, the reverse is the case. Get it clear in your mind—**CIGARETTES NEVER WERE ENJOYABLE**. Enjoyment wasn't the reason why you smoked. If smokers smoked for enjoyment, they'd never smoke more than one cigarette.

The only reason why you smoked was to feed that little monster. Just think: you had starved him for four days. How precious that one cigarette or just the puff must have been to him. You are not aware of it in your conscious mind, but the fix your body received will be communicated to your subconscious mind and all your sound preparation will be undermined. There will be a little voice at the back of your mind saying, 'In spite of all the logic, they are precious. I want another one.'

That little puff has two damaging effects.

1. It keeps the little monster alive in your body.

2. What's worse, it keeps the big monster alive in your mind. If you had the last puff, it will be easier to have the next one.

Remember: just one cigarette is how people get into smoking in the first place.

Will It Be Harder for Me?

The combinations of factors that will determine how easily each individual smoker will quit are infinite. To start with, each of us has his own character, type of work, personal circumstances, timing, etc.

Certain professions may make it harder than others, but providing the brainwashing is removed it doesn't have to be so. A few individual examples will help.

It tends to be particularly difficult for members of the medical profession. We think it should be easier for doctors because they are more aware of the effects of ill-health and are seeing daily evidence of it. Although this supplies more forceful reasons for stopping, it doesn't make it any easier to do. The reasons are these:

1. The constant awareness of the health risks creates fear, which is one of the conditions under which we need to relieve our withdrawal pangs.

2. A doctor's work is exceedingly stressful, and he is usually not able to relieve the additional stress of withdrawal pangs while he is working.

3. He has the additional stress of guilt. He feels that he should be setting an example for the rest of the population. This puts more pressure on him and increases the feeling of deprivation.

During his hard-earned breaks, when the normal stress is momentarily relieved, that cigarette becomes very precious when he eventually relieves his withdrawal pangs. This is a form of casual smoking and applies to any situation where the smoker is forced to abstain for lengthy periods. Under the Willpower Method the smoker is miserable because he is being deprived. He is not enjoying the break or the cup of tea or coffee that goes with it. His sense of loss is therefore greatly increased, and, because of the association of ideas, the cigarette gets credit for the total situation. However, if you can first remove the brainwashing and stop moping about the cigarette, the break and the cup of tea can still be enjoyed even while the body is craving nicotine.

Another difficult situation is boredom, particularly when it is combined with periods of stress. Typical examples are drivers or housewives with young children. The work is stressful, yet much of the work is monotonous. During an attempt to stop on the Willpower Method the housewife has long periods in which to mope about her 'loss', which increases the feeling of depression.

Again this can be easily overcome if your frame of mind is correct. Do not worry that you are continually reminded that you have stopped smoking. Use such moments to rejoice in the fact that you are ridding yourself of the evil monster. If you have a positive frame of mind, these pangs can become moments of pleasure.

Remember, any smoker, regardless of age, sex, intelligence or profession, can find it easy and enjoyable to stop provided **YOU FOLLOW ALL THE INSTRUCTIONS.**

The Main Reasons
for Failure

There are two main reasons for failure. The first is the influence of other smokers. At a weak moment or during a social occasion somebody will light up. I have already dealt with this topic at length. Use that moment to remind yourself that there is no such thing as one cigarette. Rejoice in the fact that you have broken the chain. Remember that the smoker envies you, and feel sorry for him. Believe me, he needs your pity.

The other main reason for failure is having a bad day. Get it clear in your mind before you start that, whether you are a smoker or a non-smoker, there are good days and bad days. Life is a matter of relativity, and you cannot have ups without having downs.

The problem with the Willpower Method of stopping is that as soon as the smoker has a bad day he starts moping for a cigarette, and all he does is make a bad day worse. The non-smoker is better equipped, not only physically but also mentally, to cope with the stresses and strains of life.

If you have a bad day during the withdrawal period, just take it on the chin. Remind yourself that you had bad days when you smoked (otherwise you wouldn't have decided to stop). Instead of moping about it, say to yourself something like, 'OK, today's not so good, but smoking is not going to cure it. Tomorrow will be better, and at least I have got a marvellous bonus at the moment. I have kicked that awful cigarette habit.'

When you are a smoker you have to block your mind to the bad side of smoking. Smokers never have smokers' coughs, just permanent colds. When your car breaks down in the middle of nowhere you light a cigarette, but are you happy and cheerful? Of course you aren't. Once you stop smoking the tendency is to blame everything that goes wrong in your life on the fact that you have stopped. Now if your car breaks down, you think, 'At times like this I would have lit a cigarette.' That's true, but what you forget is that the cigarette didn't solve the problem, and you are simply punishing yourself by moping for an illusory crutch. You are creating an impossible situation. You are miserable because you can't have the cigarette, and you'll be even more miserable if you do. You know that you have made the correct decision by stopping smoking, so don't punish yourself by ever doubting the decision.

Remember: a positive mental approach is essential—always.

Substitutes

Substitutes include chewing gum, sweets, peppermints, herbal cigarettes and pills. **DO NOT USE ANY OF THEM.** They make it harder, not easier. If you do get a pang and use a substitute, it will prolong the pang and make it harder. What you are really saying is 'I need to smoke or fill the void.' It will be like giving in to a hijacker or the tantrums of a child. It will just keep the pangs coming and prolong the torture. In any event the substitutes will not relieve the pangs. Your craving is for nicotine, not food. All it will do is keep you thinking about smoking. Remember these points:

1. There is no substitute for nicotine.

2. You do not need nicotine. It is not food; it is poison. When the pangs come remind yourself that it is smokers who suffer withdrawal pangs, not non-smokers. See them as another evil of the drug. See them as the death of a monster.

3. Remember: cigarettes create the void; they do not fill it. The quicker you teach your brain that you do not need to smoke, or do anything else in its place, the sooner you will be free.

In particular avoid any product that contains nicotine, whether it be gum, patch, nasal spray or the latest gimmick, the inhalator which is similar to a plastic cigarette. It is true that a small proportion of smokers who attempt to quit using nicotine substitutes do succeed and attribute their success to such use. However, they quit in spite of their use and not because of it. It is unfortunate that many doctors still recommend nicotine replacement therapy (NRT).

This is not surprising because, if you don't fully understand the nicotine trap, NRT sounds very logical. It is based on the belief that when you attempt to quit smoking, you have two powerful enemies to defeat:

1. To break the habit.

2. To survive the terrible physical nicotine withdrawal pains.

If you have two powerful enemies to defeat, it is sensible not to fight them simultaneously but one at a time. So the NRT theory is that you first stop smoking but continue to take a nicotine replacement. Then, once you have broken the habit, you gradually reduce the supply of nicotine, thus tackling each enemy separately.

It sounds logical, but it is based on the wrong facts. Smoking is not habit but nicotine addiction and the actual physical pain from nicotine withdrawal is almost imperceptible. What you are trying to achieve when you quit smoking is to kill both the little nicotine monster in your body and the big monster inside your brain as quickly as possible. All NRT does is to prolong the life of the little monster which in turn will prolong the life of the big monster.

Remember EASYWAY makes it easy to quit immediately. You can kill the big monster (brainwashing) before you extinguish your final cigarette. The little monster will soon be dead and, even while it is dying, will be no more of a problem than it was when you were a smoker.

Just think, how can you possibly cure an addict of addiction to a drug by recommending the same drug? One eminent and highly respected doctor has actually stated on national television that some smokers are so dependent on nicotine that if they did quit they would have to take a nicotine substitute for life. How can a doctor get so confused as to believe that the human body is not just dependent upon food, water and oxygen, but on a powerful poison?

We often have smokers attend our clinics who have quit smoking but are hooked on nicotine gum. Others are hooked on the gum and are still smoking. Do not be fooled by the fact that the gum tastes awful— so did the first cigarette.

All substitutes have exactly the same effect as nicotine chewing gum. I'm now talking about this business of 'I can't have a cigarette, so I'll have ordinary chewing gum, or sweets, or peppermints to help fill the void.' Although the empty feeling of wanting a cigarette is indistinguishable from hunger for food, one will not satisfy the other. In fact, if anything is designed to make you want a cigarette, it's stuffing yourself with chewing gum or peppermints.

But the chief evil of substitutes is that they prolong the real problem, which is the brainwashing. By saying 'I need a substitute for smoking' what you are really saying is 'I am making a sacrifice.' The depression associated with the Willpower Method is caused by the fact that the smoker believes he is making a sacrifice. All you will be doing is to substitute one problem for another. There is no pleasure in stuffing yourself with sweets. You will just get fat and miserable, and in no time at all you'll be back on the weed.

Casual smokers find it difficult to dismiss the belief that they are being deprived of their little reward: the cigarette during the canteen break of office or factory workers who aren't allowed to smoke while working, or of teachers in the staff room between lessons, or the quickie by doctors between patients. Some say: 'I wouldn't even take the break if I didn't smoke.' That proves the point: often the break is taken, not because the smoker needs it or even wants it, but because the smoker desperately needs to scratch the itch. Remember, those cigarettes never were genuine rewards. They were equivalent to wearing tight shoes to get the pleasure of taking them off. So if you feel that you must have a little reward, let that be your substitute; while you are working, wear a pair of shoes a size too small for you, don't allow yourself to remove them until you have your break, then experience that wonderful moment of relaxation and satisfaction when you do remove them. Perhaps you feel that would be rather stupid. You are absolutely right. It's hard to visualize while you are still in the trap, but that is what smokers do. It's also hard to visualize that soon you won't need that little 'reward', and you'll regard your friends who are still in the trap with genuine pity and wonder why they cannot see the point.

However, if you go on kidding yourself that the cigarette was a genuine reward or that you need a substitute to take its place, you will feel deprived and miserable, and the chances are that you'll end up smoking again. If you need a genuine break, you'll soon be enjoying that break even more because you won't have to choke yourself.

Remember, you don't need a substitute. Those pangs are a craving for poison and will soon be gone. Let that be your prop for the next few days. *Enjoy* ridding your body of poison and your mind of slavery and dependence.

If, because your appetite is better, you eat more at main meals and put on a couple of pounds during the next few days, don't worry about it. When you experience the 'moment of revelation' that I describe later, you will have confidence, and you'll find that any problem you have that is capable of being solved by positive thinking you will be able to solve, including eating habits. But what you mustn't do is to start picking between meals. If you do, you will get fat and miserable and you will never know when you've kicked the weed. You'll just be moving the problem instead of getting rid of it.

Should I Avoid
Temptation Situations?

I have been categorical in my advice so far and would ask you to treat this advice as instruction rather than suggestion. I am categorical, first, because there are sound, practical reasons for my advice and, second, because those reasons have been backed up by thousands of case studies.

On the question of whether or not to try to avoid temptation during the withdrawal period, I regret that I cannot be categorical. Each smoker will need to decide for himself. I can, however, make what I hope will be helpful suggestions.

I repeat that it is fear that keeps us smoking all our lives, and this fear consists of two distinct phases:

1. How can I survive without a cigarette?

This fear is the panic feeling that smokers get when they are out late at night and their cigarettes begin to run out. The fear isn't caused by withdrawal pangs but is the psychological fear of dependency—you cannot survive without a cigarette. It actually reaches its height when you are smoking your last cigarette; at that time your withdrawal pangs are at their lowest.

It is the fear of the unknown, the sort of fear that people have when they are learning to dive. The diving board is 1 foot high but seems to be 6 feet high. The water is 6 feet deep but appears to be 1 foot deep. It takes courage to launch yourself. You are convinced you are going to smash your head. The launching is the hardest part. If you can find the courage to do it, the rest is easy.

This explains why many otherwise strong-willed smokers either have never attempted to stop or can survive only a few hours when they do. In fact, there are some smokers on about twenty a day who, when they decide to stop, actually smoke their next cigarette more quickly than if they had not decided to stop. The decision causes panic, which is stressful. This is one of the occasions when the brain triggers the instruction 'Have a cigarette', but now you can't have one. You are being deprived—more stress. The trigger starts again—quickly the fuse blows and you light up.

Don't worry. That panic is just psychological. It is the fear that you are dependent. The beautiful truth is that you are not, even when you are still addicted to nicotine. Do not panic. Just trust me and launch yourself.

2. The second phase of fear is longer-term. It involves the fear that certain situations in the future will not be enjoyable without a cigarette or that you will not be able to cope with a trauma without the cigarette. Don't worry. If you can launch yourself you will find the opposite to be the case.

The avoidance of temptation itself falls into two main categories:

1. 'I will keep my cigarettes available, although I will not smoke them. I will feel more confident knowing they are there.'

I find the failure rate with people who do this is far higher than with people who discard them. I believe this is due mainly to the fact that if you have a bad moment during the withdrawal period, it is easy to light up a readily available cigarette. If you have the indignity of having to go out and buy a pack you are more likely to overcome the temptation, and in any event the pang will probably have passed before you get to the store.

However, I believe the main reason for the higher failure rate in these cases is that the smoker does not feel completely committed to stopping in the first place. Remember the two essentials to succeed are:

Certainty.
'Isn't it marvellous that I do not need to smoke any more?'

In either case, why on earth do you need cigarettes? If you still feel the need to keep cigarettes on your person, I would suggest that you re-read the book first. It means that something hasn't gelled.

2. 'Should I avoid stressful or social occasions during the withdrawal period?'

My advice is, yes, try to avoid stressful situations. There is no sense in putting undue pressure on yourself.

In the case of social events my advice is the reverse. No, go out and enjoy yourself straight away. You do not need cigarettes even while you are still addicted to nicotine. Go to a party, and rejoice in the fact that you do not have to smoke. It will quickly prove to you the beautiful truth that life is so much better without cigarettes—and just think how much better it will be when the little monster has left your body, together with all that poison.

The Moment of Revelation

The moment of revelation usually takes place about three weeks after a smoker stops. The sky appears to become brighter, and it is the moment when the brainwashing ends completely, when, instead of telling yourself you do not need to smoke, you suddenly realize that the last thread is broken and you can enjoy the rest of your life without ever needing to smoke again. It is also usually from this point that you start looking at other smokers as objects of pity.

Smokers using the Willpower Method do not normally experience this moment because, although they are glad to be ex-smokers, they go through life believing they are making a sacrifice.

The more you smoked, the more marvellous this moment is, and it lasts a lifetime.

I consider I have been very fortunate in this life and had some wonderful moments, but the most wonderful of all was that moment of revelation. With all the other highlights of my life, although I can remember they were happy times, I can never recapture the actual feeling. I can never get over the joy of not having to smoke any more. If ever I am feeling low and need a boost nowadays, I just think how lovely it is not to be hooked on that awful weed. Half the people who contact me after they have kicked the weed say exactly the same thing, that it was the most marvellous event of their lives. Ah! What pleasure you have to come!

With an additional twelve years' feedback, both from the book and from my consultations, I have learned that in most cases the moment of revelation occurs not after three weeks, as stated above, but within a few days.

In my own case it happened before I'd extinguished my last cigarette, and on many occasions in my early consultancy sessions, during the one-to-one period, before I'd even got to the end of a session smokers would say something like: 'You needn't say another word, Allen. I can see it all so clearly, I know I'll never smoke again.' In the group sessions I've learned to tell when it happens without individual smokers saying anything. From the letters I receive I'm also aware that it frequently happens with the book.

Ideally if you follow all the instructions and understand the psychology completely, it should happen to you immediately.

Nowadays at my consultations I say to smokers that it takes about five days for the noticeable physical withdrawal to go and about three weeks for an ex-smoker to get completely free. In one way I dislike giving such guidelines. It can cause two problems. The first is that I put in people's minds the suggestion that they will have to suffer for between five days and three weeks. The second is that the ex-smoker tends to think, 'If I can survive for five days or three weeks, I can expect a real boost at the end of that period.' However, he may have five pleasant days or three pleasant weeks, followed by one of those disastrous days that strike both non-smokers and smokers, which have nothing to do with smoking but are caused by other factors in our lives. There our ex-smoker is, waiting for the moment of revelation, and what he experiences is depression instead. It could destroy his confidence.

If I don't give any guidelines, however, the ex-smoker can spend the rest of his life waiting for nothing to happen. I suspect that this is what happens to the vast majority of smokers who stop when using the Willpower Method.

At one time I was tempted to say that revelation should happen immediately. But if I did that and it didn't happen immediately, the ex-smoker would lose confidence and would think it was never going to happen.

People often ask me about the significance of the five days and three weeks. Are they just periods that I've drawn out of the blue? No. They are obviously not definite dates, but they reflect an accumulation of feedback over the years. About five days after stopping is when the ex-smoker ceases to have smoking as the main occupation of his mind. Most ex-smokers experience the moment of revelation around this period. What usually happens is you are in one of those stressful or social situations that once you couldn't cope with or enjoy without a cigarette. You suddenly realize that not only are you enjoying or coping with it but the thought of having a cigarette has never even occurred to you. From that point on it is usually smooth sailing. That's when you know you are free.

I have noticed from my previous attempts using the Willpower Method, and from feedback from other smokers, that around the three-week period is when most serious attempts to stop smoking fail. I believe that what usually happens is that after about three weeks you sense that you have lost the desire to smoke. You need to prove this to yourself, and you light a cigarette. It tastes weird. You've proved you have kicked it. But you've also put fresh nicotine into your body, and nicotine is what your body has been craving for three weeks. As soon as you extinguish that cigarette, the nicotine starts to leave your body. Now a little voice is saying, 'You haven't kicked it. You want another one.' You don't light another one straight away because you don't want to get hooked again. You allow a safe period to pass. When you are next tempted you are able to say to yourself, 'But I didn't get hooked again, so there's no harm in having another.' You are already on your way down the slippery slope.

The key to the problem is not to wait for the moment of revelation but to realize that once you extinguish that last cigarette it is finished. You've already done all you need to do. You've cut off the supply of nicotine. No force on earth can prevent you from being free unless you mope about it or wait for revelation. Go and enjoy life; cope with it right from the start. That way you'll soon experience the moment.

The Final Cigarette

Having decided on your timing, you are now ready to smoke that last cigarette. Before you do so, check on the two essentials:

1. Do you feel certain of success?

2. Have you a feeling of doom and gloom or a sense of excitement that you are about to achieve something marvellous?

If you have any doubts, re-read the book first. If you still have doubts, obtain a copy of 'The Only Way to Stop Smoking Permanently' or contact your nearest EASYWAY clinic (details listed at the end).

Remember that you never decided to fall into the smoking trap. But that trap is designed to enslave you for life. In order to escape you need to make the positive decision that you are about to smoke your final cigarette.

Remember, the only reason that you have read this book so far is because you would dearly love to escape. So make that positive decision now. Make a solemn vow, that when you extinguish that final cigarette, whether you find it easy or difficult, you will never smoke another.

Perhaps you are worried that you have made this vow several times in the past but are still smoking, or that you will have to go through some awful trauma. Have no fear, the worst thing that can possibly happen is that you fail, and so you have absolutely nothing to lose and so much to gain.

But stop even thinking about failure. The beautiful truth is that it is not only ridiculously easy to quit but you can actually enjoy the process. This time you are going to use EASYWAY! All you need to do is to follow the simple instructions that I'm about to give you:

1. Make the solemn vow now and mean it.

2. Smoke that final cigarette consciously, inhale the filth deeply into your lungs and ask yourself where the pleasure is.

3. When you extinguish it, do so not with a feeling of: I must never smoke another, or I'm not allowed to smoke another, but with the feeling of: Isn't it great! I'm free! I'm no longer the slave of nicotine! I don't ever have to put these filthy things in my mouth again.

4. Be aware that for a few days, there will be a little nicotine saboteur inside your stomach. You might only know the feeling 'I want a cigarette.' At times I refer to that little nicotine monster as the slight physical craving for nicotine. Strictly this is incorrect, and it is important that you understand why. Because it takes about three weeks for that little monster to die, ex-smokers believe that the little monster will continue to crave cigarettes after the final cigarette has been extinguished, and that they must therefore use will-power to resist the temptation during this period. This is not so. The body doesn't crave nicotine. Only the brain craves nicotine. If you do get that feeling of 'I want a cigarette' over the next few days, your brain has a simple choice. It can either interpret that feeling for what it actually is—an empty insecure feeling started by the first cigarette and perpetuated by every subsequent one, and say to yourself: **YIPPEE I'M A NON-SMOKER**!

Or you can start craving for a cigarette and suffer it for the rest of your life. Just think for a moment. Wouldn't that be an incredibly stupid thing to do? To say 'I never want to smoke again', then spend the rest of your life saying 'I'd love a cigarette.' That's what smokers who use the Willpower Method do. No wonder they feel so miserable. They spend the rest of their lives desperately moping for something that they desperately hope they will never have. No wonder so few of them succeed and the few that do never feel completely free.

5 It is only the doubting and the waiting that make it difficult to quit. So never doubt your decision, you know it's the correct decision. If you begin to doubt it, you will put yourself into a no-win situation. You will be miserable if you crave a cigarette but can't have one. You will be even more miserable if you do have one. No matter what system you are using, what is it that you are trying to achieve when you quit smoking? Never to smoke again? No! Many ex-smokers do that but go through the rest of their lives feeling deprived. What is the real difference between smokers and non-smokers? Non-smokers have no need or desire to smoke, they do not crave cigarettes and do not need to exercise willpower in order not to smoke. That's what you are trying to achieve, and it is completely within your power to achieve it. You don't have to wait to stop craving cigarettes or to become a non-smoker. You do it the moment you extinguish that final cigarette; you have cut off the supply of nicotine: **YOU ARE ALREADY A HAPPY NON-SMOKER!!!**

And you will remain a happy non-smoker provided:

1. You never doubt your decision.

2. You don't wait to become a non-smoker. If you do, you will merely be waiting for nothing to happen, which will create a phobia.

3. You don't try not to think about smoking or wait for the 'moment of revelation' to come. Either way you will merely create a phobia.

4. You don't use substitutes.

5. You see all other smokers as they really are and pity them rather than envy them.

6. Whether they be good days or bad days, you don't change your life just because you've quit smoking. If you do you will be making a genuine sacrifice and there is no need to. Remember, you haven't given up living. You haven't given up anything. On the contrary, you've cured yourself from an awful disease and escaped from an insidious prison. As the days go by and your health, both physical and mental, improves, the highs will appear higher and the lows less low than when you were a smoker.

7. Whenever you think about smoking either during the next few days or the rest of your life, you think: **YIPPEE, I'M A NON-SMOKER!!!**

A Final Warning

No smoker, given the chance of going back to the time before he became hooked with the knowledge he has now, would opt to start. Many of the smokers who consult me are convinced that if I could only help them stop, they would never dream of smoking again, and yet thousands of smokers successfully kick the habit for many years and lead perfectly happy lives, only to get trapped once again.

I trust that this book will help you to find it relatively easy to stop smoking. But be warned: smokers who find it easy to stop find it easy to start again.

DO NOT FALL FOR THIS TRAP.

No matter how long you have stopped or how confident you are that you will never become hooked again, make it a rule of life not to smoke for any reason. Resist the millions of pounds that the tobacco companies spend on promotion, and remember they are pushing the No. 1 killer drug and poison. You wouldn't be tempted to try heroin; and cigarettes kill hundreds of thousands more people than heroin does.

Remember, that first cigarette will do nothing for you. You will have no withdrawal pangs to relieve, and it will taste awful. What it will do is to put nicotine into your body, and a little voice at the back of your mind will be saying, 'You want another one.' Then you have got the choice of being miserable for a while or starting the whole filthy chain again.

Twelve Years' Feedback

Since the original publication of this book I now have twelve years' feedback, both from my own consultations and from the book itself. Originally it was a struggle. My method was pooh-poohed by the so-called experts. Now smokers fly in from all over the world to attend my consultations, and more members of the medical profession attend them than members of any other profession. The book is already regarded in the UK as the most effective aid for stopping smoking, and its reputation is rapidly spreading throughout the rest of the world.

I'm not a do-gooder. My war—which, I emphasize, is not against smokers but against the nicotine trap—I wage for the purely selfish reason that I enjoy it. Every time I hear of a smoker escaping from the prison I get a feeling of great pleasure, even when it has nothing to do with me. You can imagine also the immense pleasure I obtain from the thousands of grateful letters that I have received over the years.

There has also been considerable frustration. The frustration is caused mainly by two categories of smoker. First, in spite of the warning in the previous chapter, I am disturbed by the number of smokers who find it easy to stop, yet get hooked again and find they can't succeed the next time. This applies not only to readers of the book but also to my consultations.

A man telephoned me a few years ago. He was very distraught; in fact, he was crying. He said, 'I'll pay you £1,000 if you can help me stop for a week. I know if I can just survive a week, I'll be able to do it.' I told him that I charge a fixed fee and that was all he need pay. He attended a group session and, much to his surprise, found it easy to stop. He sent me a very nice thank-you letter.

Practically the last thing I say to ex-smokers leaving my sessions is: 'Remember, you must never smoke another cigarette.' This particular man said, 'Have no fear, Allen. If I manage to stop, I'll definitely never smoke again.'

I could tell that the warning hadn't really registered. I said, 'I know you feel like that at the moment, but how will you feel six months on?'

He said, 'Allen, I will never smoke again.'

About a year later there was another phone call. 'Allen, I had a small cigar at Christmas, and now I'm back on forty cigarettes a day.'

I said, 'Do you remember when you first phoned? You hated it so much you were going to pay me £1,000 if you could stop for a week.'

'I remember. Haven't I been stupid?'

'Do you remember you promised me you would never smoke again?'

'I know. I'm a fool.'

It's like finding someone up to his neck in a bog and about to go under. You help pull him out. He is grateful to you and then, six months later, dives straight back into the bog.

Ironically, when this man attended a subsequent session he said, 'Can you believe it? I offered to pay my son £1,000 if he hadn't smoked by his twenty-first birthday. I paid up. He's now twenty-two and puffing away like a chimney. I can't believe he could be so stupid.'

I said, 'I don't see how you can call him stupid. At least he avoided the trap for twenty-two years, and he doesn't know the misery he's in for. You knew it as well as anyone and survived only a year.'

If re-reading EASYWAY doesn't help, read ONLYWAY or contact your nearest EASYWAY clinic. Smokers who find it easy to stop and start again pose a special problem. However, when you get free **PLEASE, PLEASE, DON'T MAKE THE SAME MISTAKE**. Smokers believe that such people start again because they are still hooked and are missing the cigarette. In fact, they find stopping so easy that they lose their fear of smoking. They think, 'I can have an odd cigarette. Even if I do get hooked again, I'll find it easy to stop again.'

I'm afraid it just doesn't work that way. It's easy to stop smoking, but it's impossible to try to control the addiction. The one thing that is essential to becoming a non-smoker is *not to smoke*.

The other category of smokers that causes me frustration is those who are just too frightened to make the attempt to stop or, when they do, find it a great struggle. The main difficulties appear to be the following:

1. Fear of failure. There is no disgrace in failure, but not to try is plain stupidity. Look at it this way—you're hiding from nothing. The worst thing that can happen is that you fail, in which case you are no worse off than you are now. Just think how wonderful

it would be to succeed. If you don't make the attempt, you have already guaranteed failure.

2. Fear of panic and of being miserable. Don't worry about it. Just think: what awful thing could happen to you if you never smoked another cigarette? Absolutely none. Terrible things will happen if you do. In any case, the panic is caused by cigarettes and will soon be gone. The greatest gain is to be rid of that fear. Do you really believe that smokers are prepared to have their arms and legs removed for the pleasure they get from smoking? If you find yourself feeling panicky, deep breathing will help. If you are with other people and they are getting you down, go away from them. Escape to the garage or an empty office or wherever.

If you feel like crying, don't be ashamed. Crying is nature's way of relieving tension. No one has ever had a good cry without feeling better afterwards. One of the awful things we do to young boys is to teach them not to cry. You see them trying to fight the tears back, but watch the jaw grinding away. As Britons, we teach ourselves to keep a stiff upper lip, not to show any emotions. We are meant to show emotions, not to try to bottle them up inside us. Scream or shout or have a tantrum. Kick a cardboard box or filing cabinet. Regard your struggle as a boxing match that you cannot lose.

No one can stop time. Every moment that passes that little monster inside you is dying. Enjoy your inevitable victory.

3. Not following the instructions. Incredibly, some smokers say to me, 'Your method just didn't work for me.' They then describe how they ignored not only one instruction but practically all of them. (For clarification I will summarize these in the check list at the end of the chapter.)

4. Misunderstanding instructions. The chief problems appear to be these.

- 'I can't stop thinking about smoking.' Of course you can't, and if you try, you will create a phobia and be miserable. It's like trying to get to sleep at night; the more you try, the harder it becomes. I think about smoking 90 per cent of my life. It's what you are thinking that's important. If you are thinking, 'Oh, I'd love a cigarette,' or 'When will I be free?' you'll be miserable. If you are thinking, **'YIPPEE!** I am free!' you'll be happy.

- 'When will the little physical monster die?' The nicotine leaves your body very rapidly. But it is impossible to tell when your body will cease to suffer from the slight physical sensation of nicotine withdrawal. That empty, insecure feeling is identical to normal hunger, depression or stress. All the cigarette does is to increase the level of it. This is why smokers who stop by using the Willpower Method are never quite sure whether they've kicked it. Even after the body has ceased to suffer from nicotine withdrawal, if they suffer normal hunger or stress, their brain is still saying, 'That means you want a cigarette.' The point is you don't have to wait for the nicotine craving to go; it is so slight that we don't even know it's there. We know it only as feeling 'I want a cigarette.' When you leave the dentist after the final session, do you wait for your jaw to stop aching? Of course you don't. You get on with your life. Even though your jaw's still aching, you are elated.
- Waiting for the moment of revelation. If you wait for it, you are just causing another phobia. I once stopped for three weeks on the Willpower Method. I met an old school friend and ex-smoker. He said, 'How are you getting on?'

    I said, 'I've survived three weeks.'

    He said, 'What do you mean, you've survived three weeks?'

    I said, 'I've gone three weeks without a cigarette.'

    He said, 'What are you going to do? *Survive* the rest of your life? What are you waiting for? You've done it. You're a non-smoker.'

    I thought, 'He's absolutely right. What am I waiting for?' Unfortunately, because I didn't fully understand the nature of the trap at that time, I was soon back in it, but the point was noted. You become a non-smoker when you extinguish your last cigarette. The important thing is to be a happy non-smoker from the start.
- 'I am still craving cigarettes.' Then you are being very stupid. How can you claim, 'I want to be a non-smoker,' and then say, 'I want a cigarette'? That's a contradiction. If you say, 'I want a cigarette,' you are saying, 'I want to be a smoker.' Non-smokers don't want to smoke cigarettes. You already know what you really want to be, so stop punishing yourself.
- 'I've opted out of life.' Why? All you have to do is stop choking yourself. You don't have to stop living. Look, it's as simple as this. For the next few days you'll have a slight trauma in your

life. Your body will suffer the almost imperceptible aggravation of withdrawal from nicotine. Now, bear this in mind: you are no worse off than you were. This is what you have been suffering the whole of your smoking life, every time you have been asleep or in a church, supermarket or library. It didn't seem to bother you when you were a smoker, and if you don't stop, you'll go on suffering this distress for the rest of your life. Cigarettes don't make meals or drinks or social occasions; they ruin them. Even while your body is still craving nicotine, meals and social occasions are marvellous. Life is marvellous. Go to social functions, even if there are twenty smokers there. Remember that *you* are not being deprived; *they* are. Every one of them would love to be in your position. Enjoy being the prima donna and the centre of attention. Stopping smoking is a wonderful conversation point, particularly when smokers see that you are happy and cheerful. They'll think that you are incredible. The important point is that you'll be enjoying life right from the start. There's no need to envy them. They'll be envying you.

- 'I am miserable and irritable.' That is because you haven't followed one of my instructions. Find out which one it is. Some people understand and believe everything I say but still start off with a feeling of doom and gloom, as if something terrible were happening. You are doing not only what you'd like to do but what every smoker on the planet would like to do. With any method of stopping, what the ex-smoker is trying to achieve is a certain frame of mind, so that whenever he thinks about smoking he says to himself, **'YIPPEE! I'M FREE!'** If that's your object, why wait? Start off in that frame of mind and never lose it. The rest of the book is designed to make you understand why there is no alternative.

THE CHECK LIST

If you follow these simple instructions, you cannot fail.

1. Make a solemn vow that you will never, ever, smoke, chew or suck anything that contains nicotine, and stick to your vow.

2. Get this clear in your mind: there is absolutely nothing to *give up*. By that I don't mean simply that you will be better off as a non-smoker (you've known that all your life); nor do I mean that al-

though there is no rational reason why you smoke, you must get some form of pleasure or crutch from it or you wouldn't do it. What I mean is, there is no genuine pleasure or crutch in smoking. It is just an illusion, like banging your head against a wall to make it pleasant when you stop.

3. There is no such thing as a confirmed smoker. You are just one of the millions who have fallen for this subtle trap. Like millions of other ex-smokers who once thought they couldn't escape, you have escaped.

4. If at any time in your life you were to weigh up the pros and cons of smoking, the conclusion would always be, a dozen times over, 'Stop doing it. You are a fool.' Nothing will ever change that. It always has been that way, and it always will be. Having made what you know to be the correct decision, don't ever torture yourself by doubting it.

5. Don't try *not* to think about smoking or worry that you are thinking about it constantly. But whenever you do think about it—whether it be today, tomorrow or the rest of your life—think, **'YIPPEE! I'M A NON-SMOKER!'**

6. DO NOT use any form of substitute.
DO NOT keep your own cigarettes.
DO NOT avoid other smokers.
DO NOT change your lifestyle in any way purely because you've stopped smoking.

If you follow the above instructions, you will soon experience the moment of revelation. But:

7. Don't wait for that moment to come. Just get on with your life. Enjoy the highs and cope with the lows. You will find that in no time at all the moment will arrive.

Help the Smoker Left on the Sinking Ship

Smokers are panicking nowadays. They sense that there is a change in society. Smoking is now regarded as an unsociable habit, even by smokers themselves. They also sense that the whole thing is coming to an end. Millions of smokers are now stopping, and all smokers are conscious of this fact.

Every time a smoker leaves the sinking ship, the ones left on it feel more miserable. Every smoker instinctively knows that it is ridiculous to pay good money for dried leaves rolled up in paper, to set light to them and to breathe cancer-triggering tar into his lungs. If you still don't think it is silly, try sticking a burning cigarette in your ear and ask yourself what the difference is. Just one. You cannot get the nicotine that way. If you can stop sticking cigarettes in your mouth, you won't need the nicotine.

Smokers cannot find a rational reason for smoking, but if someone else is doing it, they do not feel quite so silly.

Smokers blatantly lie about their habit, not only to others but to themselves. They have to. The brainwashing is essential if they are to retain some self-respect. They feel the need to justify their habit, not only to themselves but to non-smokers. They are therefore forever advertising the illusory advantages of smoking.

If a smoker stops on the Willpower Method, he still feels deprived and tends to become a moaner. All this does is to confirm to other smokers how right they are to keep smoking.

If the ex-smoker succeeds in kicking the habit, he is grateful that he no longer has to go through life choking himself or wasting money. But he has no need to justify himself; he doesn't sit there saying how marvellous it is not to be smoking. He will do that only if he is asked, and smokers won't ask that question. They wouldn't like the answer. Remember, it is fear that keeps them smoking, and they would rather keep their heads in the sand.

The only time they ask that question is when it is time to stop.

Help the smoker. Remove these fears. Tell him how marvellous it is not to have to go through life choking yourself, how lovely it is to wake up in the morning feeling fit and healthy instead of wheezing and coughing, how wonderful it is to be free of slavery, to be able to enjoy the whole of your life, to be rid of those awful black shadows. Or, better still, get him to read the book.

It is essential not to belittle the smoker by indicating that he is polluting the atmosphere or is in some way unclean. There is a common conception that the ex-smoker is the worst in this respect. I believe this conception has some substance, and I think this is due to the Willpower Method of stopping. Because the ex-smoker, although he has kicked the habit, retains part of the brainwashing, part of him still believes that he has made a sacrifice. He feels vulnerable, and his natural defensive mechanism is to attack the smoker. This may help the ex-smoker, but it does nothing to help the smoker. All it does is put his back up, make him feel even more wretched and consequently make his need for a cigarette even greater.

Although the change in society's attitude to smoking is the main reason why millions of smokers are quitting, it doesn't make it easier for them to do so. In fact, it makes it a great deal harder. Most smokers nowadays believe they are stopping mainly for health reasons. This is not strictly true. Although the enormous health risk is obviously the chief reason for quitting, smokers have been killing themselves for years and it has made not the slightest difference. The main reason why smokers are stopping is because society is beginning to see smoking for what it actually is: filthy drug addiction. The enjoyment was always an illusion; this attitude removes this illusion, so that the smoker is left with nothing.

The complete ban on smoking in London's Underground system is a classic example of the smoker's dilemma. The smoker either takes the attitude: 'OK, if I cannot smoke on the train, I will find another means of travel,' which does no good but merely loses London Transport valuable revenue, or he says: 'Fine, it will help me cut down on my smoking.' The result of this is that instead of smoking one or two cigarettes on the train, neither of which he would have enjoyed, he abstains for an hour. During this enforced period of abstinence, however, not only will he be mentally deprived and waiting for his reward but his body will have been craving nicotine—and, oh, how precious that cigarette will be when he is eventually allowed to light up.

Enforced abstinences do not actually cut down the intake because the smoker just indulges himself in more cigarettes when he is eventually allowed to smoke. All it does is to ingrain in the smoker's mind how precious cigarettes are and how dependent he is upon them.

I think the most insidious aspect of this enforced abstinence is its effect on pregnant women. We allow unfortunate teenagers to be bombarded with massive advertising that gets them hooked in the first place. Then, at what is probably the most stressful period in their lives, when in their deluded minds they need cigarettes most of all, the medical profession blackmails them into giving up because of the harm they are causing the baby. Many are unable to do so and are forced, through no fault of their own, to suffer a guilt complex for the rest of their lives. Many of them succeed and are pleased to do so, thinking, 'Fine, I will do this for the baby and after nine months I will be cured anyway.' Then comes the pain and fear of labour, followed by the biggest 'high' of their lives. The pain and fear are over, and the beautiful, new baby has arrived—and the old trigger mechanism comes into operation. Part of the brainwashing is still there, and almost before the cord has been cut, the girl has a cigarette in her mouth. The elation of the occasion blocks the foul taste from her mind. She has no intention of becoming hooked again. 'Just the one cigarette.' Too late! She is already hooked. Nicotine has got into her body again. The old craving will start, and even if she doesn't become hooked again straight away, post-natal depression will probably catch her out.

It is strange that although heroin addicts are criminals in law, our society's attitude is quite rightly 'What can we do to help the pathetic individuals?' Let us adopt the same attitude to the poor smoker. He is not smoking because he wants to but because he thinks he has got to, and, unlike the heroin addict, he usually has to suffer years and years of mental and physical torture. We always say a quick death is better than a slow one, so do not envy the poor smoker. He deserves your pity.

Advice to Non-smokers

HELP GET YOUR SMOKING FRIENDS OR RELATIVES TO READ THIS BOOK. First study the contents of this book and try to put yourself in the place of the smoker.

Do not force him to read this book or try to stop him smoking by telling him he is ruining his health or wasting his money. He already knows this better than you do. Smokers do not smoke because they enjoy it or because they want to. They only tell themselves and other people this in order to retain self-respect. They smoke because they feel dependent on cigarettes, because they think that the cigarette relaxes them and gives them courage and confidence and that life will never be enjoyable without a cigarette. If you try to force a smoker to stop, he feels like a trapped animal and wants his cigarette even more. This may turn him into a secret smoker and in his mind the cigarette will become even more precious (see chapter 26).

Instead, concentrate on the other side of the coin. Get him into the company of ex-smokers (there are 15 million of them in Britain alone). Get them to tell the smoker how they too thought they were hooked for life and how much better life is as a non-smoker.

Once you have got him believing that he can stop, his mind will start opening. Then start explaining the delusion created by withdrawal pangs. Not only are the cigarettes not giving him a boost but it is they that are destroying his confidence and making him irritable and unrelaxed.

He should now be ready to read this book himself. He will be expecting to read pages and pages about lung cancer, heart diseases, etc. Explain that the approach is completely different and that references to illness are just a small fraction of the material in the book.

HELP DURING THE WITHDRAWAL PERIOD. Whether the ex-smoker is suffering or not, assume that he is. Do not try to minimize his suffering by telling him it is easy to stop; he can do that himself. Instead keep telling him how proud you are, how much better he is looking, how much sweeter he smells, how much easier his breathing is. It is particularly important to keep doing this. When a smoker makes an attempt to stop, the euphoria of the attempt and the attention he gets from friends and colleagues can help him along. However, they tend to forget quickly, so keep that praise going.

Because he is not talking about smoking, you may think he has forgotten about it and don't want to remind him. Usually the complete opposite is the case with the Willpower Method, as the ex-smoker tends to be obsessed by nothing else. So do not be frightened to bring the subject up, and keep praising him; he will tell you if he doesn't want you to remind him of smoking.

Go out of your way to relieve him of pressures during the withdrawal period. Try to think of ways of making his life interesting and enjoyable.

This can also be a trying period for non-smokers. If one member of a group is irritable, it can cause general misery all round. So anticipate this if the ex-smoker is feeling irritable. He may well take it out on you, but do not retaliate; it is at this time that he needs your praise and sympathy the most. If you are feeling irritable yourself, try not to show it.

One of the tricks I used to play when trying to give up with the aid of the Willpower Method was to get into a tantrum, hoping that my wife or friends would say, 'I cannot bear to see you suffering like this. For goodness' sake, have a cigarette.' The smoker then does not lose face, as he isn't 'giving in'—he has been instructed. If the ex-smoker uses this ploy, on no account encourage him to smoke. Instead say, 'If that is what cigarettes do to you, thank goodness you will soon be free. How marvellous that you had the courage and sense to give up.'

Finale: Help End
This Scandal

n my opinion, cigarette smoking is the biggest scandal in society, including nuclear weapons.

Surely the very basis of civilization, the reason why the human species has advanced so far, is that we are capable of communicating our knowledge and experiences not only to each other but to future generations. Even the lower species find it necessary to warn their offspring of the pitfalls in life.

If nuclear weapons do not go off, there is no problem. The people who advocate nuclear armament can carry on saying smugly, 'They are keeping the peace.' If they do go off, they will solve the smoking problem and every other problem, and a bonus for the politicians is that there will be nobody around to say, 'You were wrong' (I wonder if this is why they support nuclear weapons).

However, much as I disagree with nuclear weapons, at least such decisions are made in good faith, in the genuine belief that they help mankind, whereas with smoking, the true facts are known. Maybe during the last war people genuinely believed that cigarettes gave you courage and confidence. Today the authorities know that is a fallacy. Just watch the cigarette advertisements nowadays. They make no claims about relaxation or pleasure. The only claims they make are about the quality of the tobacco. Why should we be worried about the quality of a poison?

The sheer hypocrisy is incredible. As a society we get uptight about glue sniffing and heroin addiction. Compared with cigarette smoking, these problems are mere pimples in our society. Sixty per cent of the population have been addicted to nicotine, and most of them spend the bulk of their pocket money on cigarettes. Tens of thousands of people have their lives ruined every year because they become hooked. Smoking is by far the biggest killer in society and yet the biggest vested interest is the British treasury. It makes £8,000,000,000 every year out of the misery of nicotine addicts, and the tobacco empires are allowed to spend £120,000,000 per year advertising the filth.

How clever that cigarette companies print that health warning on packets, and the British government spends a pittance on TV campaigns involving cancer scares, bad breath and legs being chopped off, and then they justify themselves morally by saying, 'We have warned you of the danger. It is your choice.' The smoker doesn't have the choice any more than the heroin addict does. Smokers do not decide to become hooked; they are lured into a subtle trap. If smokers had the choice, the only smokers tomorrow morning would be the youngsters starting out believing they could stop any time they wanted to.

Why the phoney standards? Why are heroin addicts seen as criminals, yet able to register as addicts in the UK and get free heroin and proper medical treatment to help get off it? Just try registering as a nicotine addict. You cannot get cigarettes at cost. You have to pay three times the true value.

If you go to your doctor for help, either he will tell you, 'Stop doing it, it's killing you,' which you already know, or he will prescribe another form of nicotine addiction that will cost you a prescription fee and actually contains the drug you are trying to kick.

Scare campaigns do not help smokers to stop. They make it harder. All they do is to frighten smokers, which makes them want to smoke even more. It doesn't even prevent teenagers from becoming hooked. Teenagers know that cigarettes kill, but they also know one cigarette will not do it. Because the habit is so prevalent, sooner or later the teenager, through social pressures or curiosity, will try just one cigarette. And *because* it tastes so awful, he will probably become hooked.

Why do we allow this scandal to go on? Why don't governments come out with proper campaigns? Why don't they tell us that nicotine is a drug and a killer poison, that it does not relax you or give you confidence but destroys your nerves and that it can take just one cigarette to become hooked?

I remember reading H. G. Wells's *The Time Machine*. The book describes an incident in the distant future in which a man falls into a river. His companions merely sit around the bank like cattle, oblivious to his cries of desperation. I found that incident inhuman and very disturbing. I find the general apathy of our society to the smoking problem very similar. We allow darts tournaments sponsored by tobacco companies to be televised during peak viewing hours. There is a cry of 'One hundred and eighty'. The player is then shown lighting a cigarette. Imagine the furore if the tournament were being sponsored by the Mafia and the player were a heroin addict, shown injecting himself.

Why do we allow society to subject healthy young teenagers, youngsters whose lives are complete before they start smoking, to paying through the nose for the rest of their lives just for the privilege of destroying themselves mentally and physically in a lifetime of slavery, a lifetime of filth and disease?

You may feel that I over-dramatize the facts. Not so. My father was cut down in his early fifties because of cigarette smoking. He was a strong man and might still have been alive today.

I believe I was within an inch of dying during my forties, although my death would have been attributed to a brain haemorrhage rather than to cigarette smoking. I now spend my life being consulted by people who have been crippled by the disease or are in the last stages. And, if you care to think about it, you probably know of many too.

There is a wind of change in society. A snowball has started that I hope this book will help turn into an avalanche.

You too can help by spreading the message.

FINAL WARNING

You can now enjoy the rest of your life as a happy non-smoker. In order to make sure that you do, you need to follow these simple instructions:

1. Keep this book safely in a place where you can easily refer to it. Do not lose it, lend it out or give it away.

2. If you ever start to envy another smoker, realize that he or she will be envious of you. You are not being deprived. The smoker is.

3. Remember you did not enjoy being a smoker. That's why you stopped. You do enjoy being a non-smoker.

4. Remember, there is no such thing as just one cigarette.

5. Never doubt your decision never to smoke again. You know it's the correct decision.

6. If you have any difficulties, contact your nearest Allen Carr clinic. You will find a list of these on the following pages.

Now at last you can say
'YIPPEE! I'M A NON-SMOKER'

You have achieved something really marvellous. Every
time I hear of a smoker escaping from the sinking ship,
I get a feeling of enormous satisfaction.

It would give me great pleasure to hear that you have
freed yourself from the slavery of the weed. Please sign
the letter and add your comments, and send it back to:

Allen Carr USA
12823 Kingsbridge Lane
Houston, Texas 77077
Tel.: 281 597-1904
Fax: 281 597-9829
E-mail: Acatt38826@aol.com

or

Allen Carr USA
St. Louis, Missouri
Tel.: 800 524-9949
E-mail: acezway@juno.com

....

YIPPEE! I'M A NON-SMOKER

....
Signed   Date
....
Name
....
Address
....
                                  Zip code
....
Comments
....

....

....

ALLEN CARR CLINICS

UK

http://www.qwerty.co.uk/allencarr

LONDON
1c Amity Grove, Raynes Park, London SW20 0LQ, Tel. & Fax: 0181 944 7761,
   Therapist: Roy Sheehan

BIRMINGHAM
415 Hagley Road West, Quinton, Birmingham B32 2AD, Tel. & Fax: 0121 423
   1227, Therapist: Jason Vale, E-mail: JASEYBEAN@AOL.COM

BRISTOL
Unit 13, The Coach House, 2 Upper York Street, Bristol BS2 8QN, Tel.: 0117 908
   1106, Therapist: John Emery

DEVON
Angel Cottage, Cutteridge Farm, Whitestone, Exeter EX4 2HE, Tel.: 01392
   811603, Therapist: Trevor Emdon, E-mail: horwell@curobell.co.uk

KENT
Tel.: 01622 679 595, Therapist: Angela Jouanneau

NORTH EAST
10 Dale Terrace, Dalton-le-Dale, Seaham, County Durham SR7 8QP, Tel. & Fax:
   0191 581 0449, Therapist: Tony Attrill

SHEFFIELD
Tel.: 0700 900 0305, Fax: 01904 340 159, Therapist: Diana Evans

SOUTH COAST
Christchurch Business Centre, Grange Road, Dorset BH23 4JD, Tel.: 01425
   272757, Fax: 01425 274250, Therapist: Anne Emery, E-mail:
   AEmery3192@aol.com

YORKSHIRE
Leeds: Tel.: 0113 235 0000, Fax: 01904 340 159,
   Therapist: Diana Evans
York: 185 Burton Stone Lane, York YO3 6DG, Tel.: 0700 9000305, Fax: 01904
   340159, Therapist: Diana Evans

EDINBURGH
48 Eastfield, Joppa, Edinburgh EH15 2PN, Tel. & Fax: 0131 660 6688, Therapist:
   Derek McGuff, E-mail: derek@djmcg.demon.co.uk

WALES
Travellers Chambers, Ludlow Street, Penarth, S. Glamorgan CF64 1ED, Tel.:
   01222 705500, Fax: 0181 940 1153, Therapist: Jim Trimmer, E-mail:
   jimtrim@compuserve.com

HOLLAND

AMSTERDAM
Pythagorasstraat 22, 1098 GC Amsterdam, Tel.: 020 465 4665, Fax: 020 465
   6682, Therapist: Eveline De Mooij

ROTTERDAM
Mathenesserlaan 290, 3021 HV Rotterdam, Tel.: 010 244 07 09, Fax. 010 244 07
   10, Therapist: Kitty van't Hof

UTRECHT
De Beaufortlaan 22 B, 3768 MJ Soestduinen, (gem. Soest), Tel.: (stop smoking): 035 60 29458, Tel. (weight): 035 60 32153, Fax: 035 60 322 65, Therapist: Nicolette de Boer, E-mail: nicolette@overtoom.com

ITALY

MILAN
Studio Pavanello, Piazza Argentina 4, 20124 Milan, Tel.: 02 29 52 9251, Therapist: Francesca Cesati

FRANCE

MARSEILLE
70 Rue St Ferreol, 13006 Marseille, Tel.: 04 91 33 54 55, Fax: 04 91 33 32 77, Therapist: Erick Serre, E-mail: ELYFRANCE@COMPUSERVE.COM

AUSTRALIA

MELBOURNE
148 Central Road, Nunawading, Victoria 3131, Tel. & Fax: 03 9894 8866, Therapist: Trudy Ward, E-mail: easywaya@Bigpond.com

USA

MISSOURI
St. Louis: Tel.: 800 524-9949, Therapist: Keith Newmark, E-mail: acezway@juno.com

TEXAS
Houston: 12823 Kingsbridge Lane, Houston, Texas 77077, Tel.: 281 597-1904, Fax: 281 597-9829, Therapist: Laura Cattell, E-mail: ACatt38826@aol.com

ISRAEL

JERUSALEM
97 Jaffa Street, Office 806, Jerusalem, Tel.: 02 624 2586, Therapist: Michael Goldman

HONG KONG

CAUSEWAY BAY
22nd Floor, A & B Guangdong Tours Centre, 18 Pennington Street, Causeway Bay, Tel.: 852 2893 1571, Fax: 852 2554 2958, Therapists: Leo Ngai & Jon Lewis-Evans, E-mail: easyway@ukwww.com

CANADA

TORONTO
461 North Service Road, Unit B7, Oakville, Ontario L6M 2V5, Tel.: 905 827 3888, Fax: 905 827 9434, Therapist: Nancy Toth, E-mail: aceasyway@msn.com

GERMANY

http://www.allen-carr.de, E-mail: info@allen-carr.de

BAD SALZUFLEN
Im neuen Land 20a, 32107 Bad Salzuflen, Tel.: 05222 797 622, Fax: 05222 797 624, Therapist: Wolfgang Rinke, E-mail: wolfgang.rinke@allen-carr.de

BERLIN
Hohenstauffenstr. 10a, 10781 Berlin, Tel.: 030 217 50488, Fax: 030 217 50489, Therapist: Regine Schoengraf, E-mail: regine.schoengraf@allen-carr.de

DUSSELDORF
Steffenstr. 4, 40545, Dusseldorf, Tel.: 0211 557 1738, Fax: 0211 557 1740, Therapist: Axel Matheja, E-mail: axel.matheja@allen-carr.de

FRANKFURT
Tel.: 06701 960673, Therapist: Elfi Blume, E-mail: elfi.blume@allen-carr.de

HAMBURG
Tel.: 040 280 510 56

MUNICH
Hochgstattweg 8, 82216 Uberacker, Tel.: 081 35 8466, Fax: 081 35 89 20, Therapists: Petra Wackerle & Stephan Kraus

STUTTGART
Heumadener Str. 11, 70329 Stuttgart-Hedelfingen, Tel.: 0711 4209154, Fax 08135 8920, Therapists: Petra Wackerle & Stephen Kraus

AUSTRIA

http://www.allen-carr.at

SALZBURG
Tel.: 662 878718, Fax: 08031 463068, Therapist: Erich Kellermann, E-mail: erich.kellermann@allen-carr.at

VIENNA
Tel.: 01 3331355, Fax: 08031 463068, Therapist: Erich Kellermann, E-mail: erich.kellermann@allen-carr.at

SWITZERLAND

http://www.allen-carr.ch

ZURICH
Bernhofstr. 34, Ch-8134, Adliswil, Tel.: 0041 1 7105678, Fax: 0041 1 7105683, Therapist: Cyrill Argast, E-mail: cyrill.argast@allen-carr.ch

BELGIUM

ANTWERP
Marialei 47, 2018 Antwerpen, Tel.: 03 281 6255, Fax: 03 744 0608, Therapist: Dirk Nielandt, E-mail: GD32280@GLO.BE

SPAIN

MADRID
C/Fernandez De Los Rios, 106, 1. IZQ, 28015 Madrid, Tel.. 91 543 8504, Therapist: Geoffrey Molloy & Rhea Sivi, E-mail: sivimoll@arrakis.es

ICELAND

REYKJAVIK
Ljosheimar 4, 104 Reykjavik, Tel.: 354 553 9590, Fax: 354 588 7060, Therapists:
    Petur Einarsson & Valgeir Skagfjoro, E-mail: pein@ismennt.is

IRELAND

DUBLIN
123 Coolamber Park, Templeogue, Dublin 16, Tel.: 01 494 1644, Therapist:
    Brenda Sweeney, E-mail: seanow@iol

SOUTH AFRICA

CAPETOWN
Western Cape, Tel.: 083 600 5555, Fax: 083 8 600 5555, Therapist: Dr. Charles
    Nel

ECUADOR

QUITO
Veintimilla 878 y Amazonas, P.O. Box 17-03-179, Quito, Tel. & Fax: 02 56 33
    44, Therapist: Ingrid Wittich

About the Author

Allen Carr became a qualified accountant in 1958. He was successful in his chosen profession, but his hundred-cigarettes-a-day addiction was driving him to despair. In 1983, after countless failed attempts to quit, by using willpower and other methods, he finally discovered what the world had been waiting for—the Easy Way to Stop Smoking. Since leaving accountancy to help cure the world's smokers, Allen has built up a global reputation as a result of the phenomenal success of his method. He is now recognized as the world's leading expert on helping smokers to quit. Smokers used to have to fly from all over the world to attend his clinic in London; now his network of clinics spans the globe. *Allen Carr's Easy Way to Stop Smoking* is an international bestseller and has been published in over twenty different languages. His second book, *The Only Way to Stop Smoking Permanently*, and video, audio and CD ROM versions of his method are also available. In his third publication, *Allen Carr's Easyweigh to Lose Weight*, he applies the same simple logic to weight loss, so that it becomes easy and enjoyable, as those attending his clinics have discovered. His latest book is *How to Stop Your Child Smoking*.

The Achievement Challenge
How to Be a 10 in Business

The Achievement Challenge

How to Be a 10 in Business

By

Don Beveridge, Jr.

and

Jeffrey P. Davidson

Dow Jones-Irwin
Homewood, Illinois 60430

This publication is designed to provide accurate and authoritative information in regard to the subject matter covered. It is sold with the understanding that the publisher is not engaged in rendering legal, accounting, or other professional service. If legal advice or other expert assistance is required, the services of a competent professional person should be sought.

From a Declaration of Principles jointly adopted by a Committee of the American Bar Association and a Committee of Publishers.

This book was set in Century Schoolbook by Carlisle Communications, Ltd.
The production manager was Carma W. Fazio.
The designer was Sam Concialdi.
The Maple-Vail Book Manufacturing Group was the printer and binder.

ISBN   1-55623-060-5

Library of Congress Catalog Card No. 87–71441

Printed in the United States of America

1 2 3 4 5 6 7 8 9 0 MP 5 4 3 2 1 0 9 8

FOREWORD

During a break near the end of reading this book, I spied a bumper sticker. Its message was: A BEACH IS BETTER ON A BAD DAY, THAN A JOB ON A GOOD DAY. I said to myself: "This bumper sticker owner needs a good dose of *THE ACHIEVEMENT CHALLENGE: HOW TO BE A 10 IN BUSINESS!*"

Don Beveridge packs his book in a coherent and compelling manner with what he has been counseling companies for years. His is no consultant-come-lately kind of counsel. It was born and bred by several decades of diagnosing and resolving problems here and abroad. The author conveys to us what he learned through protracted, firsthand experience.

This book has answers . . . lots of answers . . . for those entrapped by a marking-time business or the career blahs. Just note this sampling of Beveridge-isms representing what you are about to read . . . and enjoy:

- "Success is not a goal. Success is a *result!* "
- "The Risk Phase is the time to innovate within the firm; it's time to question existing management practices, time to review old policies and time to rewrite the procedures manual."
- "I'd much rather be at only ninety percent of an excellence standard than one hundred percent of an adequacy standard."
- "Vacillating and varying from the objective and goal . . . creates failure."
- "Quite frankly, the only difference between stumbling blocks and stepping stones is the way we use them."
- "Entrepreneurs and winners do what others won't do."
- "In conclusion . . . the non-negotiable standard to insure we achieve, excel and get ahead in business is customer focus, customer focus, customer focus."

Beveridge identifies and details the career milestones to guide, measure and assess one's achievement towards career success: Learning Phase → Leadership Phase → Risk Phase → Wealth Phase → and Security Phase. What seemingly simple yet powerful guidance this career-sequencing represents. To those searching for a blueprint, here is one meriting serious consideration. Fabled Hansel and Gretel depended on shiny pebbles to guide them through uncertainty. Too bad they didn't know Beveridge. His approach is practical and illuminating. Enviably, the author avoids blue-sky promises while nevertheless expanding our business horizons and showing us the stars.

In 1985, the author recounts that Burger King retained Beveridge Business Systems to instill Burger King employees with a new advertising campaign. The theme was a bigger and better Whopper. Beveridge's organization effectively translated that advertising theme into an employee rallying-point i.e. a bigger and better *you*. In a very real sense, that could be an unstated theme of this book . . . a bigger and better you! Through twelve, well-paced chapters that clarion message bleeds through for you, the reader.

Complementing this book's valuable message is an array of pertinent quotes and "successful person profiles." The profiles neatly reinforce Beveridge's advice with real-world insights from role-model doers. The book is highly readable and easily understood. If you decide not to do anything after you read this book, it won't be because you didn't understand it.

My final observations are these. This is not a book for all seasons. What book is? This book is for those who seek a new way to view . . . and a new way to pursue . . . business and career success. Beveridge's advice exacts commitment, energy and perseverance. Slug-a-beds need not apply! But for those bent on excelling in their business and their career, this book's for you. For you, my admonition is:

DON'T JUST READ THIS BOOK. INHALE IT!

John C. Keane
Director
Bureau of the Census
June, 1987

ACKNOWLEDGMENTS

The authors wish to thank numerous individuals for their support. Elizabeth Warren at the Arlington County Library is an author's best friend, speedily providing references and citations. As she has done so many times, Judy Dubler provided expert word-processing support. The editing assistance offered by Dianne Walbrecker and Jeanne Wolfe accelerated preparation of the final product. Dirk Beveridge was helpful in furnishing supporting data. Betty Beveridge lent her valuable insights and objectivity.

　　　　We also wish to thank Susan Glinert, Rori Rozen, and Mike Desposito for their marketing support. Finally, special thanks to Richard Staron whose unceasing efforts were instrumental in making this book a reality.

CONTENTS

Disintegrating Standards. Recapturing
Excellence as a Standard.

INTRODUCTION

We all continually face the challenge to achieve whether it's on the job, in our studies, or at home. Yet achievement is not something in which we are normally schooled. Each of us seeks our own path towards achievement, usually through trial and error; an inefficient, frustrating process mastered by few.

This book offers basic guidelines for high achievement. It is a reflection of what the senior author has learned over the past 33 years, as an executive with Mobil Oil and as a speaker, consultant, author, and successful entrepreneur in his own right.

The purpose of this book is to provide business executives and professionals with practical, implementable information and ideas to achieve great results in their own careers or businesses. Insights are offered as to what makes one successful. Working with top corporations and leading executives on three continents, the senior author has been able to succinctly capture the essence and common denominators of a successful career and a balanced life. There are critical skills and experiences that everyone who wants to achieve and be successful must acquire. If your present career track does not include or is not likely to provide them, then you must actively seek them.

Chapter One, "Promotable Posturing," provides a road map to promotability whether you're employed by a multinational corporation or self-employed as an entrepreneur in your own venture. It details the five key phases in the career of a high achiever and offers specifics as to what should happen and when.

Chapter Two, "The Continuity of Challenge," poses the question, "When were you happiest in your job?" The overwhelming response of most people to this question is, "When the job was new." This is when the job provided the greatest challenge. Chapter Two will show you how to ensure that you are continually being challenged and why it is your responsibility to stay challenged.

Chapter Three, "Expediency, Adequacy, or Excellence Standards," makes an important distinction between the standards maintained by achievers versus those maintained by the masses. The Chapter also provides guidelines by which you can determine if your standards are, indeed, excellence standards.

Chapter Four, "Why People Fail," offers three basic indicators that serve as harbingers to personal or business failure. It also provides ten common reasons why people fail and makes a strong argument that the study of failure is as important as the study of success for those who want to achieve.

Chapter Five, "A Positive Goals Attitude," focuses on goal-setting in a new way and shows why the accomplishment of set goals must be mandatory as opposed to being guidelines or targets. It also discusses how to learn from role models while not emulating them, and why a role model need not be from your own industry or profession.

Chapter Six, "Make Change an Ally," offers a strong argument as to why your ability to cope with and actually seek change spells the long-term difference between career success or failure. The chapter provides a test for tolerating your capability for change and offers several examples of corporations and individuals who use change to their advantage.

Chapter Seven, "The Orchestrators," introduces a new term and a new concept to describe how achievers are able to work effectively within their organizations or business environments. Though the road to becoming an effective orchestrator is often bumpy, the role is nevertheless necessary to generate a team psychology that gets many people working in unison toward a common goal. Orchestrators are people with vision who are able to convince others to work with or support them.

Chapter Eight, "Entrepreneurship," provides eleven characteristics of the entrepreneur based on studies conducted at the Caruth Institute. Entrepreneurism is synonomous with leadership. This chapter also discusses why entrepreneurs are "take-charge" individuals, and how to assess your entrepreneurial profile.

Chapter Nine, "Execution, The Competitive Edge," addresses a problem and makes an important distinction that affects nearly all businesses. Most communication and effort are expended upon what is perceived to be a deficiency of knowledge. For example, salespeople are trained extensively on product capabilities, performance, and specifications. Unfortunately, what is needed in most companies, and by most individuals, is not greater product knowledge but better execution of strategies, plans, and tasks. The promotable person understands that the ability to execute offers a unique competitive advantage and is a characteristic of all achievers.

Chapter Ten, "Organize, Organize, Organize," puts into proper perspective the importance of personal organizational skills and the role this ability plays in fostering an environment of achievement. If you are organized, you can take better advantage of opportunities as they present themselves. This chapter provides guidelines on how to increase your organizational capabilities. Also, it stresses that if you are overwhelmed by the responsibilities of managing and staying organized, it's okay to let others lead while you become a good follower.

Chapter Eleven, "Customer-Focused Culture," profiles the new corporate and professional mission: to produce customers that are more than satisfied. Drawing on anecdotes such as the customer focus developed by Mercury Marine, this chapter reveals why corporations as well as individuals must renew their focus on those who they serve. It also offers a broader definition of "customer." A customer is anyone to whom you must report, from whom you earn salaries or revenue, or who otherwise looks to you for help.

Chapter Twelve, "How Do My People See Me?", provides a rare look at how employees regard their supervisors. This can include being a non-manager, a policeman or policewoman, or a superman or superwoman. Yet the proper and, indeed, only way for a manager or supervisor to be perceived is as a coach. "How Do My People See Me?" offers new insights as to what your employees may be thinking, but are not apt to tell you.

A Balanced Perspective

This book provides a balanced perspective and an enjoyable way of mapping out your whole career by relying on an active, time-tested set of principles that you can readily implement. The book prescribes plans for achievement and success that don't require mortgaging one's time, energy, and outside life. Instead, it stresses maintaining a normal, balanced schedule that includes time for the family, exercise, and vacations.

The 'Excellence' books talk about companies that get ahead. The Achievement Challenge talks about the people in those companies who *got ahead*.

Following each chapter are success profiles of individuals of varying ages and occupations who have enjoyed great achievements while maintaining a balanced life. This perspective is particularly important in the late 1980s and 1990s, as so many business executives and career professionals find themselves spending more and more hours on the job while withdrawing from other parts of their lives.

Those who don't achieve a balance, and instead go all-out for their career or job, actually have less chance at lasting achievement because they fail to effectively prioritize. The profiles provided at the end of each chapter, summarized below, are real-world examples of successful individuals whose working styles and lifestyles embody the principles discussed throughout the book.

SUCCESSFUL PERSON PROFILES

Uniqueness and creativity, blended with a family atmosphere

Bernie Swain and Harry Rhoads
Founders
Washington Speakers Bureau

IBM standards and performance in the laundry business

Richard T. Farmer
Chairman and CEO
Cintas Corporation

A competitive individual in a security-oriented environment

Jim Hennessy
Executive Vice President
NYNEX Corporation

Attacking change with vigor, confidence, and results

Michael J. Friduss
General Manager, Distribution
Illinois Bell Telephone

The right man in the right place, anywhere, any time

Kendrick B. Melrose
President and CEO
Toro Company

Drive, commitment, and intuition, forming the basis of the skills necessary to succeed

Helen F. Boehm
President
Boehm Porcelain

Finding a way to do what they love doing and making a lot of money in the process

Charlie and Ginny Cary
Founders
The Moorings Group

A commitment to develop people in an industry that never does

Richard A. Ferguson
President
New City Associates

An internationally recognized leader in his industry

Richard J. Haayen
Chairman and CEO
Allstate Insurance Company

What the CEOs of today will use as a role model

J. Jeffrey Campbell
Chairman Restaurant Group
Pillsbury

Clear, concise, confident, professional management

Dale F. Larson
Group President
Continental Grain Company

Guts, glory, and the ultimate entrepreneur

W. J. (Jim) Ellison
President/Owner
Ellison Machinery Company

CHAPTER 1

PROMOTABLE POSTURING

"The men [and women] who succeed are the efficient few. They are the few who have the ambition and the will power to develop themselves."

Herbert Casson

Being successful is important to you. Whether you work for a corporation or yourself, you want to work wisely and move ahead. To do this most effectively, you must be aware of promotable posturing, the positions in which you must place yourself to succeed in a career or business. This chapter and this book will provide the information necessary for you, and a blueprint to guide you, on your quest for success.

Our task is this: To get you promoted, or to make your business more successful. We're going to assume that you have the tools, the skills, and the desire to get ahead. We're going to assume you're working in an environment that has opportunities for advancement. And finally, we also will assume that you're not the only one in your company or business who has these characteristics and ambition.

In order to accomplish our task, we are going to discuss five key phases in a system to achieve, excel, and get ahead in business. They are proven methods that have worked for others, and they will work again, but this time for you! Be forewarned that sacrifices will need to be made. We offer no magic wand. Leadership in a competitive industry is not a bed of roses. There are many trade–offs, many rewards, and some disappointments.

Management Doesn't Come Naturally to Many

Frankly, management is a most difficult task! It often involves doing things that are one hundred eighty degrees reversed from what it is you do well. It means ceasing the "doing" yourself, and instead getting productivity from other people. By anyone's assessment, that is a difficult task.

Most of us desire advancement and success—isn't that why you purchased this book? Since you have made the investment, then this is the commitment I'll make to you: If you have the tools, the skills, the opportunity, and the competitiveness required; and, more importantly, if you have the dedication to work hard for your goals, then you have my guarantee that you *will* get ahead. If you have the right prerequisites, you can do it, but it won't be easy. Attaining worthwhile rewards seldom is.

What I'm about to share with you is not drawn from the blue sky. It's the result of working with and for the managers of the world's leading corporations such as Johnson Wax in England, Dennfix in Copenhagen, Musel in France, Purolator in Canada, Endeavor in New Zealand, Ensign in Australia, and General Motors, Burger King, and Continental Grain in the United States.

My firm routinely interfaces with the managing directors, the presidents, and the CEOs, as well as the line and staff managers of the world's foremost organizations. I personally spend a minimum of two days a week, twenty weeks a year, in the field with successful and promotable people. I know, down to the marrow in my bones, that the system about to be described is effective and that the concepts are sound. The execution is your responsibility. If you follow the advice in this book carefully, you will position yourself to be a highly promotable person or the manager of a very successful business. Remember that those individuals who get ahead are those who do more than is necessary. . . and they keep on doing it!

Let me add one additional thought before we proceed. I have found that when successful or promotable people are exposed to new ideas or concepts, especially advice, they rarely become defensive and begin to question the system. Professionals just learning about promotable posturing begin by considering each new idea, and each new concept and component in our system of HOW TO ACHIEVE, EXCEL, AND GET AHEAD, on its own merits. Promotable people ask themselves:

How will I stand up in this company if my peers or my competitors follow this advice, and I don't?

How will I do in this environment if it is my competitors who do these things?

These questions allow a potential leader to logically and unemotionally sort out what it is he or she must do to achieve, excel, and get ahead. If you continually ask yourself those questions, you will position yourself to *objectively* sort out how it is you will prioritize each of the mandatory components in this system.

An attempt to sort out and follow the system *subjectively* will most certainly lead to discouragement. If you catch yourself thinking, "That would take an awful lot of work" or, "That really doesn't apply to me," stop it! Wait until you get the whole picture and gain an understanding of what needs to be accomplished before discounting any parts of it.

I suggest you read straight through each chapter the first time, then with a pad, pencil, and highlighter, go back and read it again. Stop and start as needed, but, for heavens sake, end up with a plan you are personally committed and determined to execute.

A Foundation for Advancement

You can have all the opportunity on this earth and you can have a superhuman desire to be promoted, but, if you haven't laid the foundation, getting ahead, achieving, and excelling are going to be much more difficult, if not impossible. Promotable posturing prepares one for success. It is the career plan that has been demonstrated internationally, time and again, to provide the greatest chance of success and advancement.

Promotable posturing offers benchmarks—activities you should be doing and successful business experience you should be getting—at specific identifiable phases of your career. You may find your current age or position makes a certain activity or experience unavailable or, at best, tardy. Don't let this discourage you, though. In some instances, it is possible to play catch-up. You may be surprised at how far a little polishing will go.

If you are my age, in your fifties, you could do someone else a favor (maybe your children) and share the concepts of promotable posturing with them so they do not miss out on advancement or business opportunities.

LEARNING PHASE

Promotable posturing begins with the learning phase, which takes place between the ages of seventeen and twenty-seven. About 80 percent of the preparation necessary to effectively function in the business environment occurs between the ages of seventeen and twenty-seven. Most people never realize this.

In that period of your life, it's a major fallacy to join a company or organization which is not committed to the development of its human resources. There is just no substitute for good, solid classroom training. Additionally, the management within an organization must understand that *their* number one job priority is to coach and train their subordinates.

You must develop basic business knowledge and skills. Hopefully, you either completed college on the standard path or at least found some other way to obtain college-type training. If you didn't . . . well, you have to play catch-up.

Unfortunately, most young career professionals right out of college are seeking financial rewards. I wanted a car when I was twenty-one. I wanted a large, comfortable new home for my family as quickly as I could get it.

But how many people do we all know who failed to lay their own groundwork? How many started with companies that had no commitment to the training of their personnel? How many of these people are still there, still in a similar position, or still doing the same work today? It may not seem obvious at first, but these people are numerous, because in most cases they tried to circumvent the learning phase of promotable posturing.

At this point, if you are sitting there thinking, "Well, I'm beyond twenty-seven and never graduated from college," that's a crutch and a poor excuse to ignore the learning phase. If you have to play catch-up, do what you can and start doing it now! Every city in the United States has colleges and universities within a short driving distance offering one- and two-day business programs in which almost anyone can participate and benefit from. These schools also offer numerous programs for completing an unfinished college degree and earning higher degrees, structured specifically around the busy professional's schedule.

There are also numerous management development and business skills seminars advertised by direct mail. I know you receive several each month. This time, I'd like you to actually consider enrolling!

Perhaps you have thought of continuing your education but shelved the idea because it would be a lot of work. But think of what you stand to gain—valuable, needed opportunities to upgrade your business skills. So don't tell me you missed the boat. It's never too late. You may be thirty-four or forty-four, but there is no substitute for completing the learning phase.

Make sure your children get the education and training they need. Tell your friends, too. Tell them to demand of their managers continuing learning opportunities.

If you are a field salesperson or representative, and you're not getting in-the-field monthly coaching visits from management necessary to refine your skills, either start pushing and shoving to get these, or go somewhere where you will get them.

Promotable posturing begins necessarily with the learning phase. The completion of each subsequent phase is very difficult to achieve if you have not successfully completed the right prerequisites. Do it now, and you will be on your way, or at least you will have the opportunity to get on your way. An education, formal or informal, isn't a guarantee of promotability or business success. It's a hunting license that will permit you to enter the wilderness of success or career advancement with the right tools. Happy hunting!

LEADERSHIP PHASE

The second phase is the leadership phase, the mandatory period usually initiated between the ages of twenty-eight and thirty-five. In a Bell Telephone brochure entitled, *Essentials of Leadership Training,* it says:

Supervisors must feel a strong personal responsibility to plan and direct their own program for self development. They must be willing to work at this self development and face the very real tension and sacrifice which go with outstanding accomplishment.

I don't know your unique goals for securing a position of leadership. However, in our promotable posturing system, leadership experiences must take place before age thirty-five and preferably beginning at age twenty-eight. I've found that if you have not managed others or had some leadership experience under your belt by that period of your career, you will rarely achieve business ownership or reach executive levels of management later.

The starting point to the leadership phase is to determine if you *can* develop leadership abilities. More importantly, you must find out quickly if you enjoy managing people. Many professionals don't, and to work for thirty years chasing a job, a career, or a business that at fifty you find you hate, is dumb.

Find a way and a place where you can lead and gain the experience you need. Do everything you can to get a supervisory management position early. Ask for it. Hopefully, your current employer or business situation will provide the right opportunity. At Beveridge Business Systems, our analysis has demonstrated that those who really excel will go elsewhere if necessary—to another department or another company—just to gain leadership experiences at the desired time in their career path.

Do not let anyone tell you "you're just not ready for it!" That is possible, of course, but more often it's hogwash. If I had a hundred dollars for every time a promotable individual was told they weren't ready, I'd have half the money on this earth. Naturally, you must have some skills and abilities, but most of them are gained beforehand, in the learning phase of promotable posturing. And the fact is we "learn by doing." There is no better way.

To tell you "you're just not ready" is not definitive enough. Why aren't you ready? Because management doesn't coach? Because no management preparatory training exists within the firm? Why?

Maybe *it is* because you are not prepared, but get it out on the table and make it clear that you want to know how you can get ready. Before you are in your mid-thirties, you will require several years of people-management experience to be successful in your career. So, ask for it. Demand it!

You will learn by practice once you have the responsibility. Set the goal. Let people know your objective. Begin to prepare yourself, or, if you are over thirty-five, start to play catch-up. Today is as good a time as any to talk with your boss. Tomorrow, it may be too late.

So, first complete phase one. Do everything you can to get in-depth training and education between seventeen and twenty-seven. Next, complete phase two. Find a position in which you get management experience. If you cannot find a company that will provide the opportunity, then try a community service group.

RISK PHASE

Now to phase three, the risk phase.

The risk phase normally takes place between the ages of thirty-six and forty-five. It is the time to "do your thing!" At this point in your business life, you are most often reaching the maximum of your abilities, the zenith of your industry expertise, and you still have drive and desire. Most people are still motivated to compete, so now is the time to personally capitalize on these advantages.

DO YOUR THING!

Many read that statement as suggesting that you should quit and start your own business. If that's how you define "doing your thing," then go ahead and do it. However, it doesn't have to carry that meaning. You can do your thing within a company, even your current company. The risk phase, using your gained experiences and abilities, is the time to innovate within the firm; it is time to question existing management practices, to review old policies, and to rewrite the procedures manual.

It is also the time, if appropriate, to disagree with management! If you are not comfortable discussing opposing points of view with the higher-ups at this point in your career, chances are you never will be.

The risk phase is the time to demonstrate you can do more than simply follow and execute. The risk phase is the right period to generate new, innovative programs through which the department or company can grow and benefit. It may be the time to propose to your management comprehensive ideas and plans that suggest major changes in the firm's strategies and planning. Yes, it could even be the time to take the leap into your own venture.

Whatever you choose, you incur risk. If it works out, you are still young enough to enjoy the fruits of your labor and attempt other risks. You will achieve, excel, and get ahead in business. If it does not work out, you are still young enough to recover and maybe try again later.

Remember the old adage: "Better to have tried and failed, than not to have tried at all." In my opinion, the saddest statement any businessperson, at the conclusion of his or her career, could ever make is, "Man, I wish I would have tried that."

No way! If you are ever going to do it, *now* is the time! You will never be more ready than you are between the ages of thirty-six and forty-five. Develop a strong, well-thought-out plan, and cross the T's and dot the I's. Bounce the ideas off several associates or friends you respect, and enlist the support of family or peers if necessary . . . but, GO FOR IT!

As I said, you will never be better prepared than you are during this point in your career. To procrastinate may mean you will never again have conditions that favor you more. Take the risk. It's probably not as 'iffy' as you think.

WEALTH PHASE

Let's move on to phase four, that very important period in your career that has to do with money—lots of it. In the wealth phase, it is important to get a return on your life's investment and reap the harvest you have sown through the other phases.

Most likely, you have attempted to maximize your salary and income throughout your business life and, hopefully, you have earned a series of salary or compensation increases that provide a better than average living.

However, if there exists one period in your career or business life cycle when you are most apt to achieve wealth, this is it. Whether you remain with your present company or move to a new organization, you will be able to best generate real wealth from the ages of forty-five to fifty-five.

When Yamaha Outboard Engines decided to enter the United States market and compete head-on with the big three—that's not GM, Ford, and Chrysler, but, in the marine industry, Evinrude, OMC Johnson, and Mercury—they needed someone who was an experienced and recognized leader in the business. They wanted someone who had an identity within the marine industry; who could function like a magnet, drawing the important dealer and distributor networks together to market the product successfully.

Consequently, Yamaha's choice was "Ham" Hamberger, former leader and general manager of Mercury Marine's outboard division. The company needed Hamberger to effectively develop a distribution network to market Yamaha outboards. I'm not privy to the dollars provided "Ham" for making that move. However, I do know Yamaha needed him badly and if Hamberger did not position himself for wealth when he made that move in the early 1980s . . . well, in my opinion, he never would.

That particular example is of an individual who went outside his company to accumulate wealth.

In contrast, Arnold Kuthy, CEO of the McIntosh Corporation in Pennsylvania, generated personal wealth without moving to a new organization. Kuthy had labored long and hard for the Mobil Oil Corporation and then spent many years as a vice-president for McIntosh. The promotion from vice-president to the positions of both president and chief executive officer came at the apex of an already outstanding career.

When the board of directors asked him to lead the company through troubled times, he was honored. He was confident of his ability to turn the company around and had eagerly awaited this chance. However, despite the personal triumph he felt about the board's offer, Kuthy maintained a sense of reality.

It soon was clear to him that the financial offer, although substantial, was not going to make him wealthy. You see, when

Kuthy and I were managers with Mobil Oil, and later when I was a consultant to the company, on many occasions we discussed promotable posturing and its five phases. He was aware that he was now in the wealth phase of his life and knew he had to structure his salary and benefits to achieve his monetary goals. Throughout the negotiations, Kuthy kept those goals in mind.

In the promotable posturing process, phase four is "wealth time." I do not propose you treat the wealth phase in a cavalier, superficial way. We are not suggesting that you throw your career to the wind. While some people do, most know better.

The wealth phase is the time to obtain a return on your investment and assets and "reap the harvest." Ham Hamberger and Arnold Kuthy did. Why shouldn't you? Be objective and honest and ask yourself what it is you feel you deserve. Do not sell yourself short—you have built up years of experience and knowledge.

Many go through a mid-life crisis in the wealth phase, so you must be wary of a blurred career-enhancement strategy turning to career destruction. But let's put the facts on the table. You must now tear away any hopeful facade. If you are not getting the money you feel you deserve now, between the ages of forty-five and fifty-five, you're probably never going to get it.

So now is the time. Consider your abilities, your performance, your needs, and, importantly, your alternatives. Then ask for, or seek what you think you deserve. For good reason, this period of your business career is called the "nest-egg years." Devise your strategy now to accumulate wealth to your standards, or, unfortunately, it probably won't be attained. It is your choice. Plan for getting it, require it, and ask for it now . . . or, my friend, the opportunity will be gone.

I know completing the wealth phase requires much thought. Consider what I have said carefully, because it is *that* important.

SECURITY PHASE

Now we move on to the fifth phase. You have my guarantee that after you reach age fifty-five you will begin thinking about security. I know, I'm almost there. This is the security phase, the time to actively start thinking about your future comfort and financial stability.

The number of people I have met in this world who start thinking about security when they are only in (or should be in) the leadership, risk, or wealth phases has always depressed me. What a shame. What lost opportunities! What a failure to maximize abilities. After you have reached fifty-five, you should make security your priority. AND NOT BEFORE!

Age fifty-five is the time to start thinking about planning a comfortable retirement. You will notice both your battery and your enthusiasm move to "low" more quickly. You may no longer feel convinced you can save the world or the company. You will have less tolerance for the new ideas of the firm's bright young stars.

So be it. Don't let this scare you. Let those young stars be the leaders and take the risks, while you relax and enjoy all the things you put off during the four previous phases. But this is not a time to relax completely. You need to do some important planning.

I'm not suggesting you sell your business or halt your career advancement at *any* age. But I am saying that this may not be the time to transfer to a new city with a new home and a new mortgage. Again, it is up to you—and, of course, decisions vary by individual. The important point is, in the winter of your career, your judgement and your decisions should have overtones of security considerations. It's time to screw down the hatches.

Look toward guaranteeing yourself a trouble-free, comfortable existence for the balance of your life. Have fun, and if possible, adopt my slogan for living. It's not astute or world shaking, but somehow it justifies my life today. My slogan? Simply, "I owe it to myself."

You do too, don't you? So, what are you going to do about it?

Harry Rhoads; left, and partner Bernie Swain; right, meet with newsman and author, Sam Donaldson.

SUCCESSFUL PERSONS PROFILE

Bernie Swain and Harry Rhoads

Washington Speakers Burear, Inc.
123 N. Henry Street
Alexandria, VA 22314

In November of 1979, *Fortune* magazine published an article on the lecture industry in the United States. After reading the article, Harry Rhoads contacted his friend, Bernie Swain, who was at that time the assistant athletic director at George Washington University, and they decided to form the Washington Speakers Bureau, Inc.

That decision was not a result of a marketing survey, experience in the lecture industry, or what was perceived as a golden opportunity for financial success. It was simply an opportunity to become entrepreneurs, and these gentlemen took it.

For the first six months, a lack of thought and planning proved to be disastrous. The speakers included in their first brochure were in most of the other lecture agency brochures. A lack of experience meant they did not even know which speakers were actually any good.

Shortly, with only $2,000 left from their original investment, they were faced with giving up. Fortunately, one banker, a friend, took a chance and gave them an additional $20,000 operating capital.

About the same time, an idea struck them. "What if we had a program where we *showcased* big-name speakers." This program brought them together with meeting planners who hired speakers. Their showcase was called "First Tuesday." For the first program, by a stroke of luck, they got Steve Bell, the respected news anchorman for "Good Morning America." They called association and corporate executives who had never heard of a program like this, and they persuaded over 400 meeting planners to attend that first showcase. Success quickly followed.

"First Tuesday" became a hallmark of Harry and Bernie's attitude and business philosophy. Today, after six years, over 15,000 executives have attended "First Tuesday" to preview needed speakers. The Washington Speakers Bureau, with offices on both coasts, has grown to be the largest bureau in the business.

By being unique and creative, by paying attention to the customer and the speakers, and by creating a family atmosphere, their business has achieved phenomonal success. Today they represent some of the best, most well-known speakers in America, including Peter Jennings, George Will, Art Buchwald, Arthur Miller, Robert Novak, Carl Rowan, James J. Kilpatrick, Steve Bell, Patricia Neal, Nancy Austin, Dr. Marvin Cetron, Dr. Tim Johnson, and, fortunately, myself.

SWAINISMS AND RHOADISMS

"Challenge is important to maintaining the spirit of an organization. Challenge helps define a sense of purpose. You must have continual challenge; otherwise lethargy and malaise set in and an organization disintegrates. Competition drives us each day."

"Consistency is based on the standards a company establishes and insists that their employees live up to. Without standards, inconsistencies abound and customers begin to look elsewhere."

"People fail because they are not properly self-motivated or, better yet, not driven to succeed."

"Change is crucial to the continued success of an organization or an individual. Without change, you remain stagnant and outdated."

CHAPTER 2

THE CONTINUITY OF
CHALLENGE

"The greatest thing in this world is not so much where we are,
but in what direction we are moving."

Oliver Wendell Holmes

Think back to happy times on the job. When did you jump out of bed, excited about going to work, and turn off the light in the office at the end of the day with some regret about leaving? As most people do, you will probably answer that you were happiest when the job was new.

When a job is new, there is challenge. You're not jaded by insurmountable roadblocks or the repetitiveness of the position. You're excited about possibilities. Your body is pumping with adrenalin because it's being pushed to the maximum.

You are promotable when you can ensure the continuity of that challenge; it will keep you on the cutting edge and bring life to the job. Challenge stimulates, motivates, and creates a work environment that is conducive to career advancement and enhancement.

Without challenge, the Roman civilization crumbled. Without challenge, marriages fall apart. Challenge is essential in all areas of life. I had to quit my job, and end a pleasant affiliation with Mobil Oil Corporation, to learn that lesson.

When I was a sales trainee at Mobil, there were always challenges learning new skills. During my ten-year career, I was transferred to four different states and promoted almost every eighteen months. Finally, I was promoted to district manager for upstate New York. Looking back at my career, I recall the fun and challenge that each of my advancing responsibilities provided. By God, I loved it!

However, I felt I was losing my enthusiasm during my last year in New York. Our service stations were using updated versions of old promotions, the training clinics conducted by my sales personnel were last year's version, and managing no longer took much effort. I didn't quit, though, until a suggestion brought back memories of my initial challenging times at Mobil.

During my first months at the company, my boss had a great suggestion for boosting sales. He said to me, "Don, there's a service station out there which has the potential to sell more gas. I want you to go out to a farm and buy two truckloads of pumpkins. Then I want you to unload those pumpkins at the service station and put up a sign that says, "FREE PUMPKINS DURING HALLOWEEN WITH EVERY 10 GALLONS OF GASOLINE." I did what he asked and it worked beautifully. That was in 1958.

Then I moved up the ladder and became a sales representative and a sales manager. When I was a district manager 10 years later, the manager of my sales force showed me a massive pumpkin promotion. It frightened me that we were still giving away glasses and pumpkins in 1968. I decided then to get out of the business because I hadn't grown, and it seemed the business hadn't grown in ten years, either.

So I quit my job even though I had six children, a substantial house mortgage, and an upcoming promotion. The problem wasn't the proposed promotion, my district, or the people with whom I worked. It was the business itself. While I personally had always thrived on missionary leadership assignments, the retail oil business had degenerated into a situation of mundane maintenance. The constant state of challenge was gone.

To achieve, excel, and get ahead in business, you must carefully cultivate the excitement of what you are doing. It's your responsibility as well as that of your management, to do so. Challenges don't allow for boredom, dissatisfaction, or complaints.

DISCIPLINE MAKES THE CHALLENGE REAL

When you integrate challenge with discipline, you discover that leaders are in a constant state of challenge and are disciplined to ensure the continuation of that state. It is discipline that makes the challenge real. Hopefully, discipline can come from your managers or vendors, but promotable people keep the continuity of challenge by disciplining themselves.

If I had known that when I worked at Mobil Oil, I might still be working there, because I would have known it was my responsibility to make my job exciting. Look at your own job as a challenge. Make it new again; make it come alive.

TO BE CHALLENGED, YOU MUST EXIST IN A COMPETITIVE ENVIRONMENT

My firm consults for many of the world's leading companies. In those organizations, we are continually exposed to management activities that foster competition—salesperson versus salesperson, production facility versus production facility, profit center versus branch.

Those comparison activities, standard for so long in the business community, are not the motivational carrots they are alleged to be. For such competition to succeed, the comparison factors should not be based on dollars or units. Instead, they should be based on comparing your work to your own standards. We'll discuss this in more detail later.

Judge Using the Proper Context

Any comparison of salespeople using dollar sales or the numbers of units produced or serviced is, at best, inaccurate—at worst, biased and misleading. No two sales territories are ever the same; one territory usually has a built-in edge over another.

Demographics vary. Competitive levels are different. A particular market may have a lot of similarities in terms of population, industry, or politics, but I guarantee you no two are the same. The training, expertise, and experiences of individuals working those markets also vary. It is asinine to expect the same productivity levels from a person six months on the job versus a veteran who is well-seasoned in the territory.

It is equally impossible to make an honest comparison between production facilities on the basis of units manufactured. Environments vary, the equipment used to produce each unit differs, and even the individuals who perform the tasks have different capabilities and motivations. Consequently, using a strict number-of-units comparison among widely differing environments is not accurate.

Measure in Percentage of Goals

More importantly, besides being inaccurate, dollar and unit comparisons do not introduce challenge into the job. If a comparison must be made, using "percentage of goals" as the measurement is the choice because no two goals are ever the same.

As an example, let's say Oakcrest Printing has a goal of printing 50,000 more catalogs in October than in September. If Oakcrest actually prints only 37,500 more, it reached 75 percent of its goal. A bigger printing plant, with a goal of printing 200,000 additional catalogs per day and reaching 60 percent of its goal, would be achieving less. Management must ensure that individual and facility goals are relative, realistic, and challenging, and not designed to compete directly with other individuals or facilities.

COMPETE WITH YOURSELF

In every case, however, the most effective type of competition occurs within ourselves. The average individual in business competes with other salespeople. However, for the successful business and the promotable person, this type of competitive environment is not good enough. To excel, achieve, and get ahead, the challenge and competition must be with ourselves.

Of course, excellent companies develop programs that make sure the salespeople, plant managers, and branch managers are aware of others' performance. But the most successful companies emphasize challenge and competition that the individual undertakes with himself or herself.

If your objective is to get ahead, then your challenge is to attain goals that are unrelated to the performance levels of your peers. Therefore, your standard cannot be to produce at a similar level to your peers—not if you seek career advancement or a successful business. You must develop and write your own set of performance levels and compete against *those* criteria.

At Mobil Oil, people in my district outsold and outproduced every other district in our group. Not only were we good, we were the best! Although I didn't realize it, this caused a problem. Because we were competing with other districts and beating them hands down, it soon became unchallenging. Eventually, I ended up quitting. Had I set objectives and goals that disciplined me and my staff to compete with ourselves, a different situation might have existed.

MANAGERS MUST BE COACHES

If you're a line manager, you must spend 60-80 percent of your time coaching and training your subordinates. Tom Peters calls it management by wandering around; I call it introducing challenge to the job. Managers who preplan their visits to work with employees in the field, and who predictably communicate their standards to their subordinates, generate results.

Although predictability is the key, this is not the same as simply walking around just repeating yourself. To coach people, you must give them a firm idea of what you want. The reason the manager spends time on the job or in the field is not to motivate subordinates, not to spy on them, not to surprise them or catch them doing something wrong. The objective is to bring the individuals up to acceptable standards for the job.

Communicate Your Standards

Whether the desired result is a higher level of productivity, better quality control, a sharper appearance on the job, more detailed planning capabilities, or faster typing skills, the manager must communicate standards to his employees. People working for you should never have to second-guess you. If they don't know what it is you want, it's your mistake.

Let's say you're a new salesperson and I'm your manager. We set up a schedule for monthly visits. After I observe your performance on my first visit, I say, "I like this, I like that. By the way, you do a good job of using visual aids and selling tools. But, you don't take the time to write a detailed itinerary." When I tell you about the itinerary, you become defensive, and we discuss it for quite some time. I tell you why I believe it's important and how it works for others.

Chances are, the second time I'm with you, you're still not putting together a plan. But I'm not going to fight and argue with you; that turns the visit, designed for coaching and learning, into a battle. Instead, I become predictable. During each visit I talk to you in depth about planning comprehensively.

After our fourth visit, you say to yourself, "Every time Beveridge visits me he talks about planning. I better put together a plan." The next month you show me your itinerary.

Recognize, that you have competently arrived as a manager, the day a subordinate tells you what you want to know, before you have to ask. That desirable component results because of challenge, standards and predictability.

Be Predictable

Excellent managers are predictable, repetitive, and even laborious in what business they discuss with their people. The information these managers request is challenging in and of itself. They want to know how the subordinate is doing relative to his or her internal goals.

Furthermore, my employees know the agenda that will be discussed. They know my criteria. They feel secure because they know what I am going to ask. Consequently, they can prepare for meetings and feel confident of their abilities because they know what I want.

I've never seen any purpose to management by being visible or simply wandering around. It seems like intrusion with no rhyme or reason. Instead, let your people know your standards and your ideas by repetitively talking about basics during those field visits. Like the football coach who stresses tackling, running, and blocking, you'll get results when your employees know what you want . . . and the job will be challenging!

Additionally, excellent managers are predictable about when they will return. Prior to leaving the field, the competent manager emphasizes the specific date and time he or she will return to informally review performance levels again.

GET FEEDBACK FROM YOUR MANAGERS OR SUPPLIERS

To be a "10" in business and become promotable, we must have effective stimulation. Find a way to have regular visits and reviews (both formal and informal) with your manager or business advisor. Not only is the continuing exposure to what "you're all about" important, but it will help you stay on track.

Promotable people and successful business leaders react favorably to on-the-job management visits. You must request your manager to set aside regular amounts of time to act as a mentor. Should you be in business for yourself, your suppliers can act in that role.

One of our clients, the robotics division of General Motors (General Motors FANUC, or GMF), is a good example of a company that acts as a business advisor. In addition to providing data and engineering on robotics, the company supplies business expertise and stimulation to its distributors. Because GMF provides on-site counseling, distributors find that it's a challenge to set performance standards far exceeding any comparable industry norm.

Although some GMF distributors grumble about meeting the challenge, GMF revenues in 1985 were three times what they were in 1983 prior to implementation of performance standards. The distributors with the GMF challenge marketed more units and GMF owned the dominant market share.

Take Action to Get Stimulation

As an independent business person, you should understand the need for a continuing challenge and recognize the usefulness of on-the-job coaching and training from your management and/or supplier. If you're not getting the stimulation you need, take action. First, develop a plan. Think about the kinds of information and feedback that would be useful in your situation. Whether you'd like practice at handling employee relations, or detailed comments on written reports, list alternative methods for obtaining these skills. If discussing your plan with your manager doesn't bring results, make a formal presentation of your strategy at budgeting or goal-setting time.

Rewriting your job description is another positive way to let managers know you need and want attention. Ask for a personal meeting to discuss your revisions of the job description. You should write a complete job description even if you own the company. At the least, rewrite your job description every three years—yearly is better. I've appreciated the fresh perspective I get from rewriting mine regularly ... *and,* it maintains job challenge.

Seeking periodic on-the-job management visits are an important part of moving ahead on a career path. Hopefully, your corporation is enlightened enough to mandate on-the-job coaching and challenge.

Successful business people and promotable individuals do what is necessary to remain in a constant state of challenge. It is challenge that keeps a job alive. That interest, those standards, that productivity can elevate you to a highly successful level.

ENSURING THE CONTINUITY OF CHALLENGE

Here are ten specific activities which will, in my opinion, ensure that the challenge continues. Review this list periodically.

1. Hone Your Skills
The first step is to challenge yourself to hone your skills. It doesn't matter what you produced last year or what your performance level was. THE CHALLENGE IS TO IMPROVE!

If you're a doer, good at taking action, then challenge yourself by completing management training classes. Prepare yourself for advancement at all phases.

If you're a salesperson and you lead all others in the region, then hone your skills by selling more of the product line to a broader range of customers.

You may be good, but if you're not competing with yourself, then you're not good enough. Hone your skills.

2. Sweat!

Since others seek the same goal as you, you must work hard. Promotable people universally work harder. I do not mean to eat, sleep, breathe, and live the job. What I do mean is that when you work, WORK!

At times, we've all had to sacrifice part of our personal lives. But in the end it's results, not time spent on the job or number of activities, that count. If you haven't had a vacation in five years and work 60 hours a week, there is a serious lack of balance in your life. That's not working hard, that working stupid!

Working hard means that when you're on the job, you're really there; you're achieving your objectives. Physically being in the work environment is not a standard in itself. Productivity is the real key!

3. Be Yourself

The challenge in achieving, excelling, and getting ahead in business is to use the best of your abilities, skills, and style. You must stretch your capabilities, not take on the thinking patterns and mannerisms of your leader. If you falsify or subdue who and what you are, your quest for a successful business or career advancement will short-circuit. Those around you will soon see through the facade, distrusting even your honest intentions.

Additionally, your own enjoyment will be shallow because it takes a lot of energy to maintain a constant lie. The task is to maximize your own capabilities; to learn from management but not to be its reincarnation. Although the people at IBM may be similar in appearance and dress, the employees still retain their identity. Rest assured that each employee innovates, functions, and performs in a way that is consistent with who, what, and where he or she is as an individual.

4. Maintain Your Integrity

At some point in your career, you may be asked to compromise your standards. You may be exposed to "opportunities" that are available only if you compromise your ethics. For instance, you may be asked to support untruths about your peers, or condemn the actions of others when you're not privy to the factual information regarding their cases. Don't do it.

The challenge is not to surface as your firm's Sir Lancelot, but rather to go to work unafraid and unconcerned that any actions you take may destroy a promising career. For a promotable person, ethics, business morals, and integrity are uncompromising standards. Contrary to popular opinion, among those who advance the furthest, integrity, ethics, and morals are not the exception, but rather the norm! Never compromise your ethical standards.

5. Innovate

Cream rises to the top because it's richer and thicker than milk. Likewise, the promotable individual rises to positions of power because he or she is different and better than the rest. Innovative thoughts are constantly churning through his or her mind. How can I do the job better? What systems can I execute to improve results? What new ideas can I implement to increase productivity? What old ideas can I try with a new and different focus?

The promotable individual is able to do more than execute. Proactivity has gotten a good name lately, with good reason. Implementors are reactive; innovators are proactive and continually challenge themselves to remain so.

6. Learn Your Business

How often do you interact with people who are responsible for other areas in your company, aside from quick conversations at office social gatherings or occasional forays into a different department? To maintain the continuity of challenge, you need to know as much as possible about the business as a whole. If you're a marketer, you probably have a sound understanding of long-term market analysis and similar aspects of your specialty. But do you know, understand, and have empathy for the manufacturing function? Can you relate to the administrative or financial side of the business? Although there is advancement within each discipline, it is the generalist who will achieve, excel, and get ahead in business.

The individual who can participate constructively in each of the organization's activities will ensure his business success. It isn't necessary to be a salesperson to empathize with the frustrations and triumphs of selling. You don't have to be a CPA to have the ability and skills to understand budgeting and interpret a profit-and-loss statement. Know the different aspects of your business so you can mentally generate a team psychology. Such a psychology eliminates tunnel vision and allows you to see the total picture.

When I start to build a team psychology in an organization, I recommend that every manager spend one complete day every six months in another department. I want the sales manager sitting with the comptroller for a day; I want the head engineer sitting with the production manager for a day. The engineer can then recognize the importance of the production department, while the sales manager can see the need for financial report forms.

In addition to understanding the operational details of other areas of the company, these visits help develop a sense of "we're all in this together."

7. Execute

Execution, combined with knowledge, is the strength of a leader. To be a "10" in business, you must demonstrate the ability to execute plans, programs, and strategies. Most professionals have sufficient knowledge to do a job. Not all have the ability and the commitment to use and execute that expertise to generate the desired results.

8. Pick a Field You Enjoy

Choose a field of work you enjoy. Avoid getting stuck in an industry that bores you. If you're already in a rut, find a way to get out before it's too late.

You don't have to make a lifetime choice. Although the women's retail industry may have gotten your juices flowing when you were just out of college, it may now bore you. Just as I grew tired of and left the retail oil business after 10 years, so you may also need to change fields to keep challenged and remain sharp.

Often people realize they are getting stale in their field, but they just don't know how to get out. The dedicated woman who typed this manuscript from my longhand copy called her husband after she had typed this section. She knew that the concept would hit a nerve with her husband. He had worked for some time as an engineer at Pratt & Whitney and had been thinking about looking for a new job for the past two or three years. He didn't enjoy going to work anymore. As a result of his wife's phone call he resigned the next day.

In an industry you dislike, it's difficult to be promotable and seek out additional accountability and responsibility. Being unhappy in your field affects your attitude and will eventually be reflected in your performance. Challenge yourself to find an interesting field.

9. Grab Opportunities

The merry-go-round with the brass ring of opportunity does not go on forever. From my experience, there will be only a few chances to grab the brass ring. When you sense an opportunity to achieve, excel, or get ahead in business, grab it! The promotable individual or successful businessperson is very aware of those opportunities and calculates the risks quickly. Knowing when to reach for opportunities is what separates leaders from mediocre individuals. Nothing ventured . . . nothing gained.

10. Balance Your Life

Seemingly distant from the subject at hand, the greatest challenge of the promotable person is far removed from the business environment. That challenge comes from maintaining a balance in all aspects of your life. It's the process of caring about your job and your company while at the same time caring about your family and friends.

It's unfortunate and unnecessary to achieve career goals at the expense of those you love. The words of the 1980 song, "The Cat's in the Cradle," have helped me balance career and family. In the song, written and sung by the late storyteller Harry Chapin, a little boy is asking his father to take time out to throw a ball with him. The father replies that he's too busy just then but will play later. Part of the refrain is the father's reply: "Son, I don't know when, but we'll get together then. I know we'll have a good time then." The verses follow the boy's progression from childhood to adulthood to his own fatherhood. It is then that the once-busy father calls his son, who is now too busy to spend any time with his father.

According to stories in the music industry, Chapin composed the song after his wife wrote him a verse on a napkin about the childrens' string game, cat's cradle. The verse chided him for touring so often. Chapin died in a car accident a few years later. Two of his own children were less than five years old when he died.

Caring about your job or your company more than your family is the characteristic of a limited person with the inability to balance his or her life. Such people will eventually find Chapin's message coming back to haunt them.

IT'S YOUR RESPONSIBILITY TO STAY CHALLENGED

Even if your company and managers don't challenge you, you must find your own way to stay on the edge, to stay challenged.

For example, my daughter Deborah was becoming bored with her job and was not as productive as she used to be. But, she thought, "Maybe I can't get out of this slot right now, but in four to six months I can. Until then, I must continue to challenge myself even though my managers want to leave me here in this unchallenging, unsophisticated telemarketing position." So Deborah created her own challenges and asked for new responsibilities. Today, she is one of the top sales representatives for AT&T.

If you are the top performer in your position, you must always find the challenge. The best engineer must find a way to design the water system so it adds to the architectural beauty of the building. A consultant must find a way to bring in a wider variety of clients.

Any time you're not stretched, you'll quickly become dissatisfied and bored with your job. Your managers should challenge you; it's good for their business. But if they don't, you must take action yourself. Ultimately, it is your responsibility to make sure you stay challenged.

Successful Person Profile

Richard T. Farmer

Chairman of the Board
Chief Executive Officer
Cintas Corporation
Cincinnati, Ohio

As successful as Dick Farmer is in the laundry business, it's almost a tragedy that he isn't in line to take the reins at IBM. He could handle the assignment!

Dick Farmer eats, sleeps, and breathes "standards." Although Dick believes strongly in performance standards, he takes the long-term view. He doesn't believe in judging people too harshly on a short-term basis. If a particular plant's production is standing still for a period of months, but the employees there are building a foundation for later expansion, Farmer applauds.

The corporate creed at Cintas is "mission, spirit, and growth." It's much more than a slogan. Cintas employees are taught the company culture and creed in a formalized classroom style, which is conducted by Farmer. In this day and age, it's hard to imagine the chairman and CEO of a multi-state, growing, public, profitable company teaching line employees. But Farmer, greatly furthering the success of this, his family business, believes in his training and does it well. While most companies focus on their products, product knowledge, and specifications, Farmer focuses on service. The fabric of Cintas is how the customers are served. Consequently, Cintas' mission is to identify and satisfy true customer needs and wants.

By teaching this company culture in the classroom, Farmer formalizes the importance of the mission and ensures that every employee fully understands it. At the end of training, each employee has a better understanding of how to meet customer needs.

"Mission, spirit, growth" has served the company well. From 1976 to 1985, under Dick Farmer's management, Cintas increased its revenues from $15,000,000 to $100,000,000 and increased net income from $800,000 to over $9,000,000. The company's stock earnings per share have jumped from $.16 to $1.42.

Farmer studied at Miami University in Oxford, Ohio, and received a degree in business administration. He's been a dishwasher, a truck driver, and an officer in the Marine Corps. Today he is a member of the boards of Bowne, Inc., of New York; The Fifth Third Bank, Eagle-Picher Industries, and Bethesda Hospital, all in Cincinnati; and the Cincinnati Chamber of Commerce.

Dick has also served two terms as a member of the board of directors of his industry's International Trade Association, and he has served as a member of the Dean's Advisory Council, School of Business Administration, Miami University.

Dick is 50, married, and has three grown children. His life has balance. He creates a continuity of challenge in his business and believes in coaching and training his employees. There is little doubt that Dick Farmer would have achieved, excelled, and gotten ahead in any field he chose.

FARMERISMS

*"I'm a firm believer in performance standards,
but not on a short-term basis. Great executives sometimes
look bad in the short term."*

*"Change is almost always positive. It sometimes
looks negative in the short term; but, if we keep
digging, change always opens up new doors."*

*"At Cintas, we talk about 'mission-spirit-growth',
and it's more important to know our corporate
culture than it is our product or our pricing."*

*"Our company atmosphere is conducive to the entrepreneurial
spirit. It is backed up by objectives and training,
and strongly reinforced by incentive programs."*

CHAPTER 3

EXPEDIENCY, ADEQUACY, OR EXCELLENCE STANDARDS

"I have failed to take advantage of many opportunities, but the world has not failed in offering them."

Edgar W. Howe

Each of the suggested methods for achievement must, of course, be tailored to your own circumstances. Consequently, the ages at which you reach the promotable posturing phases may not correspond to the age brackets I've used in this book. The level of stimulation you need to maintain a continuity of challenge will not be the same as that of your peers. That's expected and desirable. The key consideration in every case, however, is the *setting of mandatory standards that relate to and fit your own set of circumstances and needs*.

To be a "10" in business, we must have standards of performance, standards for functioning in our job, below which we refuse to go. These standards should be achievable, attainable, and, at the same time, stretch our capabilities to their peak.

THE JOB DESCRIPTION

In industry today, the standard job description is almost useless. Although nearly every company in America uses job descriptions, for many it is a mere formality. When was the last time you saw your job description? More telling, when was the last time you changed your job description or discussed a subordinate's job description?

If your company is like others, job descriptions are written once and placed in three-ring binders to be brought out only when a position is filled. Used in this way, job descriptions are futile and have lost their effectiveness. However, job descriptions can be living documents, the fiber of the management–subordinate relationship, used to evaluate performance and set goals.

Develop Your Own Job Description

First you must recognize that job descriptions are the basis for developing standards for your position. They can be important and useful to your organization. To ensure this, review your job description with your supervisor or partner. Does it fully outline all your responsibilities in both routine and crisis situations? Does it adequately describe what your supervisor expects of you and what you expect of yourself? If not, your job description needs to be revised to reflect the expectations of all concerned individuals.

If you're not given a job description on a new job, write one after 30 days. Since that's not enough time to understand a job completely, revise it as often as necessary. There is no way you can become promotable or successful if you don't have an in-depth concept about what is expected of you and from you. If you're an entrepreneur, the advice is the same. Whether you work by yourself or plan to employ 500 people, you still need a blueprint that lists your expectations and outlines what you do.

A job description lists the requirements of the job, but it doesn't list *how often* and *how well* to perform those requirements. Therein lie the keys to improving the usefulness of the job description.

STANDARDS OF PERFORMANCE

Job descriptions don't work unless they are combined with standards of performance. These standards outline how often a person should perform a particular task and how well that person should do the task. Good job descriptions include measurable components.

The difference between merely doing a task and doing that task three times a week with an 80 percent success rate is immense. Let's say you are in newspaper-advertising sales. Your job description states that one of your tasks is to develop a prospecting system and call companies who have never bought advertising from you. To be able to evaluate your work, however, you need more details and definition. How many such companies make up the market? How many times should you call each company? And very importantly—what is the desirable end result of a particular action? After a telephone call, what follow-up procedures must take place? Should potential clients buy advertising at the end of a sales call? Or should they ask for rate cards and a sample newspaper?

If these questions are answered fully in your standards of performance, your organization has a good understanding of the importance of performance measurement. Standards of performance are a joint decision between employer and employee. The professional manager should sit down with each subordinate to develop that individual's unique standards of performance for the job. Remember, the job description is identical for all in a similar job function, but standards of performance are never the same for any two individuals in the same job function. Standards of performance are yours, and yours alone. Ideally, setting standards is a joint decision with your manager, but the yardstick with which to compete is yours.

Unique standards of performance are the frosting on the cake, the trim tabs that allow job descriptions to work. Most of your peers have goals similar to your own; they want to achieve, excel, and get ahead in business. Each person has a job description that details what it is he or she must do to perform. However, with challenging standards of performance, the cream surfaces and the promotable or successful business person ascends to the top.

Write Your Current Performance Standards

What are *your* standards of performance today? What are those levels below which you refuse to go? Are they clear and definite? What are your own individual standards that will ensure your rise to the top in your company or business? Take the time to write your current non-negotiable standards of performance. Think about the different tasks you perform, and how often and how well you perform those tasks. If you know your standards you can judge if they strive for expediency, adequacy, or excellence.

Working Productively Versus Showing Up

I know of more than one office where employees stop work precisely at closing time, some with half-written sentences on reports on their desks. To hold a job or to make a living today is something we take for granted, generally speaking. Too many people, however, go to work merely to fulfill the required numbers of duties and/or activities.

If you look closely at the world's employed, you will find that most are working at 20 to 30 percent of their capacity. This is true of those who are considered productive and engaged in meaningful activity. Most people do not push themselves to achieve beyond their current productivity level. It's frightening to realize that we have a situation where people who are functioning at only 20 to 30 percent of potential are seen as achieving respectable standards of performance.

EXPEDIENCY STANDARDS

This inadequate standard of performance exists in almost all areas of business today and involves unskilled labor as well as highly educated personnel. For example, the airline pilot's union in the United States fought just as long and hard to keep a third, unneeded person in the cockpit of sophisticated jet aircraft as the coal miners in England fought to keep unproductive mines open.

Those battles were waged in 1985. Both groups were seeking to preserve an environment where they could illegitimatize employment so all workers could produce at half-pace. It's called "feather-bedding," and it falsifies productivity. Many countries of the world today not only condone feather-bedding, they practically require it. It's difficult to remove redundant personnel in England because the laws make it very difficult. Many third-world countries—Haiti, the Mid-East, Kenya, for instance—have excessive levels of civil servants. In the United States, some railroads continue to employee "firemen" on diesel engines.

Performing at a minimum level and just getting by in business are not the promotable posturings of the achieving individual. I call those minimal, "just-get-by" standards of performance *expediency* standards. Although performing merely at an expedient level ensures that you will maintain your job, it does not serve the productivity or continuity of the business. Those who use expediency standards perform quickly at minimally acceptable levels of performance . . . and then stay there.

ADEQUACY STANDARDS

Adequacy standards are just one step above expediency standards and are slightly more than "just scraping by." As a standard, adequacy ensures only that you're performing at a level equal to your peers; secure, perhaps, but not successful or promotable. Those persons who have established a merely adequate level of productivity or craftsmanship are less acceptable for promotions and not competitive as businesses. For example, some years ago a retailer raised industry standards by developing a policy that if you bought something and you didn't like it (for whatever reason) you could bring it back. It was a creative, innovative, unique competitive advantage and, for the time, an excellent standard. Today, almost all retailers provide that option. What was once an excellence standard is now simply adequate. Retailers must offer that option today simply to get by.

EXCELLENCE STANDARDS

To advance in your career and be promoted, you must use *excellence* standards, rather than expediency or adequacy standards. Excellence is the standard for people who will be selected to lead. Excellence standards enhance productivity, attitude, performance, quality . . . even your appearance. Having excellence as your standard almost ensures that you are one of the people who achieve, excel, and get ahead in business. Understanding this component of promotability is mandatory!

As a consultant, I continually ask managers if they have a role model for themselves, and another role model for their business. It is not necessary to reinvent the wheel to be a promotable person or develop a successful business. Many simply seek out a role model and pattern their career or business after that person or company. The key is the *selection* of the role model.

If you select another business or individual in *your* industry, then I suggest your standards are too low! I'm not condemning or ridiculing your industry. I am suggesting that by selecting a role model in your industry, you accept, as your standard, only to be "as good as" that other person. Such a standard will not get you ahead or help to achieve! Today's winners and business successes most often select role models outside their sphere or industry. This correctly and competitively positions you to be better than anyone else with whom you compete, while recognizing that you can compete only with the best that is within you.

In my consulting activities, I am constantly amazed at the number of managers who fail to understand the concept of targeting excellence as the standard. They tell us excellence is unrealistic and unattainable. Nonsense! Using excellence as a standard motivates an individual to stretch to his maximum level of productivity and craftsmanship. I would much rather perform at 90 percent of an excellence standard than 110 percent of an adequacy standard. Likewise, I would rather work with and for people who use excellence to measure performance.

SMOKING OUT ADEQUACY STANDARDS

When we are hired to help companies improve their performance and productivity, we move quickly to "smoke out" adequacy standards. Some years ago, on assignment for Harley Davidson, we were asked to help the field-marketing representatives increase their productivity and performance. At that time, Harley Davidson was plagued by a cancer of adequacy standards in their field operations.

Hours of Operation
Most Harley Davidson motorcycle dealers were functioning with adequate hours of operation. But the 9:00 a.m. to 5:00 p.m. hours seemed designed more for the convenience of the dealers than for the customers. How many customers could take off work to shop for motorcycles? Remaining open at least one or two evenings during the week might have attracted more customers.

Buildings
The location of the Harley Davidson stores was another example of adequacy standards. Although each building seemed adequate, and all had a prescribed number of square feet and appropriate display room footage and decor, 78 percent of the stores operated in secondary locations and secondary buildings. Rather than renting or buying buildings in well-lit, high-traffic shopping centers, over 75 percent of the dealers were located on hard-to-find side streets or hidden in substandard buildings. The locations and buildings were adequate, but far from excellent.

Merchandising
Likewise, the bike inventories were only adequate. Although the merchandise was displayed adequately and the stock was kept reasonably current, Harley dealers couldn't compete with the excellence standards of the Japanese bike dealers. Their merchandise quantities, their customer-focused hours of operation, and the well-lit, high-traffic shopping-center facilities were important factors in the "battle of the bikes" that the Japanese companies won.

I do not suggest that the quality, design, pricing, and engineering of Honda, Kawasaki, and Yamaha motorcycles weren't factors—they were. The Japanese-built motorcycles were of excellent quality, design, and engineering. And they were priced with a careful eye to the American market. But the Japanese companies did not win merely with the quality of their motorcycles alone. They took the top market share with excellence standards—attainable, achievable excellence standards

Image

Here, adequacy standards went even deeper in the Harley Davidson organization. During our research, we talked to potential
motorcycle buyers who were frightened to go into a Harley
Davidson store. Whether these concerns were unrealistic didn't
matter, because potential customers were worried.

Unfortunately for the entire Harley Davidson organization,
image was a problem. The organization used adequacy standards
for its image and identity. Try to picture a gentle, bespectacled
man astride a Harley Davidson. If you're like most Americans,
the picture probably will not come to mind. Harley's adequacy-
standard image allowed for this perception to exist.

I don't believe the company ever placed advertisements
showing a Harley owner such as Al McGuire, the well-re-
spected Marquette University basketball coach, riding the back
roads of Wisconsin on his Harley Davidson to relieve the ten-
sions of his job. I never saw advertisements showing Malcolm
Forbes on his Harley; or, more accurately, on his Harleys.
According to published reports, most of his 72 motorcycles
were Harley Davidsons. This business tycoon, worth an estimated $400 to $600 million, toured the world on his Harleys.
The owner and editor of the highly respected *Forbes* magazine
rode across China on his Harley, sporting a flag with the
motto, Capitalist Tool.

Harley Davidson could have used an Al McGuire or Malcolm
Forbes to help develop a more acceptable image to a greater
share of the market place. At the time the company seemed
resistant to changing its image. Harley Davidson had adequate
dealers, adequate products, and adequate markets. But it didn't
have excellence standards for its image. Consequently, the company never targeted a Malcolm Forbes or an Al McGuire to help
change its long-held identity.

Dealers

The cancer was deeper. In our consulting activities, we approached many of the Harley Davidson field marketing representatives and asked this question about their dealers: "Have
you had any turnover?"

"Yes!" most representatives shot back. "Two or three of my dealers quit. Some are going out of business, and one or two are changing over to Yamaha or Kawasaki."

We explained that we were not asking about cases where the dealer chose to terminate the relationship. Instead, we were asking the representative about dealers terminated by Harley Davidson. We asked if there has been cancellations of a dealer relationship because of a failure to move toward or achieve excellence standards.

You should have seen the stunned, amazed looks on the faces of some of the representatives.

"Cancel a dealer? You're crazy. They're switching to sell the Japanese bikes so fast we don't have a chance to terminate."

We then asked each of the representatives if that bothered them. Most said, "no," and the surprised looks on their faces indicated they had no idea what we were talking about.

"If you had challenging standards, excellence standards, rather than just adequacy, doesn't it stand to reason that not every dealer could meet those standards?" we asked.

"If you used excellence as the Harley standard for decor, location, marketing, merchandising, inventory levels, and customer-focused features such as hours of operation, then you would have some turnover of distributors, dealers, or staff. But it would be generated by the company."

DISINTEGRATING STANDARDS

When management-generated turnover doesn't occur, it quickly tells you that the company has lowered its standards to adequacy levels so that everyone fits in. Many businesses begin with well-developed standards. But these standards are compromised in the face of competition or changes in the market. What were once excellence standards shortly become expediency standards or adequacy standards. Soon after, the company starts to go down the tubes.

At Harley Davidson, a paramount reason for the company's major loss of market share was a well-entrenched adequacy stan dard level among sales personnel in the field.

RECAPTURING EXCELLENCE AS A STANDARD

Eventually, Vaughn Beals headed a group of investors who purchased Harley Davidson from AMF. Today Mr. Beals, as president, battles against well-entrenched Japanese motorcycle dealerships that are managed, disciplined, and motivated to have excellence as their standard. Yet Harley Davidson is starting to recapture its lost market share.

When the U.S. government moved to control motorcycle imports, Vaughn Beals leased the large Performing Arts Auditorium in Milwaukee and brought in every Harley Davidson dealer. The audience included the entire Harley staff, from marketing to manufacturing. Beals even invited each one of Harley's suppliers and financiers to sit in on the meeting. I cajoled, threatened, and hopefully imparted to the gathering that their expediency and adequacy standards were no longer viable.

The story is yet to be finished, but Harley Davidson is regaining its market share. Their successes and rebirth were amplified when in May of 1987 Vaughn Beals petitioned the government to actually remove the U.S. import restrictions against large Japanese mortorcycles . . . one year ahead of schedule. The news was so startling President Reagan visited the Harley Davidson manufacturing facility in Pennsylvania to personally compliment the group on excellence performance, excellence standards and a new, desirable competitive posture. Now, they battle with a complete arsenal. Harley's very fine motorcycle is only one weapon in that arsenal; excellence standards complete the package.

Excellence standards allow profitable businesses, competitive companies, and promotable people to continue to perform. To achieve, excel, and get ahead in business requires a commitment to an uncompromising set of excellence standards and the skill and tenacity to see that they're achieved. Use excellence standards as the level below which you simply will not allow your skills, productivity, or attitude to slip. Promotable people stretch to the maximum level of their capabilities and are unfailing in their quest for that skill and performance level.

To start, dig out your job description. After you've dusted it off, tear it apart. Write down every required activity for your position. Then honestly assess and reevaluate what you have consciously or subconsciously established as your standard for each.

If your standard is expediency, you lose. If your standard is simply adequacy, you will probably be secure in your position, but you will not be promotable or successful. Each of us who accepts the challenge to achieve wants and needs excellence standards for each job activity. Remember, the challenge is not to be "as good as;" the requirement is to be "better than."

Successful Person Profile

James E. Hennessy

Executive Vice President
NYNEX Corporation
New York

Jim Hennessy spent most of his professional career in the Bell System, which educates its managers to be humanists, attentive to and sensitive about feelings. In line with that organizational focus, Hennessy believes the criteria for managing people is to "help them develop goals. Help them see *what* is needed and *why*. Let *them* develop *how*. Serve them well and thereby lead well."

Before divestiture of AT & T, Hennessy had nine different posts ranging from supervisor of the plant department with New York Telephone to director of organizational planning.

Fortunately, considering his various positions, Hennessy says, "I always see change as positive."

Jim Hennessy continues to do well and achieve. He was appointed vice-president of business marketing and later given the additional title of vice-president for sales, responsible for 4000 sales and support people in NYNEX, the company resulting from the merger of New York and New England Telephones. More recently, Jim is challenged with numerous responsibilities. As corporate executive vice-president, his long-term responsibilities are for both the company's strategic marketing and strategic planning for science and technology. In the short-term, he functions as president of NYNEX Business Information Systems, which consists of 93 locations nationwide including its acquisitions from IBM.

A business professional with a passion for performance excellence, he has a unique personal philosophy of life based on the five "Ls"—Learn, Labor, Laugh, Love, and Live. Jim Hennessy does all five well; he is a living symbol of an excellence standard.

HENNESSYISMS

*"Performance standards must be tough,
but attainable with extra effort."*

*"People fail because they don't think through carefully and
explicitly their own personal goals, and therefore there is
no determined commitment to a direction to one's life."*

*"Almost everything requires team play, but there are
many positions on the team; not every person can be a
quarterback or a coach or team physician."*

"Learn, labor, laugh, love, and live."

CHAPTER 4

WHY PEOPLE FAIL

"People can be divided into three groups: those who make things happen, those who watch things happen, and those who wonder what happened."

John W. Newbern

To succeed at a career or business, we must create circumstances which maximize our opportunities to achieve, excel, and get ahead in business. Focusing on the methods used by promotable, achieving individuals is only one way to understand success. It will also serve us well, however, to analyze factors which cause other people to fail.

The phenomenally successful business books of the eighties, such as *Theory "Z"*, *Megatrends,* and the series on excellence provided insights on effective Japanese and U.S. management practices. The authors described certain indicators that could accurately predict the future; and they explained how businesses such as the Disney organization, Hewlett-Packard, A.B. Bradley's, and Delta Airlines strived to be effective, efficient, and profitable.

Marketing Mistakes by Robert F. Hartley approached the subject matter from an entirely different point of view. The approach of this book was to discuss the details of why carefully designed marketing campaigns and strategies fail. Although *Marketing Mistakes* never hit the *New York Times* bestseller list, it is as informative as the books that describe success factors.

Examining the criteria for both failure and success is equally important. We learn well from the successes of others; we can learn even more from their mistakes. For example, the failure of the great Atlantic and Pacific Tea Company should be taught in every freshman-level business course as a case study on how not to run an enterprise. By understanding the factors behind A & P's failure, or any other venture gone astray, we can avoid similar decisions and activities which would affect our own planned growth.

The national grocery chain dropped from a total of 15,738 stores to less than 500 in 1985. How did A & P fail? At one time the chain possessed a dominant market share and had immense buying leverage and established distribution systems. By the 1970's, the chain had been plagued by years of lethargy. Innovation was an unknown term. Profits were falling.

In 1972, bolstered by initial success at test locations, A & P's new leadership made the decision to convert the chain to super discount stores. The stores were called WEOs—"Where Economy Originates." However, throughout the country, the chain's new image did not appeal to young suburban families with substantial purchasing power. Instead, stores were attracting more elderly consumers with limited incomes. A & P's lower prices helped them to gain an increase in total volume, but profits dried up. Spurred on by lower prices, competitors followed suit. Industry-wide price-cutting meant large losses for A & P. Consequently, they were forced to forgo paying a quarterly dividend to shareholders for the first time since 1925.

The company had little cash to carry it during a period of what became intense competition. Like a sputtering giant, the company saw smaller, leaner competitors grab market share.

A & P never completely recovered from the WEO strategy. Whether they will ever recapture the markets represented by their previous 15,000+ stores is doubtful.

THREE INDICATORS OF FAILURE

Let's first discuss three basic indicators of impending failure. Then we'll list and examine ten primary reasons why people and businesses fail. As you read this chapter, examine your attitudes, postures, and activities (or those of your employees) for these indicators of possible failure.

Individuals who resist change, who are untrainable, and who are not going to succeed generally (1) act as prima donnas, (2) think they're a horse of a different color, or (3) too readily accept the status quo.

The Prima Donna

"I wonder what this company would do if I ever left," is a strong indicator of a loser. People who make such statements have concluded that they are indispensable. They believe it is *their* skills, *their* knowledge, *their* expertise, and *their* customer contacts that enable the company to survive. Once an employee becomes a prima donna, both the company and the individual's career are in jeopardy. When an individual wonders how the company would do without him or her, there's trouble further down the line. In over 80 percent of the cases on which my consultants have worked, the answer is that the company would do better without the individual.

When one reaches the state of prima donna, that person no longer strives for improvement, growth, and challenge in his or her job. Earlier, I wrote about my resignation from Mobil Oil Corporation. Unfortunately, I personified a typical prima donna. While I was resigning, I asked my wife to retrieve all our Mobil shares from the safety deposit box. Then I instructed her to call our stockbroker and sell the stocks. Extremely foolish in hindsight, my strategy was to sell the stock before I resigned; my thoughts then were that Mobil Oil would be in big trouble if I left. I believed that without my skills and leadership abilities, the company would certainly suffer! How immature and naive.

Instead, the value of the stock went up several points and, on more than one occasion, split two or three for one. I could be replaced, I was not indispensable, and the firm survived (quite well, I might add) without me.

When we identify individuals who both consciously and subconsciously believe that the company will fall apart if they leave, we have identified either untrainable, unpromotable potential losers, or "stars" with lots of talent who can cut corners and still do a good job, but who may negatively influence the procedures of those fellow employees not as gifted.

The Horse of a Different Color

"I'm different" is another indicator of a nonpromotable person. When you hear that statement from anyone in your company, recognize that individual uses a crutch to rationalize a lack of performance. Suggesting to others and, more importantly, believing that we are different demonstrates that we cannot learn from the successes, strategies, and failures of others. A person who believes he or she is different will expend all efforts attempting to reinvent the wheel.

A classic example of such a situation was an article titled "What Makes A Good Salesman" in *Harvard Business Review,* July–August 1964. Written by David Mayer and Herbert M. Greenberg, that short but important piece of business literature was read by thousands of business managers throughout the United States. However, the article did not cover the specific markets, products, industries, and situations of each of the readers. The important strategic information it contained was probably discarded by many with the superficial crutch, *"We're* different."

But they're not THAT different! Unfortunately, too many people convince themselves that it's necessary to reinvent the wheel. The systems, concepts, techniques, and strategies you require to become promotable and that companies need to become emerging IBMs are there for the asking. Search for tried and true methods in books, articles, and seminars. It doesn't matter if you are selling kites in a tourist shop or microchips to foreign countries. Basic strategies that make sense in one business or geographic area often make sense in another.

I have a strong hunch that one or more executives at Xerox in Rochester, New York, read the *Harvard Business Review* article, "What Makes A Good Salesman." And I suspect these executives did not cast aside the information in the article, claiming to be different. Instead, I'm sure they asked themselves the classic question, "What will happen to our business if our competitors follow this advice and we ignore it?"

The concepts expounded in the *Harvard Business Review* article must have been tested and executed as a sales strategy in progressive companies. I'll bet that some concepts Xerox used in their sales strategies also originated in the selling "bible" of the day, *Consultative Selling,* by Mack Hanan.

Both the article and the book broke away from the typical image of the salesperson as a hustler, or a peddler. Hanan's book introduced the concept of the salesperson as problem solver. "How can I answer a customer's needs?" became the successful salesperson's question.

Companies that avoid failure often do so because they realize they are no different from other companies. Even the most profitable corporations are not afraid to use good ideas to grow and change. Sustained growth is due only in part to the actual product or service, and more largely due to sound concepts and philosophies such as those detailed in the 1964 *Harvard Business Review* article and the book *Consultative Selling.*

As Xerox began leasing machines and selling copying supplies, the techniques and systems used were so effective that their executives recognized still another revenue-generating opportunity and established a wholly owned subsidiary, Xerox Learning Systems. The flagship product of that group was PSS—Professional Selling Skills—a comprehensive sales-training program focusing on customer needs and wants. The program encompassed many of the principles detailed in the Hanan book and *Harvard Business Review* article.

Losers philosophize "we're different" and drain their energies trying to reinvent the wheel. Conversely, individuals who achieve, excel, and get ahead in business recognize that they can learn much from the successes, failures, and experiences of others . . . and they do!

The Status Quo Is Fine with Me

"I do the best I can" is another sure-fire indicator of a loser. If you hear that from an employee, you'd better be satisfied with that individual's performance level; you'd better be content with his or her skills; and you'd better pray that your competition doesn't become any more sophisticated, aggressive, or covetous of your market share. When those people—certainly no longer promotable people—exclaim, "I do the best I can," recognize that they are really saying, "I'm not going to do any more." The loser will fight to maintain the status quo and resists having your markets and product line change when faced with continuing challenges and demands for excellence.

The psychology of this concept can even be applied to raising children. It doesn't matter whether the challenge to your child is football, English, hockey, or music. When your twelve-year-old walks through the door and dejectedly offers, "I did the best I could," most of us wrap our arms around the child to console him. This isn't the time to console! Your child will not survive on this earth with twelve year old skills. This is the time to *challenge*! What we are really saying, though, is, "We're both losers. It's okay to lose." For that reason, I would not allow my child to use that rationalization anymore than I would permit myself an excuse for failure. A better response would be, "I didn't get the results I wanted, but I learned something of value."

Previously, I asked when you were happiest in your job. We concluded that most people are happiest when the job is new because it contains a challenge. The same applies to the coaching, training, and the guidance of our children. When your child offers, "I did the best I could," honestly understand what your child is really saying. He plans not to try, not to compete, and not to win anymore.

I would push the child to fight for better skills because I could not watch my son or daughter attempt to survive in this world with only a twelve-year-old's skills. Allowing children to get by without challenge stunts the growth of their coping mechanisms and skills and removes their ability to compete.

Likewise, the individual in business who claims, "I do the best I can," is communicating that he or she is not going to grow. Without a doubt, that person is not promotable and has only a limited chance of business success.

Losers undertake an action that goes hand-in-hand with the statement, "I do the best I can." This action indicates their lack of desire and/or motivation to perform, to achieve, and excel. It demonstrates that those individuals want to rest squarely at a comfort level.

For evidence of this among your own staff, call a meeting of your employees. Ensure that you are the first to arrive so you can observe your employees as they enter the meeting room.

Although it may seem simplistic, notice which people in your group are without note paper. Their action illustrates a lack of accountability to perform; in fact, they only perform within their comfort level. In their thinking, they have successfully transferred responsibility to the person who is running the meeting. It is then the leader's responsibility to perform, not the attendees. But they're wrong.

Attending a meeting without note paper also suggests that these people feel they have nothing more to learn. The day the doers, the individuals in your company who must execute the plans, appear for meetings without note-taking materials, you've got a problem.

If you have heard yourself utter any of the three loser's songs discussed above, you will need to change your job, or at least your attitude, to become promotable. If, as a manager, you hear your employees utter any of these three excuses you must take decisive action.

In the case of the prima donna, call the individual in on the carpet immediately. The majority of the time, the answer to the question, "What would this company ever do if I left?" is, "I don't know but I have a feeling we're going to find out."

Because of his successes, the prima donna is often serving as a role model to others in the corporation. The prima donna may have well-developed skills and abilities and may be doing very well without preplanning his activities. Others in the company observe this type of behavior and believe that they, too, can achieve success without preplanning their activities. Obviously, this is not a desirable situation.

Though you may be quaking in your boots at the prospect of having one of your stars leave, you must tell him or her, "As much as it scares me to think about having you go, I believe that with your attitude, we will actually be better off." This is so because when the prima donna leaves, the deterioration of the entire unit begins to reverse itself. This is particularly true in selling, where the prima donna might not be using the proper sales aids and is significantly influencing the professionalism of others in the department.

When one of your staff members utters the phrase, "I'm different," your task is to demonstrate graphically how your organization or your department is similar to that of others. This can be done by doing a comparison of corporate literature, specification sheets, and other printed literature.

I once arranged to have a sales demonstration made to my staff by someone from another organization. I wanted my staff to observe an effective sales presentation and to note the common denominators. I wanted them to see the selling techniques employed by a person working for another company offering a product completely different from ours. Ostensibly, this individual was making a presentation to sell my staff on the benefits of his product. My goal, however, was to have my staff realize that there were fundamental, transferable components of an effective sales presentation.

One of my key tasks when I was a sales manager was to continually demonstrate to my staff that what we were charged with doing was not so different from any other effective sales organization. Thus I constantly displayed competitors' literature, and I solicited sales presentations from outside sales representatives so that my staff got a clear message—"I am different" or "We are different" when used as justification for non-performance is losers' talk and has no place in an effective organization.

What about the situation when one of your staff members says, "I do the best I can?" At that point, drop everything and meet with this individual outside the office environment so you are free from phones and interruptions. Once alone, tell him or her, "That concerns me. Look how much this company has changed. Look how much this industry has changed. Look how much this market has changed." Then bring the comparison closer to home by saying, "And look how much the other staff members have changed. What concerns me is that if you and I remain at the skill level where we are today the world around us will continue to change without us."

I would then tell the employee, "I am willing to share all of my experience with you so that together we can move you from "I do the best I can" to "I am challenging myself for great achievement."

A long time ago I heard two sayings which have meant a lot to me. One is "Grow or go," and the other is "Pull with or pull out."

TEN REASONS PEOPLE FAIL

Now that you can identify people headed toward failure, we will discuss ten of the most basic reasons for failure.

Lack of Preparation

The primary reason people fail in business (and life, as well) is a lack of preparation. Poorly educated, poorly prepared, and poorly trained people fail because they do not have the skills or expertise to perform. Inadequate financing, the number-one reason businesses fail, can also be traced to a lack of preparation.

Adequate preparation doesn't require a formal education or a lengthy apprenticeship. But it does require a complete awareness and ability to perform the skills required in the business. How you prepare can vary from attending school to swinging a bat a thousand times. If you practice daily, your chances of hitting a home run increase dramatically over those of the batter who rarely swings the bat. Preparation dramatically increases your chances of achieving, excelling, and getting ahead in business. If you shortcut preparation, you've got a very good chance of striking out. Preparation is the most important component of success. Without it, you won't even play the game.

Lack of Focus

The second reason people fail is a lack of focus on their goals. I had a friend and fraternity brother in the fifties who was killed in pilot training just after the Korean War. His plane crashed while he was practicing bombing runs. The cause of the crash was a phenomenon known as "target fixation." On the final target approach, my friend became so focused on his objective that the plane *and* the explosive crashed on-target.

Unlike my friend's fatal mistake, "target fixation" in business is mandatory and desirable. Vacillating between different objectives causes failure. Achievers establish goal-oriented activities and attitudes. Their thought processes are directed consistently toward a well-defined goal. The goal itself is not as important as your daily progress toward achieving it. Target your decisions and skills squarely on that mark.

Lack of Discipline

A lack of discipline and/or commitment also causes failure. When you would rather be playing golf, it takes discipline to work hard. It takes discipline to maintain a successful business image. Someone once said to me, "To be successful, do the things you don't want to do." That takes discipline and commitment, but you will eventually get ahead. A successful person has non-negotiable standards which he will not fall below.

Let me give you an example in selling. A non-negotiable standard would be to require that all sales presentations include the use of some selling tools. Moreover, each and every customer contact should involve the use of some selling tools. Studies show that people remember less than 10 percent of what they are told, but a far greater percentage of what they are told and shown. Thus the effective salesperson offers a presentation which is a blend of both verbal discussion and illustration of points using graphs, pictures, charts, spec sheets, samples, slides, video, etc.

The type of selling tool used is a varying standard. One sales representative may find it highly effective to use a yellow marker to underline key points in a brochure that specifically apply to a prospect. Another sales rep may find some other technique to be highly effective. However, the non-negotiable standard is that selling tools must be used with each customer on each call.

The day you start winging it, by showing up with no selling tools and making a presentation that is just talk, is the day on which you have set out down the road to failure. Why is this so? Without using selling tools you can't be assured of offering a chronological approach, the customers cannot retain what you have presented, and you have diminished the "perception of value" and your ability to effectively close the sale.

Lack of Execution

While long-range planning and analysis are vital parts of business life, you've probably known individuals who never surpass that stage. These people fail because they put all their efforts into preparing for work and precious little energy into actually doing the work. A case-in-point is the many professional students at colleges and universities who, I believe, never really plan to work. That same type of individual exists in business.

Although some individuals are very adept at developing, designing, creating, or studying problems and opportunities, they never execute what they've developed. Failures always have another project or a new idea that allows them to shelve their most recently planned program. These people are "committee" types who study a need to death and eventually fail, or else move on to still another project because they never perform. It takes drive to succeed and energy to achieve. To avoid this problem in my own company, I've instructed the marketing people not to develop a new program until they've made their last one work. Resultantly, we're developing better programs.

Lack of External Focus
Many people fail because they are strictly internally motivated, completely lacking the ability to focus on what the customer needs and wants. Engineers love to design, CPAs love to generate the bottom line, and bakers love to bake. That's great, but loving what you do doesn't sell the service or the product. All business revolves around customers. People in their own comfort zone can drown in their specialty, remaining unaware of customers' needs.

Customer focus is an external, empathetic approach which ensures that engineering, accounting, or baking are focused at identifying and satisfying a client or customer need. Unless you can create benefits to customers from your own abilities and expertise, you'll have problems succeeding. (We'll discuss this in more depth in Chapter 11.)

Lack of Tenacity
Failure also results from poor follow-through and a lack of tenacity. Unless you're a genius, you probably won't achieve your objective the first time you try. It usually takes at least six sales attempts to bring a new customer on-board. Unfortunately, most salespeople stop after the third rejection. Failure results from giving up before achieving the objective.

Many businesses fail because they are undercapitalized. However, money isn't the only culprit—equally important is the inability of company owners to hang in there. If you want to achieve, then you better have staying power.

Lack of Willingness to Handle All Aspects of the Business

Another reason people fail is that they no longer want to handle certain areas of the business; they don't want to get their hands dirty. Some people consider selling to be beneath them. Business is supposed to come to them, so they don't pursue contracts. These unfortunate individuals have elevated themselves to feel that they are above performing all the tasks necessary to achieving a goal.

Some years ago, I entered into two different partnerships with people in England. Both failed because my partners considered themselves to be above certain types of work. My first partner was a retired military officer. My days with this man included making sales calls in a chauffeur-driven limousine. The "major" wouldn't think of asking for a sale; he merely visited clients. Logically enough, he didn't sell and the business failed.

I recently reached the end of an unfortunate five-year agreement with another United Kingdom executive. I knew we were in trouble four years ago when my partner stood, leather attaché case in hand, totally removed from an immediate problem. The meeting room and product display for our new business in London's World Trade Center had not been properly set up.

We were scheduled to present a seminar about our services to a group of 75 potential customers. When I walked into the seminar room 40 minutes before its starting time, my partner was standing in the middle of the boxes and books I had shipped to the site. Chairs were folded and leaning against the back wall. I asked what was going on and he said he was waiting for someone from the facilities department (already hours late) to put up the chairs and display cases. My partner could not bring himself to open a box, organize a shelf, or set up a chair. As an "owner," he considered himself above those tasks. Both he and the business failed.

Dependence on Networking

Of the ten reasons for failure, this is probably the saddest. If you plan to change jobs today, most self-help books suggest "networking." Although there is nothing wrong with networking, a *dependency* on social contacts can be harmful. Relying on personal and business relationships is a short cut to failure. First, you can't count on every person you believe to be your friend. Second, if someone suspects that an association with you (because of your needs or unemployment) might reflect negatively on his or her own career, he or she is gone! You'll get verbiage, you'll get sympathy, but you won't get help. If networking help comes, consider it a bonus. But do not depend on friends and relatives for your success.

Lack of Generalist Skills

People fail to get ahead when they are unable to make the transition from specialist to generalist. If your goal is to remain a specialist, a "doer," that's your decision. However, it is the multi-skilled person, the generalist, who most often moves up through the ranks. When you first join an organization, your ticket for success is to learn your job well. You may come on board as a specialist or learn from experience. But, once you've learned your job, make sure you're becoming knowledgeable or skillful in other areas. If you expect to achieve, excel, or get ahead in business, you must be aware of all the activities that are necessary to make the business as a whole successful.

Lack of Character

Finally, many people fail because they lack character. You've probably met them along your path. You've known people who constantly find fault with others but are incapable of recognizing their own deficiencies; people who do as little as possible yet reach for all available credit. You've listened to people whose ambition is so intense they habitually talk long, loud, and negatively about their peers in a vain effort to better themselves. The woods are also populated by deceitful individuals, those who believe they can harvest rewards before sowing the seeds of honest service. Those who lack character are void of the basic fabric of individuals who are promotable.

A leader demonstrates uncompromising character over the long-term. Integrity and moral strength generate an environment where people *want* you to lead them. People want a strong, clear direction. They do not want to wonder if their leader is taking unprofessional, illegal, or unethical actions. If you lack character, your peers will find a way to sink your ship.

LISTENING TO THE GURUS

Listen to ten different business-oriented tapes or read ten books on business success. You'll end up with twenty different lists of steps to take. The next time a business author makes suggestions or recommendations, don't act on that information until you have examined that person's skills, qualifications, and successes (or lack of successes).

For years, we have been led to the slaughter, instructed by scores of motivational speakers who are, in fact, "successful failures." Their successes are in their writing and/or speaking skills, but they can demonstrate little, if any, results in performing the activities of which they speak so eloquently.

Answers to our questions on getting ahead from the business gurus have become the mystic "positive mental attitude." If we stand before the mirror and tell ourselves long enough and hard enough that we are the best salespeople on this earth, we can *will* it into being. Not so!

People take this kind of advice seriously. They stand in front of their mirrors, psyching themselves into quixotic business adventures. Turned down by potential customers on their very next sales call, these same people are devastated. All too frequently, they are turned aside because they lack the necessary training, the necessary education, and the necessary skills with which to perform.

There is no magic wand! If you don't first possess the skills and abilities to accomplish the task, there is no positive mental attitude in the world that will carry you through to success. Inadequate preparation, commitment, and follow-through will quickly lead you to failure. So will an unwillingness to become a generalist, to learn and handle all aspects of the business.

People fail and will continue to fail. Obtaining an awareness of why most people fail will give you a unique, competitive edge over your peers, and a solid basis upon which to achieve.

SUCCESSFUL PERSON PROFILE

Michael J. Friduss

General Manager—Distribution
Illinois Bell Telephone
Chicago, Illinois

Mike Friduss thrived on the responsibility and challenge of thrusting an 8000-person division into the competitive environment. He attacked change and the divestiture of AT & T with vigor, confidence, and results.

Mike graduated from the Illinois Institute of Technology with a degree in industrial engineering and obtained an MBA from Northwestern University. In 1963, he joined the Bell System and has been there ever since.

His first management assignment came at age 27. At 30, he was promoted to division manager, corporate planning, in New York. At 33, he returned to Chicago as a division plant manager and at 35 was division corporate planning manager. By age 40 he became general manager—distribution service. In an industry that has been categorized as reactive, divestiture has provided the stage for a proactive, skilled manager to take charge and demonstrate leadership and "make-it-happen" capabilities.

"At Illinois Bell, we must achieve corporate success in the short term, while preparing for the long term with vision. There is a never-ending focus on this month and this quarter. Unfortunately, we tend to look towards the future only a few times a year."

Married with two children, Mike Friduss had a crystal-clear vision of his role and assignment, which included a recent transfer. Mike is helping to achieve a transformation that benefits the entire system at Bell. By and large the Bell companies are still staffed with monopoly-experienced leadership . . . Mike Friduss as a skilled, results-focused individual, could be perceived as a 'threat' to many. The man achieves and excels within the environment.

FRIDUSSISMS

"A promotable person is, among other things, a change-maker; someone who makes things happen; an innovator."

"We are in the midst of an unprecedented refocusing of the manager's attention on our customers. We have recently instituted customer councils, customer champion awards, executive visits, and an extensive customer-based measurement system. But . . . we still have a long way to go."

"An organized manager keeps several balls in the air at a time and has the ability to take the pulse of a multitude of activities around the organization."

"People fail to progress further in business not because they reach a level of incompetence, but rather because they reach a level of 'caretakership'."

CHAPTER 5

A POSITIVE GOALS ATTITUDE

"The person who gets ahead is the one who does more than is necessary—and keeps on doing it."

Anonymous

In sports, goals are clearly established and understood by all players. How would a football, hockey, soccer, or basketball game be played if one were to remove the goalposts or nets? The answer is obvious—without the goal, there is no game. This same premise applies to all aspects of life—without a goal there is no method of measurement, no way to keep score.

SETTING GOALS

In 1954, Yale University conducted a study on goal-setting as a determinant of future performance. Members of the Yale graduating class were asked if they had identified their goals for future financial worth. Three percent of the students had written goals clearly identifying a dollar value; 11 percent had formulated goals in mind; while the remaining students, 86 percent, had no definite financial goals in mind.

A followup was conducted in 1974, with astonishing results. The three percent of those 1954 graduates with clearly defined, written financial goals had a combined net worth that exceeded the combined total of the remaining 97 percent. Although setting goals will not guarantee success, you are far more likely to succeed if your goals are clearly identified and serve as a focus.

Your goals should be realistic and attainable, and stretch your capabilities. Your goals should challenge you to produce more and higher-quality work.

I marvel at the number of companies who proudly proclaim that the majority of their people are performing at 120 percent, 150 percent, and as high as 200 percent of goals. Such ridiculous claims merely confirm that challenging goals were not set. If everyone is achieving his or her target, you'll find that the goals were set too low and are void of challenge—the most important motivator of people.

Following a lecture I gave recently, one of the program participants handed me his business card. Four thoughts were written on the back:

1. Decide exactly what you want as your life's goal.
2. Intensely believe you will reach that goal.
3. Want that goal enough to pay the necessary price.
4. Use proven success methods to achieve the goal.

Those four points are right on target. We're going to isolate and then analyze each point to show how it can help you become a "10" in business.

Decide Exactly What You Want As Your Life's Goal

How many people drift through life aimlessly, trying on different careers and businesses like so many pairs of shoes? How many people haven't been able to decide on a life goal? If you are vague about your life's goal, you certainly are not alone. The sooner you decide what you want from life, the better your chances of accomplishing that objective.

In most cases, people fail to set a life goal because they look too far to the future, strategizing about a grandiose plan. For the long term, think initially about generalities, such as working in a certain industry or working with different types of activities, as opposed to a specific goal such as becoming president of General Dynamics by 2008.

For the short term, however, specific targets are appropriate and useful. Plan some targets for this year. A short-term objective, for example, could be to learn about selling. A short-term goal could be to work in a service industry. These are targets that will help you discover where you want to be and decide exactly what you want as a life goal. All achievers in life have a goal!

Intensely Believe You Will Reach That Goal

Since you went to the trouble of establishing a goal in the first place, you must feel capable of achieving it. Winners and promotable people "buy in" to the goal. After all, it's their goal, their objective, their target. In a classic comment, Arnold Palmer said it best: "Winning isn't everything, but wanting to win is." If you don't believe you *can* win, then you really do not *want* to win.

Motivation has a lot to do with how your goals are set. How are goals set in your company? In sophisticated organizations, goals are not sent down to the subordinates like commandments from on high. Goals are mutually established criteria, with both manager and subordinate participating in the activity. Any leader commits a grave error in passing down a set number of goals to achieve. Those goals become the objectives of management, a management "wish list," and not those of the people who must conform to the goals. Employees will not be committed to a goal decided by management and may not be convinced the goal can be achieved.

A story will illustrate the problem with management setting the goal. It's about Dick McClain, a sales manager who worked in Moline, Illinois, for F. W. Means and Company. At the time, I was director of sales for the company. I organized a sales managers' conference at Kentucky Dam Village. Over drinks one evening, McClain asked the sales manager in Chicago, our most populous location, what each of his five salespeople were averaging in sales weekly.

The Chicago sales manager shot back a figure that astounded McClain. It was so far above the productivity of Dick McClain's own group that you could almost see McClain's mental wheels turn. "Wow!" he thought. "That's three times what my people are producing."

For the sake of illustration, let's say that the Chicago sales manager's employees sold $5,000 per week. McClain couldn't wait to get back to Moline. He was anxious to line up his entire sales team and communicate this new figure as a goal. When McClain asked, "Do you know what the reps in Chicago are selling?". The sales representatives in unison answered "no." "Five thousand dollars per person, per week!" McClain said. "You know what that means, don't you?"

"No," again was the reply. McClain walked toward each of those salespeople, pointing a finger at each and declaring, "$5,000 for you, $5,000 for you, $5,000 for you, $5,000 for you, and $5,000 for you!" Dramatically, emphatically, and with determination, Dick McClain was dispensing the new goals for the F. W. Means Moline sales team.

The key to understanding the situation was the response of his sales force. The first salesperson was really bothered. He had never in his life sold over a thousand dollars a week. He paled, became exceptionally quiet, and you can bet he was thinking, "$5,000 a week!? That's crazy, impossible! I can't do that! I won't even try."

Dick McClain lost the productivity of that salesperson for two reasons. First, he didn't allow the individual to participate in determining the objective. Second, McClain didn't get the salesperson to "buy in" to the commitment. The salesperson did not "intensely believe he could do it."

Forcing a person to accept a goal he doesn't believe in will never work, no matter how you rationalize the process. It is counterproductive.

What followed McClain's tirade about goals was even more alarming. As an observer, I had been watching the concerned reaction of most of the sales force, not even paying attention to the smile on the face of another sales representative, Don Brown. For several years Don Brown had been Moline's top-producing sales man. When Dick McClain set the new goals of $5,000 a week, Brown sat back, grinned, threw up his feet, placed his hands behind his head, and declared, "No problem. Hell, I've been selling $10,000 a week, but I can cut it down!"

No two goals are ever the same. Goals must be based on the potential of the territory, unit, or salesperson to which they apply. Develop criteria that are realistic and attainable, but keep in mind that goals should stretch one's capabilities and skills. "Buy in" to the commitment! Once someone intensely believes he can achieve the goal, he will be on the path of the promotable person and have a good chance to become a "10" in business.

Want the Goal Enough to Pay the Necessary Price

How many times have you heard someone say, "I worked all weekend on this project," or "I haven't had a vacation in four years?" Do you think that person does a better job than the person who goes home at a reasonable hour and vacations with the family twice a year? Although many speakers and business gurus advise making sacrifices to achieve our life's goal, I think that advice is superficial.

It is very difficult to define "sacrifices," to spell out precisely what is a price and what is a reward. In fact, what is a sacrifice for one business person may be the essence of life for another. I've had problems for years with those managers who never take vacations, who continually work 80-hour weeks and who always have desks piled high with reports, printed matter and publications.

If they think it's necessary or even fun to work that way, I have no objections. But I do mind that these workaholics are providing role models for young people. Sure it takes hard work to achieve, excel, and get ahead in business. But it also takes balance in one's life.

Use Proven Success Methods to Achieve Objectives

This thought reinforces the earlier admonition about reinventing the wheel. You and your company *are not different*. Becoming familiar with the profiles of successful companies and the people who made them work is a great place to begin your ascent to success. Find out how they prepared themselves, what training they obtained, and how they planned their career paths. Successful people have already made the laborious journey. Learn from their triumphs as well as their defeats.

The person you choose to emulate does not have to be from your business, your company, or even from your industry. The key is to select a role model or models who closely parallel your own concepts of the professional; then learn all you can.

Many potential role models are excellent subjects in the business environment, but are less than adequate with their family and personal lives. Seek role models who embody a balance between work and family. Be selective; add and discard role models from time to time as you learn from them.

The key point is not to spend your energies trying to reinvent the career path to promotability. If you are interested in becoming a "10" in business, *use proven success methods* to achieve your objectives.

Further, the suggestion to locate several role models does not propose that you elevate those persons to sainthood. You seek *education from* your role models, not *adulation of* them.

I once reported to Ed, executive vice-president of a firm for which I worked. On the credenza behind Ed's desk was a walnut-framed photograph of the firm's president, Sam. Sam's office was immediately adjacent to Ed's. Although I wasn't immediately sure why, that center-stage picture bothered me.

Soon I recognized that the company president had been positioned far above Ed's family in Ed's mind. Ed had elevated Sam to sainthood; in effect, Sam's picture had become a psychological shrine.

Ed was not a teenager admiring a professional quarterback, but rather a skilled, intelligent executive vice-president, and an experienced leader of a one-hundred-million-dollar-a-year corporation. However, the company was in trouble; corporate sales results and performance continued to be far less than projected. Consequently, Sam found it necessary to terminate Ed.

I had several conversations with Ed in the next 30 days because he was given an office next to mine. (The company provided Ed the opportunity to seek other employment at its expense.) Each of our conversations ended with Ed emotionally and dramatically asking, "How could he do it to me?" Ed felt that his hero had forsaken him. He hadn't, but Ed remained hurt and bitter . . . and eventually took his own life.

Another factor in choosing a role model is to pick an individual who complements your skills and strengths. For instance, you may have a weakness in communicating assignments but not in marketing your company's services. In that case, find a role model who is successful in your area of weakness. More importantly, seek to emulate a system for career advancement that has worked for an individual. Do not seek to emulate personality traits of that individual.

The maximum benefit in your quest for advancement will result if you generate a composite of the most successful people. It is not necessary to expend energy reinventing the wheel. Instead, utilize those energies to perform tasks.

A CLEAR PERSPECTIVE ON GOALS

Here are four distinctly different definitions for the word "goal." As you read them, select the one definition that most accurately describes a goal.

Definition #1: A Goal Is A Target
According to this definition, setting goals is not an exact science. In fact, what we do is obtain the best possible data and information, acquire the most accurate demographics, review the results of previous years, and make projections (ensuring they are communicated to all). After all those criteria are analyzed, the number becomes the target.

Definition #2: Goals Are Mandatory
Goals are mandatory and it is our responsibility to find a way to reach them. The goals that we've set are what we will achieve—coming close is not satisfactory. This definition implies diminished concern with any particular unique advantages the competition may have and is instead based on your own capabilities.

Definition #3: Goals Are Guidelines
Using this definition, a goal is a guideline for all to incorporate on the company's path to productivity, and into each individual's planning process. Goals are broad parameters used to track productivity. They are sufficiently broad to provide direction and allow for flexible approaches toward their accomplishment, while encouraging progress towards desirable results.

Definition #4: Goals Are Something The Company Would Like Me To Hit

The conclusion behind this definition is that workers are unable to formulate their own goals since they are not aware of the complexities of the business. Employees are not privy to the required return-on-investment or return-on-assets criteria. As a result, goals are positioned as "something the company would like me to hit."

Now, consider all four definitions and choose the most accurate, sensible one. In my opinion, the only possible selection is number two—goals are mandatory.

To illustrate the logic of defining goals as mandatory, imagine this situation: The next time you're boarding an airplane for a vacation or business trip, lean into the cockpit. The pilot is likely to be checking flight plans, the weather, and his or her gauges. Ask the pilot how he or she feels about flying the airplane safely back to its destination. Is arriving safely a target? If so, the pilot is only promising to do the best possible job with all available information. Is a safe, accident-free flight a guideline? Or is a safe flight something the airline would like the pilot to accomplish?

If the pilot answers that goals are either targets, guidelines, or the desires of the company, I'd advise you to find a parachute or disembark immediately. The pilot must reply that the goal of arriving safely is mandatory! Professional pilots believe they must land their planes safely 100 percent of the time.

Likewise, promotable professionals and successful business people recognize that goals are mandatory. Nothing less than 100 percent of a goal is acceptable to any business professional hoping to achieve, excel, and get ahead in business. Have you ever heard a medical doctor lean over a patient going into surgery and reassuringly say, "I'm going to do the best I can"? If you ever hear that, run away and hire another doctor.

Promotable people want to reach their goals and regard them as mandatory. Through training, education, retraining, and years of practice, they transfer their knowledge into workable, professional skills. GOALS MUST BE MANDATORY!

DEVELOPING A PROPER GOALS ATTITUDE

A proper goals attitude involves recognizing that professional, promotable people and successful businesses really have no other alternative—their goals are mandatory! The day you discard all of your justifications for inadequate or sloppy work is the day you begin to have the proper attitude about goals. A proper goals attitude is really knowing and understanding that "IF IT IS TO BE, IT IS UP TO ME."

In addition, a proper goals attitude includes being accountable and taking responsibility for your actions. A proper goals attitude is a non-negotiable standard for the individual who accepts the challenge to achieve.

SUCCESSFUL PERSON PROFILE

Kendrick Bascom Melrose

President
Chief Executive Office
The Toro Company
Minneapolis, Minnesota

There's little doubt that in business Ken Melrose is the right man. With Toro on the brink of disaster in the early 1980s, Melrose tackled the difficult and disagreeable task of cutting corporate costs. After two years of losses totalling nearly 22 million dollars, the Toro work force was drastically reduced and plans for a new office building were scrapped.

Today, those profit-losing years are history because the company has turned around. Ken Melrose was the man who made it happen. "I'm a conduit. I believe in participatory management, in letting people who have the responsibility make the decisions that otherwise I have to make," Melrose claims.

Factually, tough calls were his only choice. Educated at MIT's Sloan School of Management, with a cum laude degree from Princeton, and an MBA from the Graduate School of Business at the University of Chicago, Melrose was prepared for the challenge. He got his practical experience as a market analyst for IBM, marketing manager for the Pillsbury Company, part-owner of Bayfield Technologies, and president of Game Time, Inc.

Melrose is described as "tough-minded" by some and "sensitive" by other people. One Toro board member, Stephen Keating, describes Melrose as a "very honest man of great integrity." Keating added, "He just stood there and battled it out. You find out who's a leader when tough decisions must be made."

Today the only thing in better health than Toro is Ken Melrose. Active, athletic and married with three children, he could still compete in football, basketball, and track, sports in which he lettered. Melrose serves on the boards of directors for the Valspar Company, Churchill Scientific, First Bank of Minneapolis, and the Minnesota Symphony Orchestra.

Additionally, Kendrick Melrose was the 1984 recipient of the MIT Corporate Leadership Award. He is a supreme role model for both business and private life and how to strike the balance between the two.

MELROSEISMS

"People have the potential of doing much more than they do. My job is to facilitate that potential."

"Our achievements are directly related to our own expectations of ourselves."

"People fail because they do not believe in their God-given potential to become better than they are."

"Organizations merely clarify the distribution of work, but most organizations are wrong. They don't recognize the true boss (the customers), and they reinforce the erroneous notion that management has the power. The rank and file have the power."

CHAPTER 6

MAKE CHANGE AN ALLY

"No one ever got nervous prostration pushing his (or her) business; you get it only when business pushes you."

Elbert Hubbard

After you've determined your direction and have a positive attitude toward your goals, someone changes the rules. The change could be as minor as new titles for all employees or as major as a complete corporate reorganization. For the balance of your work life, you're going to be confronted with the need to function in a continually changing environment.

How you react to change is your choice. You can either embrace, welcome, and learn to cope with change, or you can divorce yourself from any possibility of real achievement.

The challenge to promotable people is to do more than merely exist or function in the environment of change. The ticket to success is to become *proactive* about change—to think ahead, and to make forthcoming events both an asset and an ally. Anticipating how change will affect your life offers an extra advantage. Unlike the majority of people, you will be looking ahead and preparing for the future. Then change will work for you rather than against you.

Let's look at change in its broadest context by reviewing some startling facts. Joe Powell, a futurist and admired lecturer, describes change in terms of the speed at which we're able to travel. He notes that for most of the last 10,000 years, the maximum speed for travel was 40 miles per hour. At the time of the Pharaohs, who used horses for travel, the maximum rate of travel

was still 40 miles per hour. A thousand years later, during the
time of Jesus, the rate of travel remained constant. It didn't
speed up in George Washington's time.

But rate of travel was not the only constant. Interestingly,
George Washington heated his home using the same methods as
the Pharaohs. Change came slowly, if at all.

Yet in today's environment the ability to welcome and cope
with change is a critical factor in getting ahead. In the last 100
years, humans have progressed from a maximum rate of travel
of 40 miles per hour to what would have been unimaginable to
our ancestors. From the locomotive to the automobile, to the
propeller-driven airplane, to the jet, to rockets, to the space cap-
sule, today's speed is 18,000 miles per hour. In a few years, it's
bound to go higher.

This phenomenal increase in speed is reflected in other activities. Thirty-five percent of the supermarket products that
generate sales today are products that did not exist 10 years ago.
Eight out of ten new products fail, often because they're *too* new.
Even the first cold cereals didn't sell—consumers rejected them.

Change in the rate of consumer acceptance can profoundly
impact the success of products. Volkswagen sold only two cars
in its first year on the U.S. market. Today, it would be unusual
if you didn't see a Volkswagen on almost every street in the
country.

Change in corporate policy can make a once strong company,
strong again. Milton S. Hershey built the largest candy business
in the world without advertising. However, because he would
not alter his policy on advertising, Hershey almost lost the market. Several years after his death, management recognized that
they had better adjust to changes that had taken place. Consequently, they began to advertise. As a result, sales of Hershey
chocolate bars burgeoned, including an increase in sales of 66
percent for Reese's Peanut Butter Cups. By 1980, Hershey was
spending a whopping 42 million dollars a year on advertising.
It proved to be a sound investment.

If you're to be a promotable person or if your business is to
grow, adjusting to change is mandatory. Frankly, the only difference between stumbling blocks and stepping stones is the way
we use them. When Robert Hutchins was president of the University of Chicago, he was asked, "If you could have students

leave this great institution after four years with but one lesson firmly planted in their minds, what would that lesson be?"

Without a moment of hesitation, he replied, "I'd teach them to cope with change, which is inevitable."

TEST YOUR TOLERANCE FOR CHANGE

Dr. William Brown, author of the book, *Welcome Stress—It Can Help You Be Best,* offers a short quiz (see next page) to evaluate your tolerance for change. Using a scale from 1 to 5, indicate whether you agree with the statement or disagree. Number 1 indicates strong agreement while number 5 indicates strong disagreement. After you've completed the quiz, I'll provide Dr. Brown's evaluation of your tolerance for change.

After you've responded to all the statements, add your agreement/disagreement ratings together. A total score of 44 to 50 means that change doesn't bother you. A total score of 37 to 43 is favorable, meaning that you are not traumatized by change. A total score of 36 or less is considered poor—coping with change is exacting too high a price from you. Dr. Brown points out that it's doubtful you would find peace of mind in a career or business position where change can be expected regularly. Since there are very few positions in management where change is not a constant factor, you will need to adjust your coping mechanisms.

Change is inevitable. If you're going to achieve you will *have* to perform well within a changing environment. Dr. Brown's self-help test allows you to initially determine the degree to which you are psychologically compatible with change. If a tolerance for change is present, then perhaps you can make change an ally.

Regardless of the above, it even makes sense in business to change periodically merely for the sake of change itself . . . right or wrong!

COCA COLA'S CHANGE

To illustrate this point, let's examine Coca Cola's decision to introduce a new Coke. Every business analyst has an opinion, but not even Coca Cola can ascertain if discontinuing the

Your Tolerance for Change

Statements	Agree/Disagree
1. Whenever change is initially proposed, I feel threatened. (Grade yourself #1 if you feel very threatened, #5 if you are totally free of trauma.)	1 2 3 4 5
2. In general, I prefer things to continue the way they are. (Be honest, you're only kidding yourself.)	1 2 3 4 5
3. I get annoyed when asked to follow a new route to a usual destination. (Grade yourself #1 if a new route would bother you, and #5 if you might even enjoy a different route.)	1 2 3 4 5
4. I would be happiest if my family could stay exactly as it is today.	1 2 3 4 5
5. Our family vacations follow a predictable course and have for the past five years (with one or two exceptions.)	1 2 3 4 5
6. I prefer to continue with the tried and proven than to experiment with new ways of doing things.	1 2 3 4 5
7. My style of dress has not changed appreciatively in the last 10 years.	1 2 3 4 5
8. I become anxious whenever other people suggest office changes.	1 2 3 4 5
9. Even when I have ideas for improved work procedures, I'm very reluctant to voice them.	1 2 3 4 5
10. My biggest concern is whether I can continue in my job until retirement and then be free to do what I want. (Look at this question with all its complexities—it's a difficult one to answer accurately.)	1 2 3 4 5

Welcome Stress © 1983 William D. Brown, Ph.D. CompCare Publishers, Minneapolis, MN. Used by permission.

"original" Coke was the smartest step a marketer ever took, or if it was a monumental mistake.

But Coca Cola changed. Even though the company had 63 percent of the U.S. soft drink market, it changed aggressively. Although the "Pepsi Challenge" series of commercials blanketed the country, they were merely an irritant to Coke. Right or wrong, Coca Cola brought out a "New Coke" with a sweeter, Pepsi-like flavor.

As a result, Coke received millions of dollars of free television exposure for their product. Coke's new soft drink was the lead story many times on all three major-network morning news shows.

Other less obvious benefits also came from the change. I conducted seminars for the Coca Cola organization and saw the company's employees become rejuvenated after the new Coke was introduced. I saw an emergence of excitement, aggressiveness, and determination; a re-awakening of the need to fight for supermarket shelf space. Since getting more supermarket shelf space is the overriding objective of the company, the proactive change helped the entire company. Coke put into battle a re-kindled army of marketers.

Within a month after dropping the old Coke, it was renamed "Classic Coke" and reintroduced to the market with the new Coke. Now there are two brands, requiring more supermarket shelf space. Consequently, a food merchandiser is almost forced into selling both types of Coke.

I believe the decision to change by bringing out a new soft drink was a good one. But I'm not referring strictly to adding the new product. I'm suggesting the decision was right because the entire organization required a kick in the seat of the pants. Due to its overwhelming percentage of the soft drink market, complacency had set in. The employees' standards of performance and willingness to compete required stimulation.

BURGER KING'S CHANGE

Successful business leaders make change an integral part of their management and marketing tools. In 1984, for instance, Jeff Campbell was chief executive officer of the Burger King organization, a wholly owned subsidiary of Pillsbury. Burger King did not have a sizeable portion of the market share; in fact, next to McDonald's' 10,000+ stores and 36 percent of market share, Burger King was much smaller, with fewer units and only 16 percent market share.

Campbell elicited participation throughout the organization to set a key goal. He did so by ensuring that everyone at Burger King from top to bottom participated in determining that goal. At its 1984 franchise convention in Reno, Burger king decided to expand to over 4,000 Burger King stores by 1987, as well as substantially increase sales.

The greatest obstacle in achieving this objective was the competition—Burger King customers would first have to drive by at least three or four McDonald's to buy a "Whopper." To achieve its objective, Burger King used the same strategy as Coca Cola and made change an ally instead of an enemy. Burger King spent $35 million in the summer of 1985 promoting the new "Bigger and Better Whopper." Although the bun was reformulated and the condiments were rearranged, the hamburger was essentially the same, and somewhat larger.

While Mr. T, Loretta Swit, and Lyle Alzado emphasized a new, bigger, and better hamburger on Burger King's commercials, the real campaign was being launched on the frontline. Through research and analysis, Burger King officials learned that the necessary change was not with the menu. Instead, they needed to improve the customers' dining experience. The battle of the burgers, as the public believed it, had to do with the hamburger itself. It didn't! In reality, the problem consisted of three separate issues.

One important issue was to ensure that the bigger and better "Whopper" was served with courtesy by the Burger King personnel. Another part of that necessary change was to find a way to guarantee that the "Whopper" was served at the correct temperature. (One survey indicated that as many as 70 percent of all industry hamburgers were served at temperatures lower than the standards.) Keeping the restaurant clean and the restrooms sanitary were a third factor adding to the customers' pleasant dining experience.

My company assisted the Burger King operation in communicating these needed criteria. I was privy to the renewed commitment, involvement, and overall desire of the Burger King restaurant crews to compete successfully and beat McDonald's at Q.S.C. (Quality, Service, and Cleanliness).

Mr. T, Loretta Swit, and Lyle Alzado were the talents featured in the commercials on local television. I was the individual featured in the videotape series shown throughout the system to the restaurant crews. The three stars encouraged the public to try the bigger and better "Whopper." Meanwhile, in my videotape discourses, I discussed developing a bigger and better "you." I suggested to the employees that their strength and their new unique competitive edge were positive changes *they* could effect in Q.S.C.

The ability to see change as an ally, instead of an adversary, is an integral component in the career-advancement system of the promotable person and successful business owner. Change, right or wrong, good or bad, may seem too far-fetched as a strategy for most people. If your objective is to achieve, excel, and get ahead in business, then you might well consider the positive benefits of change.

DON'T FIX IT

A well-worn cliche that has misled business leaders is, "Don't fix it if it's not broken." Perhaps this statement makes sense on an intuitive level. But stagnation can occur without change, leading to blind maintenance of the status quo. During the 1970s, for example, the U.S. automobile industry enjoyed record sales, revenues, and profitability year after year. Instead of looking ahead and foreseeing trends, Detroit patted itself on the back. The United States auto industry didn't change because its leaders believed themselves to be secure. In fact, American manufacturers owned the major share of the market in the 1970s. But after the oil crisis, they lost a 22 percent share of that same market. And current projections predict that more than 50 percent of the United States automotive market will be lost to foreign manufacturers by 1990.

I had the opportunity to write, produce, and be featured in a business-training film for Chevrolet that communicated many of the same concepts featured in this book. I found it especially interesting that after titling the film *Survival,* General Motors saw fit to distribute the program to nearly every Chevrolet dealer in this country.

"Don't fix it if it's not broken" is not a success posture. If you live by this admonition, you become vulnerable to staying in the same place and watching your peers advance. With that attitude, your business becomes vulnerable to the changing distribution and marketing strategies of your competitors. You can't do anything but lose. There is simply no way to avoid change; consequently, the achiever understands it, seeks it out, and even creates change.

CREATE CHANGE

Creating change can energize you, leading to useful thoughts and an enthusiastic attitude. Many years ago, as a sales representative for Mobil Oil Company, I attended a workshop where I was asked to place a solitary dot on a piece of paper. That dot represented me. At the time, all I knew was the retail service station side of the oil business in St. Louis. I was secure; I knew the territory extremely well. When I finally realized how small the dot was, it hit me like a ton of bricks.

"Hey," I said to my supervisors at Mobil, "teach me more. I'll go anywhere and do anything but please help me enlarge that dot." Mobil transferred me to Tennessee. Then, as I was coached to do in the workshop, I drew a tiny circle around that original small dot. I'm more now; I know more and understand more. I know the retail service station business in St. Louis, and now I have experience in western Tennessee as well.

Over the years, I've added many circles around that original dot. The dot and circles are symbols of my expanding professional growth and development. Now when I give speeches and seminars, the audience is hearing the results of the enlargement of that tiny dot first drawn in 1959.

The importance of seeking challenge and change can be illustrated using a personal example. Eugene Burroughs and I were both born on September 10, 1932. We started kindergarten together at Irving School in North St. Louis, Missouri. We were often referred to as "the twins"—we looked alike and palled around together. We seemed inseparable.

Gene went to work for a public utility in St. Louis when he was 17. He wanted the security of the utility company. Physically and mentally, Gene never left North St. Louis. Of course, Gene took vacations occasionally, but at least half of those vacations resulted from my challenges to him to see New York, or to learn to ski or to fly. As much as I cared for Gene, I must say he was uninteresting; he never really tried to improve in his life.

I recall having a beer with him at age 35. He proudly announced that he had turned down a promotion opportunity at Union Electric. Gene Burroughs maintained his solitary dot and his security environment.

It seems to me that there were very few highs in his life. Unfortunately, he died of cancer at the age of 48. As I gazed down at him that last day, I saw the full lifespan of Eugene Burroughs, starting from Irving School, North St. Louis, Missouri, until his death—no change, no risk, little improvement. I cared for him deeply, but my friend Gene Burroughs never got beyond that single, solitary dot on the paper.

Change is a key component of achievement. Enlarge *your* dot or be comfortable with the fact that you simply are not promotable or your business will not progress.

SUCCESSFUL PERSON PROFILE

Helen F. Boehm

President
Boehm Porcelain
Trenton, New Jersey

In 1950, in a basement in Trenton, New Jersey, Ed and Helen Boehm started a business to manufacture and sell fine porcelain figurines. Neither was trained in the discipline. Ed, who was to design and make the art objects, knew nothing about ceramics and had little formal art education. It is phenomenal that they were able to produce works of art that are on exhibit today in the White House, the Vatican, and the Great Hall in Peking. This outstanding success occurred because of the determination and abilities of Helen Boehm, who, though never trained in the marketing and promotional skills necessary to accomplish the objective, recognized the need for developing these skills in making Boehm porcelain a valued name in the art world.

Helen Boehm, born Helen Franzolini, in Brooklyn, New York of parents who had immigrated to the U.S. from Italy in 1911, had several things going for her, not the least of which is a belief in the work ethic. And work she did! In the earliest days of the Boehm company, the sales force consisted of . . . Helen.

She logged many hours and miles in search of customers. She had no formal sales training, yet she had an astute manner of prospecting and selling. Helen instinctively knew the future of the company rested in (1) recognition of the superb quality of the porcelains which Ed was creating, and (2) sales. She also knew that to be successful in finding customers at early stages of the company's growth, she could not wait for them to find her; she must find them!

She made 18-hour day-long sales trips. As a fledgling art entrepeneur she had the audacity to telephone the Metropolitan Museum of Art and in return, receive a commission from that prestigious organization. Helen had no fear in seeking the sales and recognition that would lead the struggling company to its premier position in the art world today.

With Ed's untimely death in 1969, Helen was again placed in a take-charge, decision-making posture. She was a risk-taker with considerable dedication and determination. Helen's drive, commitment, and intuition formed the basis of the skills necessary to succeed. As a result, today she enjoys the fruits of the labor she and Ed sowed in the early days of their business and marriage. Helen Franzolini Boehm today graces the homes and organizations of the world's most famous people. Boehm Porcelain continues to succeed and grow because Helen Boehm continues to succeed and grow.

BOEHMISMS

"I need people! People are my energizers. People inspire me to do a good job, force me to stretch."

"One learns great lessons when one is young. My mama's philosophy was that perfection is the only thing to strive for . . . and perfection, as she showed me, requires perseverance."

"If youthful enthusiasm, determination, and the ability to work seven days a week would help assure success, then we (Ed and I) would succeed."

"If the definition of marketing is 'wanting to get somewhere in a hurry,' then I had a talent for it from the start."

CHAPTER 7

THE ORCHESTRATORS

"Do what you can, with what you have, where you are."

Theodore Roosevelt

Individuals or, for that matter, companies that are able to enjoy outstanding achievements have mastered the ability to orchestrate all elements in their environment to produce a unified, synergistic support system. What is orchestration and how is it used to achieve results? To answer, let me begin by offering a detailed example of an industry that kept shooting itself in the foot because of a fundamental inability to orchestrate.

There are many companies in the linen supply and industrial laundry industry with a history of sizeable profits. Though they have done well for many years, these companies have never been able to achieve their true potential or equal the profits and revenue growth of other businesses also classified as members of the service sector.

As management consultants to the industry, our firm was able to identify many reasons for the inability of businesses in the industry to achieve their true profit potential. The companies repeatedly failed to attract, retain, and train competent first- and second-line supervisors. Top management also strongly resisted adherence to basic marketing principles. This way of operating permeated companies and filtered down into the ranks of the line managers.

Worse, the industry suffered from what I call the "them-syndrome"—an avoidance of accountability and responsibility in the face of blatant non-performance. For example, rather than work together to achieve organizational synergy, individual departments—service, production, sales—accuse and cast aspersions on one another as to why desired levels of customer service cannot be achieved.

When you always have "them" to blame you are able to enjoy several benefits:

1. You may continue to claim that "We are doing our part."
2. You have established a perfect excuse not to work in harmony with other elements of the organization (and thereby avoid taking responsibility to orchestrate).
3. You can maintain a comfortable posture by doing business as usual.
4. You feel free of any accountability for self-improvement.

The success of a business can be illustrated by mentally picturing a three-legged stool. One leg is the sales department, another leg is the production department, and the third leg is the service distribution department. The stool remains strong and usable as long as all three legs are firmly in place. If one of the legs is a little wobbly, the overall stability of the stool suffers.

National Linen is a subsidiary of National Service Industries, a large U.S. corporation headquartered in Atlanta, Georgia, and one of many sizeable textile-rental companies throughout the United States. You may have seen National Linen's distinctive red trucks and prominent logo in your town. Every evening, thousands of those trucks filled with large white canvas bags containing soiled linen from hospitals, restaurants, nursing homes, and businesses head back to their respective industrial laundry plants. For the most part, each truck is filled to capacity—the large canvas bags are packed in tightly and held in place with the distinctive National Linen red net.

Traditionally, sales departments in the linen industry feel very strongly that the real reasons for marketing nonperformance are due to ineffective production departments. In the case of National Linen, those in sales claimed that production standards did not meet customer needs and were in fact unacceptable. Many people in the sales department felt that people in the production department were not interested in maintaining satisfied customers.

The sales department's accusations regarding the non-performance of the production department was so intense that when our consultants were first called in, we immediately went to the production department, hopefully to determine the core problem and learn why production could not perform up to more desirable industry norms.

Working with the production department, we quickly discovered that their dissatisfactions were no less intense than that of the sales department. The production department loudly and indignantly told us that the company's cancer was with the service distribution department. It was suggested that the route-service personnel functioned at such a minimal, undisciplined level that they could not meet the basic needs of the customer and caused considerable problems for the production department.

In our quest to get at the heart of the company's problem, we called upon the service department. As you may have guessed by now, they were very vocal and very concerned about the shortcomings of the company. However, they were quick to point out that they were doing the job. Now, if they could only get the proper support from the sales department . . .

Unfortunately, that scenario is typical of most companies in this industry and represents the antithesis of orchestration. Though this self-destruction exists to some degree in most companies, in the linen-supply and industrial-laundry industry, the lack of interdepartmental orchestration is a growth and revenue tumor. Everyone seems to be spending full time attempting to unscrew the other department's leg on that three-legged stool.

Working in Unison

The highly promotable person, much like the winning company, sees the need to generate and orchestrate the individuals within a department or company into a team so that everyone is working for the same common goal. Visit the Indianapolis 500, or a rock concert—it doesn't matter which. At the raceway, before the race begins and whenever the driver needs to make a "pit-stop," a highly professional crew, working in unison and demonstrating a team psychology, speedily prepares the driver and vehicle to start or get back into the race. There is no time and effort expended on destructive behavior, blaming, and non-cooperation of team members. To do otherwise would ensure that that driver and team would not be successful.

At a concert, if you go early enough you will hear the dissonance of musicians, stage managers, and others, tuning and gearing up for the performance that is about to occur. When the singer or maestro walks in and steps up to the microphone or raises the baton, all the noise and clamor suddenly become music. The drummer doesn't try to drown out the bass player. The woodwind section doesn't undermine the performance of the string section. Rather, all play their part to present the customer (members of the audience) with the desired product (a pleasing sound).

Similarly, the promotable person or the successful business strive to orchestrate the various elements of the business environment to profitably maintain a customer focus. The attitude, activities, and communication of the orchestrator are such that he or she is able to generate, motivate, and extract the best possible performance from the entire team. The orchestrator is not internally motivated by the specific interests and needs of his or her own department or group. Instead, the orchestrator has developed the capacity to empathize with the needs of the whole and to feel accountable and responsible for the activities that take place.

Pull With or Pull Out

At Beveridge Business Systems, my consulting firm, our standards are such that if you plan to be employed with our firm and enjoy advantages and opportunities for career advancement you must either *pull with or pull out*. This concept represents another non-negotiable standard for the professional who hopes to achieve, excel, and get ahead in business. Not many have the motivation or desire, perhaps even the patience, to become orchestrators. It is a unique, desired skill which requires the ability to generate a team psychology.

THE ROCKY ROAD TO BECOMING
AN ORCHESTRATOR

Your attempts at orchestrating will be met by other managers and departments that are instinctively suspicious of your motives. Most people are so busy guarding their own turf that they can't believe anyone else could be interested in what is good for the whole, as opposed to what is good for themselves.

When my daughter Deborah completed her studies at Miami University of Ohio, including a year of international business at the University of Copenhagen, she went to work for AT & T Communications in the Chicago office. This was just after the period of divestiture and breakup of the company's monopoly position in the telephone industry. Over the years, most of the individuals who joined AT & T did so because it represented a secure position in a stable industry. With divestiture came a new environment of competition and stress.

The environment in Deborah's office at that time was particularly stressful. I suggested that if the opportunity presented itself, Deborah attempt a bit of orchestrating. It sounded reasonable to her. The first time the opportunity presented itself, Deborah approached one of her peers in Selected Account Sales and offered to help. She was rebuffed immediately by a fellow employee who said, "Deborah, I don't want your help!" This incident rattled Deborah, and for some time she lost interest in attempting to orchestrate.

This story illustrates an important point. The promotable person must continue to be motivated as an orchestrator even if the effort is not welcomed.

Let's look at the situation when your attempts to orchestrate are initially resisted. The first step is to win or earn the confidence of the person or the department involved. I know of no better way than to totally discard your needs, interests, and motives for a time and become totally immersed in the interests, needs, and activities of your peers.

If it was desirable to develop a team psychology with the Selected Account Sales unit, I would first confess to those people that I didn't feel I knew as much as I should about the activities, problems, and difficulties that they experience. I would tell them that I would sincerely welcome the opportunity to spend some time with them to learn about their job or department. Further, I would suggest that if I had the opportunity I would try to find a way for my own department to do things in ways that would support the needs of both departments and the entire organization.

To formally arrange a time at which I could attend another department's meeting, I would suggest two different dates on which I was available. Thus their choice would not be yes or no, but rather which date would be more preferable. I would be outwardly appreciative and the most interested, attentive, empathic, and sympathetic business associate they ever encountered.

Does all this sound like a bit of fluff? It isn't—promotable people do what is necessary, within limits, to build a cohesive team psychology. Once you have demonstrated your sincere interest in the functions of another person or group, you have positioned yourself to extend a non-negotiable reciprocal invitation.

As others learn what you and your department do and the problems and challenges you face, you have effectively initiated a system of mutual support. However, this can only occur by first sticking your neck out a little, seeing beyond your own immediate needs and concerns, and mentally and emotionally supporting those who ultimately see the benefit in such orchestration.

Nurturing Environments

I know of corporations where managers are required to spend a minimum of one day every six months in each of the other departments. One company even made it against policy to be promoted to subsequent line or staff positions. The career path at this company *had* to be line to staff, staff to line, line to staff. This policy was enacted in the attempt to generate a team psychology within the company.

All successful companies are blessed with one or more effective orchestrators. Management consultants who have had the opportunity to work with a wide variety of organizations have known for years that it is the orchestrators who spell the difference between success and failure in an organization.

One of the best orchestrators I have encountered is Keith Krach. Keith is a Harvard MBA and a senior level executive at GMF, the robotics company of General Motors in Troy, Michigan. He is not yet 30 years old. I recall his very serious efforts at the many meetings in which I participated to sell the concept, "IT'S MY JOB!" That slogan formed the basis for generating an interdepartmental cooperation effort that built customer focus to its zenith. Today, as the robotics industry and GMF suffer through tough times, "IT'S MY JOB!" remains in place, solidifying a team effort by orchestrator Keith Krach.

Testing Yourself

How can you determine if you are an orchestrator? First, you'll want to consider how you view your company's organization chart. Are you in the habit of perceiving and contemplating the responsibilities and functions of employees several stations above and below your current position? The orchestrator always sees his role with a broad view. He accepts responsibility to inform, communicate with, and advise those in his environment—tasks necessary to meet organizational objectives. If you have what it takes to be an effective orchestrator, then you are most likely to have a clear focus as to where you are going, and the ability to persuade others to go with you.

Here is a thirty-day analysis you can undertake to determine the degree to which you are perceived as an orchestrator. Draw a line down the middle of a blank piece of paper. About one-half inch down from the top draw a line from left to right across the page. In the upper left-hand corner write the word "product or service." In the upper right-hand corner write the word "help." Each time any of your peers, line, staff, management, or any other group within your organization asks you for a product or service that is normally expected to be provided by someone in your position, note it in the left-hand column.

For the same thirty-day period, whenever you are requested to offer "help"—something associated with your expertise but not normally associated with your position—note it in the right-hand column. This simple log enables you to track, measure, and monitor the communication coming to you from others.

At the end of the thirty-day period count up the entries in the left and right columns. A highly promotable person receives more requests for help—assistance not normally associated with his or her position—than requests for a product or service—assistance with those items normally associated with his or her position.

I can honestly say that the client requests made to our own organization relative to interest in our products—our consulting services or our meeting presentations—are more often for help than they are for specific items. We feel we're in good company—I once heard an IBM executive proudly state that in his operation over 62 percent of client requests were for help as opposed to requests for product information.

In a similar manner, you can test whether a business is successfully orchestrating. Design a similar form and continually monitor and track any communication from business prospects, customers, or clients. If the majority of entries are on the left-hand side after a thirty day period, the business is in serious trouble because the market "sees" you as your product. It's a fact of business life that the day your identity is synonymous with your product line, you're beginning to lose your business. Conversely, if there are numerous requests for help, the business is postured for success because prospects and customers perceive it as being customer-focused, with the motivation and expertise to tailor solutions to individual customer needs.

The orchestrator is able to coordinate and orchestrate the attitudes and activities of the entire organization to achieve those standards.

Product or Service	Help

SUCCESSFUL PERSON PROFILE

Charlie and Ginny Cary

The Moorings Group
Roadtown, Tortola
British Virgin Islands

It's almost taken for granted that a Harvard MBA, seasoned with 25 years of corporate executive experience, will get ahead. In this case however, the founders of the world's largest yacht-charter company did it by "deep-sixing" the corporate environment and living their dream.

Charlie and Ginny Cary have done what everyone wants to do—find a way to do what you love doing and make a lot of money in the process. It couldn't have happened to two finer people than Charlie (he's got the MBA) and Ginny, who has exceptional operational expertise. At age 68, both are actively involved in a business that has seen revenues soar to $20 million since 1981, and which now operates yacht-chartering businesses in Florida, Tortola, St. Lucia, the South Pacific islands of Tahiti and Tonga, and Mexico.

Eighteen years ago, Charlie and Ginny decided to pass up his promotion at Freeport Minerals. This would have involved transferring to New York from New Orleans. Instead, this team, which started as high-school sweethearts, initiated a chartering business that is acknowledged to be the role model for the entire industry and is now two-and-one-half times larger that the closest competitor.

Today, The Moorings Group, is a sizeable organization of some 400 employees serving over 20,000 customers a year. The effort required to deliver "paradise" to their customers would seem well worth it. Revenues for 1986 increased over 30 percent from the previous year and conservative projections for 1987 indicate another 15 percent increase. Net profits in 1986 exceeded one million dollars.

Visit the Moorings in the British Virgin Islands and you'll still see Charlie and Ginny. On rare days they'll take off and sail the *Flying Ginny,* a 51-foot craft, to Virgin Gorda for a few hours of rest and recuperation.

"CARYISMS"

"We loved sailing, so we decided to make our hobby our work."

"Our business plan is as carefully organized and plotted as a sailor's navigational chart."

"Perfecting pleasure and maintaining a customer focus is the mission of the Moorings."

CHAPTER 8

ENTREPRENEURSHIP

"The business world does not want specialists, but broad men [and women] sharpened to the point."

Nicholas Murray Butler

To many, the word entrepreneur evokes images of dashing, courageous young professionals striking out on their own to create businesses that will set the world on fire. But the definition should be broadened. To be successful, the entrepreneur also requires several other personality and skill factors besides being adventuresome, having guts, or having the opportunity to go into business. For instance, several corporations now have in-house entrepreneurs, people with the freedom to create new ideas within the security of an established company. *Webster's Dictionary* suggests that an entrepreneur is a person who manages a business. Interestingly enough, Webster doesn't say they must own their own business; instead, entrepreneurs must function in their jobs as if it was their own business. That's important to understand!

ELEVEN CHARACTERISTICS OF THE ENTREPRENEUR

Much research has been undertaken by academic institutions which have set up separate departments and majors to study entrepreneurship. A case in point is the Caruth Institute, the business-focused division of Southern Methodist University in Dallas, Texas. Research there isolated 11 characteristics of the entrepreneur. As we discuss these definitions, please remember that the list is applicable to both the person in business for himself and the corporate in-house entrepreneur.

1. Entrepreneurs Are In Good Physical Health

One reason entrepreneurs are in such good physical health is that entrepreneurs frequently feel they are the only ones who can complete the job. Consequently, entrepreneurs take care of their health and remain in good physical condition.

For more than 20 years, I've been speaking to conferences, conventions, and business groups. That type of work requires scheduling engagements far in advance, especially when there are over 175 engagements each year. Yet in 20 years I have never missed a program. At our house we joke that I get sick on weekends and I'm fine on Mondays.

When my son was a sales representative for the H. B. Fuller Company, I learned that he was quite ill but had procrastinated about getting medical attention. When he failed to act upon my advice to see a doctor, I sent him a letter that said, "If you hope to achieve your life's goals, you must first take care of your health, then you take care of your business, and then you take care of your family, in that order."

Some people would disagree with those priorities, but I learned long ago you must take care of health and business so you *can* take care of your family. Entrepreneurs and promotable people are, for the most part, in good physical health. Take the necessary steps to ensure that you continue to stay that way.

2. Entrepreneurs Have Superior Conceptual Abilities

Entrepreneurs are able to see the big picture. Although entrepreneurs must have technical skills, they must also be able to conceptualize the requirements of the entire business. An entrepreneur in St. Louis, for example, was able to see the potential in some run-down warehouses located next to the famous arch, the Gateway to the West. Tourists frequently visited the Arch and then went shopping and dining in other parts of the city. As a result of that entrepreneur's foresight, those warehouses were remodeled and now contain some of St. Louis' best restaurants and shopping. Similar revitalizations are occurring in other run-down sections of cities across the country.

3. *Entrepreneurs Have the Broad Thinking of the Generalist*

You may be a very successful individual within a company. When you are motivated to become a self-employed entrepreneur, however, you must acknowledge that there will no longer be a marketing department to develop promotions or an engineering team to redesign a product. You'll be on your own. For this reason, many entrepreneurs have failed. They couldn't (in their opinion) lower themselves to handle all aspects of the business. The true entrepreneur has the broad thinking of the generalist and is willing to perform all necessary tasks to achieve objectives.

4. *Entrepreneurs Have High Self-Confidence*

Entrepreneurs believe in themselves and what they do and can do. Because of their high self-confidence, they have little doubt of their ability to excel.

5. *Entrepreneurs Have Strong Drive*

Entrepreneurs do not need starters, such as alarm clocks. They don't need bosses policing their activities or motivating them to go to work. Instead, their drives to participate, to produce, and to perform are so strong that they seem to be inborn.

6. *Entrepreneurs Need to Control and Direct*

In addition to strong drives, entrepreneurs have a need to control and direct the situations around them. They search for these opportunities. As a result, accountability and responsibility pose no problems for these people. Entrepreneurs look for, seek out, and crave opportunities to control and direct.

7. *Entrepreneurs Have Only Moderate Interpersonal Skills*

In view of all the positive characteristics we've discussed, entrepreneurs were found to have only moderate interpersonal skills. They don't get along with everybody! This suggests that the entrepreneur's drive, ability to see the big picture, and high self-confidence doesn't sit well with everyone.

The entrepreneur's drive leaves little room for the required niceties of a democratic environment. The entrepreneur and the promotable person recognize that they can't please everyone; in fact, they don't even try to. To be a "10" in business, entrepreneurs know they can't be the most popular kid on the block.

8. Entrepreneurs Are Moderate Risk Takers
The entrepreneur must take qualified risks to achieve, excel, and get ahead in business. In other words, the statement "no risk, no reward" is applicable. In fact, I wouldn't even qualify risk-taking with the word "moderate." I would have chosen the prefix "calculated."

9. Entrepreneurs Have a Realistic Outlook
Entrepreneurs must maintain a balance between stretching their capabilities and overextending themselves. If it's possible to shoot for the stars, they will; if not, they'll look around for a mountain they can climb. Entrepreneurs maintain their sense of realism and develop a grandiose plan only if such a plan is realistic for the business.

10. Entrepreneurs Have Sufficient Emotional Stability
Entrepreneurs are people who don't give up when confronted by obstacles, yet they don't bang their heads against large brick walls.

There are two extremes on the emotional stability scale. On one end, people are overwhelmed by seemingly insignificant obstacles and don't attempt to jump over them. On the other end, people become so blasé that they don't demonstrate enthusiasm or emotion about what they're doing. An entrepreneur must strike a balance between handling roadblocks and demonstrating the enthusiasm needed to stimulate other people.

This story will illustrate what happened to a person who was "too cool" for his own good.

When I was a salesperson in St. Louis, the sales representative in the neighboring territory was a former B-29 pilot. Dick Knapp was the most stable, calm, and consistent individual I had ever met. I used to sit dumbfounded as he told me of the many bombing missions he had flown over Germany in 1944. I'll never forget one particular story he told of a bombing run during which his co-pilot was killed by anti-aircraft fire in the seat just inches away. Dick continued his mission, attacked the target, then coolly returned to England.

Nothing excited Dick. And that lack of enthusiasm, which may have allowed him to perform bombing missions in war, caused him considerable difficulty in becoming promotable in business. You see, when I knew him, Dick couldn't generate the enthusiasm to foster an innovative, creative environment. He was stuck in a "super-cool" mode that was uninspiring to others. Consequently, Dick was a marginal salesperson and the poorest candidate for entrepreneur I've ever met.

11. Entrepreneurs Have a Low-Level Need for Status

Status prerequisites, such as an expensive company car, are not important to entrepreneurs. Instead, they focus on the end result rather than the niceties that come with certain positions. Entrepreneurs within an organization, however, need status prerequisites more than independent business people. This is the only component of the list that differs for in-house entrepreneurs and individuals in business for themselves.

ENTREPRENEURS ARE LEADERS

To achieve, excel, and get ahead in business, entrepreneurs must seek out, recruit, and bring on-board entrepreneurial types. These individuals will function in their jobs as if the company is their own business.

Entrepreneurs and winners do what other workers will not do. They understand that there is no heavier burden than a great opportunity. Ready, willing, and able to take on challenges, entrepreneurs seek and find stimulation.

Sky, an in-flight magazine published by Delta Airlines, featured an article in August 1985 written by Dr. Michael Mescon, dean of the College of Business Administration at Georgia State University, and Dr. Tim Mescon, associate professor in the School of Business at the University of Miami. The article[*]—"What

[*]© 1985 The Mescon Group, excerpts reprinted courtesy of Halsey Publishing Co., publisher of Delta Airlines *Sky.*

Makes A Leader?"—is applicable to our discussion of the entrepreneur. The authors wrote:

> Great leaders can do great things. Great leaders can incite
> people to build great organizations. Great leaders are visionaries
> of mountains, not molehills.

Later in the article, they continue:

> It is the smothering of the leaders' drive that makes some com-
> panies all too lethargic. Leaders energize and electrify people and
> these very same individuals energize and electrify organizations.
> And guess what? These same people and companies love it! There
> is something about extraordinary leaders that is infectious. Good
> leaders are made, not born, and these good leaders make good
> people in good organizations . . . great.

Other Characteristics of Entrepreneurs

In over 20 years of speaking engagements, one of the reasons
why I've never missed a speaking date is because I feel a "crisis-
to-perform." I feel a sense of urgency about the tasks I undertake.
The Mescons agree that this characteristic is vital to entrepreneurs. In describing leaders, they talk about the achievements
of Robert Woodruff:

> They never say never. They said you cannot introduce a new
> soft drink in 18 months. (He introduced four.) They said you ab-
> solutely, positively cannot alter a time-tested formula that had
> been in the family for a century. (He said we can and we must.)
> Robert Woodruff brought one kind of romance to Coca Cola. . .
> Great leaders can take great corporations on great journeys. You
> can never say never to a great leader and succeed. Never!

Entrepreneurs have other characteristics that are shared by
the promotable person and the successful business leader. Here's
a checklist of factors, some of which relate directly to the earlier
definitions. Evaluate yourself against this list to see if you have
what it takes to achieve, excel, and get ahead in business.

1. Strongly Competitive
A competitive environment is the spice of life for the entrepreneur. It's fun to achieve and win. If you're not competitive, your
promotability may be threatened.

2. Aggressive

"Aggressive", in this sense, doesn't mean loud or obnoxious. Instead, it means aggressive when pursuing goals and markets. Entrepreneurs are proactive, and they "step out" for what they want.

3. Adventuresome

Entrepreneurs are willing to take risks. Leaders of successful businesses are adventuresome, and they venture easily into new areas of interest or endeavor.

4. Decisive

To achieve, you must be decisive and communicate that confidence to your entire team. You must be committed, confident, and steadfast in your direction.

5. Impatient

The entrepreneurs' crisis-to-perform has been proven. Promotable people and owners of successful businesses are impatient and operate with a sense of urgency. Achievers want to get on with goals and programs.

6. Action-Oriented

In some companies where I've worked, we studied plans to death. We were the greatest meeters, the best planners, the most outstanding analyzers in the industry. Unfortunately, no one executed the plans. Entrepreneurs are action-oriented and make things happen. Anything less is unacceptable.

7. More Autocratic Than Democratic

Entrepreneurs and promotable people are authoritarian and have a "do-it-my-way" leadership style. I believe the person who achieves, excels, and gets ahead in business is a very self-confident individual and possibly a bit arrogant!

Entrepreneurs Take Charge

Who wants to commit their work life to a company lead by an indecisive, passive, "let's-vote-on-it" individual? The competition will eat you alive. Who wants to be managed by an individual whose empathy is, in fact, sympathy? Or whose inability to discipline non-performers lowers performance standards to such a level that the whole company goes down the chute?

Successful businesses are owned and staffed by entrepreneurial types who feel a crisis-to-perform. Leaders understand that problems and obstacles are the reason they are in a leadership position and are on-going facts of business life. Promotable types solve problems and attack obstacles creatively, whether or not they have the corporate staff to come up with solutions for the problems.

Frank Seiberling was broke and out of work when he founded the Goodyear Tire & Rubber Company. He lived to see that firm become the world's largest tire and rubber company. Seiberling was known as the "Little Napoleon" of the rubber industry due to his unremitting determination to succeed. Unfortunately, during the Depression he lost control of the company he had started and built. Perhaps he could have retired at that point. But Seiberling was innovative, creative, and a survivor. He bounced back and started the successful Seiberling Rubber Company.

Frank Seiberling is credited with one of the rubber industry's greatest creative minds. He developed the first tire-building machine and was one of the first five people ever inducted into the industry's Hall of Fame.

After reading this chapter you may think you don't have the characteristics to become an entrepreneur. But take heart. You can work on developing them. After all, entrepreneurs/leaders/promotable people are made, not born.

SUCCESSFUL PERSON PROFILE

Richard A. Ferguson

President
New City Associates
Connecticut

"In the last few months, this company clearly picked up a momentum that is moving it with ever-increasing speed into becoming a real customer-focused operation." Those are the words of Richard A. Ferguson, one of the new owners of New City Associates, formerly known as the Katz Broadcasting Company.

Dick Ferguson is a skilled leader who feels that "an excellent manager looks to the individual's needs, in effect treating the people he manages as customers, and works to satisfy those needs in the context of achieving the overall goal."

His interest in broadcasting started in high school. In college he led the effort to build a radio station on the Skidmore College campus. He also has worked in a variety of different cities and held every conceivable position in the business and management of broadcasting. Dick has achieved phenomonal success due in no small part to the fact he has always worked and functioned as an entrepreneur. There aren't many who move from employee to owner of a major business in a period of less than ten years. Dick Ferguson did!

In addition, his outside service reflects his involvement, concern, and availability to his community. As an example, Ferguson provides both financial and leadership support to Junior Achievement. He also teaches the Project Business Course, a Junior Achievement project, to eighth graders. Talking with him, you will note a pleasant, intelligent, empathetic individual who has drive, commitment, and determination to become even more successful. More importantly, Dick Ferguson is most committed to training his people and developing human resources.

FERGUSONISMS

"Keeping this organization and its people focused on the company mission statement is my responsibility."

"Leaders set performance standards by their actions and deeds as much as by their words and plans. To keep an organization vital and moving forward, standards must continuously be raised."

"Many talented people fail because they have the misfortune of working for a non-manager."

"People who set out to achieve something are in fact setting out to change something."

"The single most important ingredient as to whether or not you will achieve a goal, is commitment."

CHAPTER 9

EXECUTION, THE
COMPETITIVE EDGE

*"The difference between doers and dreamers is that the latter wait for the
mood before taking action while the former create the mood by acting."*

Daniel Gerson

In August of 1985, I made a keynote address to the world's
foremost advertising people in New York. Organized and sponsored by *Advertising Age,* the annual conference was targeted
to both agency and in-house advertising personnel. My message
was a departure from their standard fare. I suggested that there
was little difficulty in finding someone to design print advertisements or television commercials. Instead, the difficulty was
locating individuals who felt accountable for the success of the
advertisement.

In our own firm, for years we felt strongly that strategically
placed advertisements in the business section of city newspapers
and city business journals were perfect vehicles for marketing
our goods and services. Since assumptions are weak until research proves them correct, I decided to conduct a research project. I offered a blank check to advertising departments of target
publications to pay for any ad campaign they wished to run. I
gave the salespeople carte blanche; they could select the advertisements, choose the number of insertions or formats, and decide
the rates I offered the deal to city business journals in Kansas
City, San Jose, Sacramento, Milwaukee, Portland, and Honolulu.
We offered the same deal in Louisville, Columbus, and Buffalo.

My only requirement was that the sales department would guarantee our company a return on our investment.

Not one of the papers accepted! No one would accept the challenge. None of the papers was willing to stand behind its advertising.

Having already approached newspapers and business journals, we decided to take a different route. We approached advertising agencies saying that we had opportunities to use cable TV as a marketing vehicle or to buy radio or television commercials. Although I indicated that we needed to promote and advertise, our primary concern was to develop a partnership with an advertising agency which was capable and able to stand behind its recommendations. Again, not one agency accepted the challenge to deliver the "sales promise."

At the *Advertising Age* conference, our presentation was titled "A Unique, Competitive Edge." While most seminar participants expected new graphic techniques, new copy ideas, and a new use for four-color brochures, we addressed our remarks in an entirely different direction. We targeted our message to the center of the bull's-eye; and for those who want to achieve, excel, and get ahead in business, the center is EXECUTION!

By putting ideas, programs, and concepts into effect, people have a unique competitive edge that can lead to a real opportunity for success. Can the advertising agency help the client execute the sales promise detailed in the advertisement? Do the advertising representatives know enough about your business to help you execute their program? In the late eighties and early nineties, they better learn how. Can the corporate manager execute the strategies and policies of the company? Managers who can are promotable people. The greatest obstacle to success in business today is not a deficiency of knowledge—it's a deficiency of execution.

Deficiency of Knowledge versus Deficiency of Execution

From my 30 years of experience, I've found that most people *do* have a working knowledge of the information you think they require. The problem is not deficiency of knowledge—"D.K."—

but rather "D.E."—deficiency of execution. To be promotable, to own or operate a successful business, you must be able to make the written programs and policies work. Execute the marketing programs and the motivation specifics you learned at last year's conference. Execute the marketing plan, the procedure manual, the five-year plan, and those skills you learned in training or from previous experiences. Execute! The ability and motivation to execute is the ticket to getting ahead in business.

William Francis O'Neil headed General Tire and Rubber Company from its beginning capitalization of $200,000 to a corporation with more than $750 million in sales. When we consider that during this same 45-year period more than 350 other tire-manufacturing companies started and failed, General Tire's accomplishment is even more astounding. Is it possible that those 350 companies didn't know how to make tires? Or is it more realistic to attribute their failure to a deficiency of execution?

In its seventh year, profit for General Tire reached one million dollars. General Tire's corporate executives executed their way to success! In fact, under the executive management of William O'Neil the company made a profit every year except one. O'Neil was an executor, a merchandising originator. In the early years, he purchased $5,000 (in 1950 dollars) full-page ads in the *Saturday Evening Post* to form a strong dealer organization and push the company's state-of-the-art products.

In addition, O'Neil was an innovator in employee-relations programs. He started a stock purchase plan for employees and removed mandatory time clocks, one of the first in the industry to do so. Because O'Neil executed, he was able to make outstanding achievements in business.

O'Neil put into action the words of Goethe: "Knowing is not enough; we must apply. Willing is not enough; we must do."

How One Industry Came Back

Not all business people have the interest or capability to become executors. In the late 1970's and early 1980's, college admissions declined, causing problems for college and university budgets. Some universities had to become commercial to survive. Many even advertised for students.

They weren't alone. Businesses and services that profited from the academic community were also experiencing declining revenues. Jostens, the major marketer and manufacturer of yearbooks and class rings, suffered. So did the developers and administrators of college entrance tests such as SATs and ACTs.

At that time, American College Testing (ACT) was closely reviewing its systems, products, and revenues. The company had an extensive investment in physical facilities and computer systems to serve the university community, and a large staff of PhD-level people to develop and service the product. Unfortunately, the declining enrollment situation was affecting ACT revenues. Therefore, solutions were needed.

Our firm was retained to analyze overall sales and marketing and suggest ways to maximize revenues. During this assignment, we found a new product that seemed to fit like a glove. But, as we shall see, the problem became a lack of execution.

The product we wanted ACT to implement was "The Student Talent Program," designed and developed by Lloyd Dill, a former Iowa football coach. His concept was based on the fact there were many schools looking for student athletes who were not of the superstar caliber. Those schools would accept weaker athletic skills combined with tenacity, opportunity, and leadership.

Dill's idea was to provide a standardized form, for a fee, to coaches of selected sports to list their needs and indicate their minimum standards for skill, speed, reach, and height. The lists would be submitted to a clearinghouse, such as American College Testing. Meanwhile, the parents of high-school seniors would receive another standardized form on which they would indicate their child's preferences in sports, geographic locations, and other factors. Then the needs of the coaches would be matched with the sports and skills of the students.

Many high schools use a similar system today. Students can match up their academic qualifications against the grade standards of a desired college. Lloyd Dill and ACT's vice president of marketing, David Crockett, suggested the idea to the president of American College Testing, Dr. Oluf Davidsen. His response was, "Dave, that is too far a departure from academia."

Consequently, the program and the idea were dropped. ACT passed up an excellent chance to create revenues. Even after the idea was rejected, Dave Crockett was confident of the potential and the possibilities. So he later returned to the president's office and asked permission to independently buy and execute the idea. Permission was granted, and Dave Crockett did just that.

Unfortunately, his attempts to execute the Student Talent Program were unsuccessful. The failure was for a variety of reasons—problems such as lack of tenacity, not enough time for involvement, and high costs. However, the idea was entirely sound, the market was well-defined, and there were identifiable customers with need.

Next in line was coach Lloyd Dill. Even though he had little business training, Dill's entrepreneurial spirit spurred him into action to make the idea work. Dill was ready to execute despite one manager's failure and one company's refusal to implement the idea.

Lloyd Dill made it happen. He marketed the program nationwide, concentrating on football and women's basketball. In 1986, he successfully marketed the product in 15 states, a 50 percent increase from the previous year. Dill is an intelligent, seasoned individual, but certainly there were individuals with PhDs at ACT with more knowledge than this Iowa football coach. However, once the basic design of the concept was in place, Dill *sold* the program—on the phone, through letters and printed literature, and with a lot of personal contact. Dill placed great emphasis on executing, and a determination and commitment to make it happen.

Many people believe the most difficult part of operating a successful business or functioning as a manager is the development of new programs and systems. It's not! The individuals who achieve and get ahead in business are those who have the talent to put those ideas to work. The people who can make it happen are more of a rarity than the dreamers.

We have all heard the unfair statement that "those who can't do, teach, and those who can't teach, teach others to teach." I am personally involved in teaching and in teaching teachers. I have found that thousands of college and university graduates simply cannot apply what they have learned. The problem is not a deficiency of knowledge, or a lack of expertise, but rather an inability to execute the knowledge.

Promotable people have demonstrated an ability to execute. Successful businesses are more often owned or managed by individuals who have a talent for executing rather than originating. The boom in the franchise business, for example, could only have happened with implementors and executors. The person who can take the procedures, systems, standards, and policies of the franchise and execute them stands a good chance of becoming financially successful. They are executors!

In your lifetime, how many conferences, training programs, or seminars have you attended? As a result of attending, what did you do differently? Our survey estimates that only 13 percent of all individuals attending such programs really change their behavior. And most people mistakenly said they didn't need or require the training in the first place. To increase the execution factor, conferences or training systems should be taught at a university level to increase the challenge. Because a lot of meetings and training activities lack stimulating, skilled presentation, they should require the participant to be the performer in place of the instructor. We should discipline or excuse those who attend the activity superficially.

If we initiated discipline and non-negotiable standards and emphasized applications and skills for training programs, the performance and productivity factors would greatly increase for the trainees. Instead, we target the instruction totally on complex policy and product knowledge because we incorrectly believe the problem is a deficiency of knowledge. Correcting the deficiency of execution is *the opportunity*. Execute well and you will more quickly become a "10" in business.

Practicing Execution

"How to execute" is not as difficult a challenge as it might seem. Simplistically, it centers around the fact that you can't just perform a goal. Goals, quantified and qualified, must have plans of action and activities to execute. While working through this exercise, list your goals. List what you want to achieve personally and professionally. Do it as fast as your goals come to mind; write them down quickly. You can always go back later and delete those of a lesser priority.

As an example, let's say our goals are as follows:

1. To increase revenues 20 percent.
2. To develop more professionalism in our personnel.
3. To take all vacation owed.
4. To improve profits 10 percent.

Next, develop activities and executions that will ensure you achieve your goals. Using our examples, here are several typical activities and suggested execution steps:

1. To increase revenues 20 percent.
   - Salesforce to call on other types of businesses that may use our services.
   - Execute product line extension. Add two new products by January 1.
   - Increase prices 6 percent across the board.
2. To develop more professionalism in our personnel.
   - Identify outside industry role model, such as IBM. Communicate its standards and examples.
   - Select upgraded training programs of university-level instruction with a challenging format. Ensure all departments have exposure to some developmental activities annually.
   - Improve recruiting, selection, and hiring process. Raise standards for employment within our company.
3. To take all vacation owed.
   - Immediately talk with spouse, select vacation spot, select specific dates (both summer and winter), send deposits.
   - Delegate, delegate, delegate.
   - Appoint acting manager for that period. Tell him or her they are in charge. Under no circumstance are they allowed to call you.
   - Conceptually perceive that your vacation is mandatory!
4. To improve profits 10 percent.
   - Change salespersons unlimited-commissions plan to a fixed bonus for goal attainment.
   - Increase prices 6 percent across the board.

- Execute a program where everyone—sales, service, production, and management—has the responsibility for retaining existing customers.
- Acquire newer punch press with increased production speed.

Execution requires that for both business and an individual to achieve, activities must be developed to move them toward the desired result. When you have both a commitment to execute and the development of activities targeted at your own objectives, you will have execution.

Execution in the Automotive Business

In 1984, automobile dealers in the United States spent well over one million dollars for advertising. Yet U.S. domestic car dealers still lost over 22 percent of their markets that same year. Even new options such as talking dashboards, sophisticated car clocks that tracked travel time, and new sporty models, couldn't regain that lost market share. The automobile manufacturers blamed the Japanese for unfair government subsidies, the Arabs for cutting off the oil supply, and U.S. bankers for raising the interest rates to 20 percent. Yet the market share continued to erode.

United States manufacturers knew how to make automobiles. They knew how to promote and advertise. The problem wasn't knowledge, but rather execution. The real problem in the industry is a lack of standards and skill among dealer salespeople. Today, as the loss of market share exceeds 40%, automotive salespeople still sit in a showroom waiting for you to walk in. When was the last time a new-car salesperson came and knocked on your door? New-car salespeople are too unmotivated, undisciplined, and poorly managed. They do not execute the fundamental skills of good salesmanship.

In November of 1985, the president of Toyota North America came to this country to visit automobile dealerships. Afterwards, several newspapers interviewed the president. He described the dealers he had seen as "passive and unimaginative." In fact, many seemed to be financially fat entrepreneurs who had lost the desire to compete and lobbied for legislation in their favor as a security blanket. As a result, today it is almost impossible for any factory to discipline a dealer's nonperformance. Conversely, most dealers are frightened to discipline their own staff's lack of productivity because of the difficulty in maintaining staff.

So we continue to lose market share. Further demonstration of our failure to execute in auto sales is the fact that in the following weeks the same Toyota president sold cars door-to-door. He sold seven cars.

The problem is that the industry and, in particular, the dealers haven't recognized that execution is the key to stabilizing and then regaining market share. If I were to suggest one single factor to ensure your success in business, it would be to learn how to execute.

SUCCESSFUL PERSON PROFILE

Richard J. Haayen

Chairman and Chief Executive Officer
Allstate Insurance Company
Northbrook, Illinois

Success. The very word inspires the ambitious and evokes images of a life and a career at the top. Yet what it takes to move up is as diverse a formula as the standards by which people measure success. What works in one company may not necessarily work in another. Still, people who possess enough smarts, savvy, and diligence will tend to rise to the top.

In his 36 years with Allstate, Dick Haayen has risen to the top. A graduate of Ohio State University, Haayen joined Allstate in 1951 as an underwriter trainee. Since then, he has held a number of management positions with the company, culminating in his election as chairman and chief executive officer on October 7, 1986.

In 1982, when Haayen was president and chief operating officer of Allstate, he helped introduce their "New Perspective," a blueprint for the Future to reorganize the company and make it a more market-driven firm. Said Haayen: "In order for the Allstate Insurance Company to grow, we need, first, to 'open up' the company. We need to place responsibility for its full development, not in the hands of a few at the top, but in the creative energies of each and every employee who is willing to become committed to the challenge that we face. It is obvious that the majority of our growth will have to be taken from our competition and, at the same time, our competition will be striving to take business from us."

The goal of Allstate's New Perspective was simple yet ambitious: to become the most successful insurance company in America. Marketing territories were reconfigured, layers of management were trimmed, some positions were eliminated while new ones were created, and reporting relationships were dramatically altered.

The results speak for themselves. In 1986, Allstate recorded its most successful year in history. "Right now, I'm in a position to do something about all the things I've hoped for and dreamed about for the company," Haayen says. "I used to think it was money that motivated people in my position, but it isn't. Making a difference keeps me coming here every day."

Haayen is an internationally recognized leader in the insurance industry. He is the former chairman and a current board member of the Insurance Information Institute, chairman of the Insurance Institute of America, and a member of the Property-Casualty Insurance Council. He is also a member of the board of directors of Sears, Roebuck and Co., and is actively involved in leadership positions in several community organizations. On top of that, he's a nice guy.

HAAYENISMS

"To be successful in management, you are responsible for two things: solving problems and motivating. Nothing in this world goes exactly as planned, and problem-solving and motivation are big challenges. But when handled right, they make the manager and his or her department more successful."

"Successful managers don't all fit the same mold. But one thing they have in common is integrity. Dependable people of high character, who won't compromise their standards, are destined for success."

"I would caution managers against continuously looking to their next promotion. Once the staff detects that its manager's interest lies more in the advancement of his own career than in the tasks at hand, distrust grows."

"People who discover innovative ways to solve problems, increase efficiency and improve business get rewarded. In general, promotions go largely to people willing to take risks."

"In order to build a sound organization, first of all, you must have a sense of purpose. Second, your management style must emphasize a sense of teamwork. Third, you must foster a sense of commitment. Finally, and above all, your management style must be built on a sense of integrity."

CHAPTER 10

ORGANIZE, ORGANIZE, ORGANIZE

"I attribute my success to always requiring myself to do my level best, if only driving a tack straight."

Russell Conwell

How many times have you worked for someone you believed to be less intelligent than yourself? How many of your neighbors are more successful than you, with resources to satisfy all their needs, yet they don't seem extraordinary?

Dig into your list of successful people and you'll begin to discover that many are not "I.Q." stars. There are brilliant individuals who had a 3.9 average on the 4.0 grade-point scale, so intelligent they have more knowledge in the tips of their fingers than most of us have in our entire bodies. But they're the exception rather than the rule.

Persons who achieve, excel, and get ahead in business do not have to be intellectual giants. In fact, many achievers in the world of business actually lack extensive experience in their industry or field. Even those with only a limited formal education still get ahead by satisfying the learning phase of promotable posturing in alternate ways.

The United Technologies Corporation placed a series of advertisements in the *Wall Street Journal* in the early 1980s. One of those thought-provoking ads had a message very relevant to "succeeding-in-spite-of." The advertisement read:

> If you sometimes get discouraged consider this fellow. He dropped out of grade school. Ran a country store. Went broke. Took 15

years to pay off his bills. Took a wife. Unhappy marriage. Ran for House. Lost twice. Ran for Senate. Lost twice. Delivered speech that became a classic. Audience indifferent. Attacked daily by the press and despised by half the country. Despite all this imagine how many people all over the world have been inspired by this awkward, rumpled, brooding man who signed his name simply . . . A. Lincoln.

Any number of examples can be presented to demonstrate that extreme intelligence and exhaustive knowledge of an industry or business aren't major success factors. Ray Kroc, the founder of McDonald's, and Jim MacLamore, the founder of Burger King, are prime examples.

Organizational abilities and capabilities far outrank exceptional intelligence as criteria for getting ahead. If I had to choose, I would select a person with good organizational skills over someone with 20 years experience in the field, or eloquent verbal-communication skills. Organize . . . organize . . . organize is a primary key to becoming a "10" in business!

The Importance of Organizational Skills

The organized individual gets more work done and can be depended upon to meet project deadlines. In addition, well-organized people don't interfere with the activities and work patterns of other people. Instead, the well-organized individual complements the efforts of other people and contributes to a smooth work-flow. Organizational abilities are always a cornerstone to business success.

Disorganized people frequently work late and on weekends to cover up the fact that they are having difficulty completing their work. If your desk remains covered with paper and you have to work every Saturday to complete it, then the problem is you! You're a poor role model and the people who work for you won't be motivated to perform at superior levels. You may blame the problem on the business or the boss, but I suspect it could be your inability to organize.

Organizational skills are so integral to the abilities of the successful business person that it is difficult to conceive of an individual succeeding without organizational capacity, except in a small retail store. We all know of local merchants who have little control of their time or inventory, yet still succeed because of the small scope of the business.

To be successful in business, you must be able to juggle several balls at a time. You must be capable of working on a multiplicity of projects and control your time so that you can manage the crisis; the crisis should not and cannot manage you.

In the following example, organizational skills saved a company from an impossible work load and generated a great deal of profit.

Banta Company is a book and manual printing firm in Menasha, Wisconsin. Laura Haley, 22, was the salesperson for Banta, working out of New York. For some time, she was trying to sell an account which would require Banta to produce large quantities of a new game. The prospective buyer was unconvinced the company could accomplish the mammoth task. Laura Haley was persistent though—she continued to demonstrate the capabilities and organizational abilities of her firm. She finally won the account by displaying admirable ability and selling skill. The account Laura gained was for the production of the game *Trivial Pursuit*.

At the time of this huge order, Banta was already producing their primary products near capacity. Yet the Banta Company produced, assembled, and delivered over 18 million *Trivial Pursuit* games, within the specified 12-month period—one game for every 13 people in the United States. Moreover, Banta accomplished that feat by early identification of the potential magnitude and scope of the opportunity. To accomplish this, a highly committed task force, under the direction of Executive Vice President and Chief Operating Officer, Allan J. Williamson, assumed responsibility for the project and, by assigning it top priority, was able to dedicate the appropriate people resources to this phenomenom. A very small administrative group handled the paperwork for this significant logistical effort that involved out sourcing and numerous locations of manufacturing and materials supply. Productivity, skill, and organization were the keys to Banta's success.

Organization not only improves morale and productivity; but it is a characteristic of individuals who enjoy great achievement. Moreover, being organized is profitable. The company produced over 90 million games of all kinds during one year. Banta more than doubled their earnings. Because of their outstanding management of the Trivial Pursuit project. It pays to be organized!

Components of an Organizational System

If you're not an organized person, there are books and other resources to assist you. The best book I've seen on the subject is Alan Lakein's *How to Get Control of the Time of Your Life!*, which outlines a complete, useable organizational system. To achieve, excel, and get ahead in business, you must have the capacity to do many projects and yet still plan, lead, organize, control, and staff each project.

In observing companies like Banta it is apparent that there are as many different organizational systems as there are individual companies. All of the systems, however, have some basic components to ensure that the business is organized and under control.

1. Prioritize Your Activities
Whether you prioritize your activities mentally or in writing, it is vital to decide which activity is the most important. Furthermore, all tasks—minor or major—must be prioritized. It is a continual process. Business leaders prioritize each duty in their job description. Promotable people prioritize their time and tasks.

2. Stick to the Plan
There will always be other activities you'd rather do, and projects less difficult and easier to complete. But at the chosen moment, they're not the activities or projects that are going to move you toward the desired objectives. What you spend your time working on is not optional. To be a "10" in business, you've got to stick to the plan! It is foolhardy to spend your time designing new products if the plan and priority are to penetrate the market and sell the existing product line. It may be more comfortable to handle paperwork in an air-conditioned office, but if the plan calls for coaching activities with the sales team in the field, that is where you need to be.

3. Think and Organize in Departmentalized Terms

When you have a large project, the total number of activities necessary to complete the job may be overwhelming and confusing. To attempt to attack the whole project without separating it into manageable tasks may make the project seem beyond your capabilities.

So don't attack the whole project. Think instead of each separate business function or individual challenge. For example, first deal with the selling effort. If revenues or profits are below projections, temporarily put aside all competing pressures. Later on, you can focus on other concerns.

If you can departmentalize your tasks for minutes or hours, you will be able to better organize your approach to the project. Learn to zero in on one function until the solutions begin to materialize. Organized individuals do so consistently.

4. Manage Your Paperwork

Most time-management consultants will also advise people to prioritize their paperwork. Lakein suggests you divide paperwork into A, B, and C groups. Work hard on the As, make the Bs either As or Cs, and put all Cs into a drawer where you'll forget them.

I have my own version of Lakein's concept. I propose that you handle your *entire list of responsibilities* in a similar way. Organize your projects, reading priorities, meetings, and field activities into A, B, and C groups, and instead of naming them A, B, and C, use more descriptive classifications such as MUST DO, SHOULD DO, and DON'T DO. By doing so, you'll be using the principles of efficiency, good management, and organization.

5. Delegate Responsibility

To get ahead in business, you must delegate. There isn't a justifiable cause for not delegating. If you don't delegate, you're limited; you become the bottleneck in your business. Your employees' growth will be stunted because they won't have the opportunity to learn and develop new skills, and that is unforgiveable.

6. Consistently Ask and Listen

You must first stop giving your people answers to their problems. When you provide all the answers, you've accepted full responsibility for the success of that decision. Avoid solving the problems of your subordinate customers. Even if you have the answer on the tip of your tongue, don't provide the solutions for your sales representative's clients.

Your subordinates must be seen as problem-solvers and perceived as the customers' sustaining resource. The day clients phone and ask for you by name, you're in trouble. When you personally solve those customers' problems, you're heading for major organizational difficulties.

It's a fact of business life that you never promote people who bring you problems. You only promote people who bring you solutions to problems. Ask and listen! Your subordinates do have skills, abilities, and problem-solving capabilities. Let them use those abilities.

When your people bring you problems, delegate the problem-solving. Ask your employees how *they* plan to solve the problem. Delegate the responsibility for generating solutions to your subordinates and discover a world of new freedoms, where you can become even better organized. You must learn to delegate or even the most efficient organizational abilities will not be enough to achieve, excel, and get ahead in business.

7. Do It Now

Organize now, not this afternoon, not tomorrow, not next month. Successful people cannot physically or mentally afford the repetitious handling of day-to-day tasks. Organize now, act on it, delegate it, write a note on the bottom of correspondence and return it. More jobs will come your way tomorrow, and you'd better be ready and have time for those new projects. If you haven't moved along, you'll be in an environment of constant crisis.

8. Develop Systems to Retain Data

Organizing a library with past projects and programs will prevent you from redoing something you have done before. In business, very little is really totally new. If you've developed a program, written a report, or designed a display, photograph and keep it. One day, there will be a need for that analysis and those systems. With slight changes, they can be used again.

Develop a system for retaining major projects that you've worked on while managing your business. Find a way to collect, file, and retain the programs, displays, and systems that other people have executed; that information will stimulate you at a later date. Because of the availability of the information, you'll find that your programs, systems, and designs improve. If you organize to retain data for reuse, you'll have better programs for less effort.

If You Feel Overwhelmed, Get Out!

Finally—and perhaps most important—recognize that IF YOU FEEL OVERWHELMED, GET OUT!

Not everyone has leadership or organizational skills. When I discussed this book and its intended contents with my wife Betty, she had an excellent suggestion. Betty proposed I include an additional section entitled, "It ain't half bad to be an indian brave." The American Indian tribes are composed of two basic leadership roles—the chiefs, who provide top management, and the Indian braves, who represent the balance of the tribe and offer a supporting role to the chiefs. Individuals who achieve, excel, and get ahead in business are able to do so only because they are supported by other competent people.

A chief cannot perform or has little purpose without a tribe. The general cannot dare great feats without the foot soldier.

"It ain't half bad to be an indian brave" is Betty's phrase. With the understanding of a leader, she knows that a support person's role is important and one of respect.

You don't have to lead. You don't have to crave responsibility. If you find yourself in a position of high responsibility and the accountability overwhelms you, be honest with yourself and get out. "It ain't half bad to be an Indian brave."

SUCCESSFUL PERSON PROFILE

J. Jeffrey Campbell

Chairman-Restaurant Group
Pillsbury
Minneapolis, Minnesota

What were you doing at age 38? (Or what do you hope to be doing by age 38?) Jeff Campbell—competitive, demanding, and skilled—was chief executive officer of the Burger King Corporation. Campbell is also a visionary. He was the primary strategist in Burger King's continuing battle with McDonald's. Initiated by Jeff, the "battle of the burgers" generated the greatest increase in consumer awareness in history, according to *Advertising Age.*

That same year, Campbell was named Outstanding Corporate Advertising Executive by the *Gallagher Report.* He has a degree in psychology and a master's degree in marketing from Columbia University. A former paratrooper in the 82nd Airborne, Jeff brings that same aggressiveness and confidence to the business world. He's been very successful using planned risk-taking.

While CEO at Burger King, he was working on an additional master's degree in history from the University of Miami. In April of 1987, at age 43, Jeff Campbell moved to Pillsbury's Minneapolis headquarters. His new position with Burger King's parent company represents another big leap up Pillsbury's corporate ladder. Campbell oversees the operations of the company's largest division, which includes seven restaurant chains—Steak and Ale, Godfather's Pizza, Bennigan's, QuikWok, Bay Street, Key West Grill, and Burger King.

If those responsibilities were not challenge enough, this corporate executive and highly skilled leader jogs and lifts weights. I have heard people say that Jeff Campbell is what many future CEOs will use as a role model.

CAMPBELLISMS

"My challenge is to achieve balance between responsibility to my business 'constituencies' and my family."

"Stretch-goals, painted in exciting terms, work like hell."

*"Change must not only be expected,
sometimes it must be induced."*

"Our organization's customer focus is only about 50 percent of what it should be . . . but we're getting better at it."

"The ability to organize and use time, funds and/or people with a sense of what is decisive/essential and what the priorities ought to be is a major key to success."

CHAPTER 11

CUSTOMER-FOCUSED CULTURE

---

*"Trade could not be managed by those who manage it
if it had much difficulty."*

Samuel Johnson

Promotable posturing, continuity of challenge, adequacy standards, and making change an ally are as applicable to employees as they are to the employer; as pertinent to the person in a small business as to the executive in a large corporation. Bear this in mind as we discuss customer focus in this chapter.

Many business professionals recently have gone through a dramatic and even painful transition from a product focus to a customer focus. If you don't believe it, talk to all those employed in businesses recently deregulated. The mission statements of both large and small companies reflect this change. Today they focus on market-driven criteria rather than product-identified images.

An excellent example of this change in focus occurred at Wayne Feeds. The company previously had a variety of advertising slogans used on their packages of feed and on company promotional materials. By and large, their slogans all related to making pigs fat.

Such slogans are product-focused, emphasizing how good, strong, or beneficial the product is. In today's business world, that product focus is both dangerous and unacceptable. Wayne Feeds' new mission statement more accurately positioned the firm as serving the customer's needs and maintaining a customer focus. As expressed by Dale Larson, the group president of World Milling Industries, a subsidiary of Continental Grain, their new message is: "We won't ask for your business unless we can help improve it."

That statement is customer-focused. To succeed in business an understanding of the concept is critical.

Job Priority One

What is your number one job priority? If your response is "design," "budgeting," "profitability," "selling the product line," "accounting," "administration," or something similar, then your understanding of your number-one job responsibility is incorrect. For all disciplines, the premier responsibility is to first identify and then satisfy the customers' needs profitably. Customer focusing dominates the thinking of the promotable business person.

Some years ago in a production facility of Musel Company in Dijon, France, two signs were posted prominently. The first said, "Safety pays." The second said, "Our number one job priority is to identify and then satisfy the customers' needs profitably." The concept is universally applicable and works just as well in the United States as it does in France.

More Than Satisfied

I witnessed a presentation by Barry Clark, president of IBM Canada, for the managers of the commercial division of ESSO Petroleum, Ltd., in Toronto in September 1985. Clark detailed the intricate systems and strategies of IBM and spoke of the changes in IBM's selling posture. Throughout the program, he continually discussed IBM's uncompromising commitment to identifying and satisfying the customers' needs at *all* levels.

By Clark's declaration, all IBM salespeople and support and administration personnel "own" the accountability for customer satisfaction. In light of this customer focus, it was exceptionally interesting to learn about IBM's commission plan. "If an account is ever lost," Mr. Clark said, "commissions are *deducted* from the earnings of the marketing representative in that territory at the time, regardless if it is the third, fifth, or tenth salesperson in the area since the original sale." IBM is market-driven *and* customer-focused.

The IBM standard for satisfied customers is a commitment to produce "*more* than satisfied customers." Allow me to explain. To compete effectively today, a desire or policy to simply produce satisfied customers is inadequate. All businesses face similar standards—the customer in this country takes for granted guaranteed satisfaction for whatever it is he or she purchases. Moreover, the standard has been pushed to a more demanding level, the IBM level. This standard dictates that customer focus be characterized by clients who are not simply satisfied that they did business with you and received value. Today your clientele must be *more* than satisfied that they did business with you.

Mercury Marine's Customer Focus

Our clients sometimes describe what my company teaches as "Beveridge-Think." It's the point within the planning stage where the need to identify and satisfy the customers' needs profitably becomes the focal point for policy decisions.

Mercury Marine's experience is further evidence of the need for customer focus. In recent years, Mercury Marine's management has done an exceptional job of combating offshore imports in its business. Especially noteworthy are the comments of Richard Jordon, president of Mercury Marine, a division of the Brunswick Corporation. In a videotape directed at all Mercury Outboard dealers, Jordon said:

> Two years ago we had some problems. Now, Mercury Marine is more profitable than all other companies, more profitable than OMC (Outboard Marine Corporation, manufacturers of Johnson Outboard Engines), more profitable than Yamaha. Our market share has steadily increased in spite of the added competition. That's what I call excellence, that's what I call winning the race.

Jordon made those remarks with pride and with pleasure. After all, there aren't too many U.S. equipment companies who have competed successfully with offshore manufacturers. Jordon continued:

> Today, if Yamaha was an American company, judged by American standards, they would be bankrupt. In Yamaha's last fiscal year

ending in April, 1984, Yamaha lost 152 million dollars, and as of today, are almost a billion dollars in debt. Looking back, the best thing for the marine industry was the Japanese threat. I know it gave Mercury Marine the reason to shape up and leave the Japanese and everyone else in our wake.

How did Mercury Marine achieve that objective? Harley Davidson couldn't fend off the Honda, Suzuki, and Yamaha challenge until years later. RCA, Zenith, and other television manufacturers in this country couldn't conquer the offshore manufacturers. Certainly, the losing streak of America's automobile companies has been documented.

Mercury Marine fought hard and is winning because of its customer focus, good leadership, and execution by a committed management team. Mercury was like any other outboard manufacturer, constantly searching for product, price, and technological advantages over its competition. That's a tough road and a formidable task over the long haul. Long-term, a company will maintain a competitive edge only with a customer-focused posture.

For years, Mercury Marine brochures were product-focused, featuring engine cutaway photos. Technical data on fuel consumption and drive capability of the engine were played up. But the new strategy targeted the needs of the customer instead of focusing on the "nuts and bolts" of the motor. I'm not suggesting that the excellent defense mounted by Mercury Marine to combat competition was solely based on a new customer-focused approach, but it was a vital component.

Mercury Marine started a marketing program centered on the theme, "Possible Dream." Dealers were encouraged to remove new motors from display pedestals common in marine showrooms and to place those engines on fully rigged boats. The boats included cruising vessels, fishing boats, and boats fully equipped for water-skiing. When displayed fully rigged, including a new Mercury outboard, the whole package was marketed as a "Possible Dream." Mercury Marine was able to generate more orders than they could fulfill in 1984.

Comprehending that a customer-focused position is mandatory, as Mercury Marine did, will help all who want to advance in their careers.

Customers Go in the Top Box

Individuals who own their own businesses, and who took on such a venture because of a particular expertise, will not be successful for long if they cannot refocus direction. Managers must understand and tend to the engine that drives the business. That engine is customers; the customer is king. The customer's needs and our ability to relate to and satisfy those needs is the mission statement of those who will achieve and excel.

Picture an organizational chart on which a company places names and titles of the individuals on the team. It has a box at the top designating the top person, then it descends through the lesser ranks. What title do we place in the top box? President? CEO? General Manager? Owner?

Though many people would place anyone of these titles in the top box, most astute, aware, promotable people would not. The professionals who achieve great results place "Customer" in the top box. Because those companies are market-driven and customer-focused, nothing less is acceptable. It is the non-negotiable standard of the promotable person and of the successful business.

Business professionals are often divided into three groups: those who make things happen, those who watch things happen, and those who wonder what happened. Customer-focused, promotable people fall into the first category because they identify and satisfy their clients' needs profitably.

Broadening the Concept of Customer Focus

Customer focus does not always have to relate to a buyer-seller relationship. A customer is any individual who looks to you for support, problem-solving, expertise and, of course, goods and services. The staff-support people in a company have the line or field personnel of the firm as *their* client. The customer of the administrator may be the firm's salespeople. The client of the engineer may be his company's manufacturing group. The promotable individual easily sees and perceives that form of customer-focused relationship which is relative to him or her.

Some support people constantly crank out new programs, pouring them out to the field without ever going into the field to listen to their customers . . . the company's line personnel. For years, I have demanded that twice annually my support groups leave all their programs, all their new designs, all their developed systems back at the home office and get out into the field to be with, observe, and listen to the people they support. I have required that they accept as their standard of performance the effective execution as well as origination of new programs.

Now we achieve more goals and penetrate more markets.

THE CUSTOMER IS THE BOSS

It's important to remember that the customer is the boss. At times government agencies lose sight of that fact, doing everything they can to convince us they do not understand the concept.

In 1983, Federal Express, the profitable package-distribution company, took millions of dollars of revenue away from the United States Postal Service. The company ran television commercials that portrayed postal workers as people who didn't care about their customers. (Beginning in 1985, postal workers started training in how to be courteous and how to handle customer complaints with discretion and charm.)

Federal Express didn't advertise speed of service or bigger planes or trucks. In fact, the U.S. Postal Service had more and bigger trucks. Instead, Federal Express advertised customer focus.

The principle of customer focus is universal, regardless of the business or the job. The companies, departments, businesses, industries, and individuals who move ahead are those who identify and then satisfy the customers' needs profitably.

We recently made a presentation to 220 store managers of the large Canadian retail chain Zellers. One hundred and seventy-five management and head-office staff personnel were also in the audience. It was common knowledge that the different groups or departments within the company blamed each other for the company's failure to implement a stable replenishment program that would keep shelves stocked and hopefully generate more revenues.

They debated the effectiveness of the advertising program. They actively discussed the recent change from a decentralized to a centralized form of organizational structure. Each of those factors, in turn, was an issue that had to be resolved. Yet they were not the issues that had created flat sales for the previous two years.

The issues eating away at Zellers ability to compete with aggressive marketers such as Big Top, The Bay, and Simpson's were customer-focused issues. A 1985 survey of all Zellers stores revealed that the cleanliness of the Zellers public washrooms was "a near tragedy" (those are the words of Zellers operations manager). In addition, the analysis showed that it was very difficult for customers to return unwanted merchandise. Even though the chain blanketed most of Canada with 220 outlets, one store would not accept the merchandise of another Zellers store. Moreover, check-out time at the stores was unreasonably long. While the managers debated product-focused issues, the customer-focused issues were left to slide.

Conversely, Northern Illinois Brass Company (NIBCO), headquartered in Elkhart, Indiana, became a customer-focused company. This well known manufacturer of PVC valves, pipes, and fittings was a product-focused organization. Today, their advertisements are void of the traditional valve photos and technical descriptions of other products. Instead, the advertisements feature sales personnel as problem-solving business professionals with a high degree of expertise.

The headline on their ads suggests that the customer "TAP OUR RESOURCES," referring to their sales personnel dressed in conservative business suits. The ad copy details both the depth and range of NIBCO capabilities and has the tag line below their company name: "More than just a source. A resource." NIBCO's customer-focused advertising is now doing a fine job of marketing brass pipes and fittings.

Having a large competitive advantage in product or price is becoming less likely. To succeed, a business must bring empathy, expertise, and problem-solving skills to its customers.

TAP OUR RESOURCES.

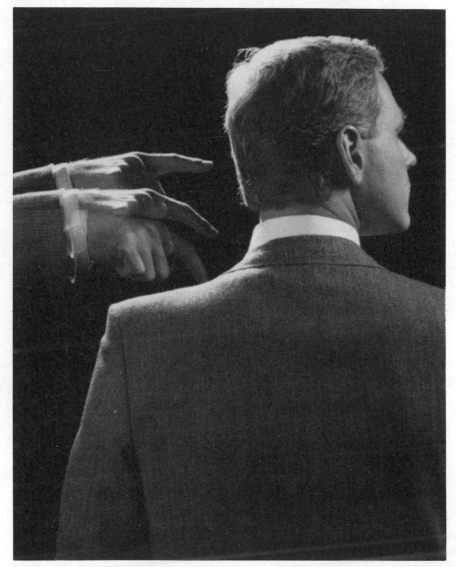

NIBCO, Inc. Reprinted with permission.

NIBCO'S Customer Needs Analysis can put answers at your fingertips.

Don't think of us merely as a source for quality plumbing products. Consider NIBCO a qualified *resource* for your business.

Because we'll put our best people to work for your company, free.

It all begins with a Customer Needs Analysis.

Your NIBCO salesman will visit your facility and spend time learning about your operation.

You tell him what will make your business more successful.

Together we'll provide customized solutions to help make it happen.

The NIBCO team can help you enter new markets. Provide training. Help improve your turns. And more.

If you need specialized help, your NIBCO salesman will tap the professionals from NIBCO's headquarters.

They can help with inventory control, product knowledge, sales, marketing, and informational equipment. Just part of the unique NIBCO system.

All the resources of America's No. 1 piping products company, at your fingertips.

All dedicated to your prosperity.

Which is not to minimize the importance of the products we provide.

NIBCO is still your source for plastic and copper fittings, faucets, and plumbing valves.

Available from 13 warehouses nationwide for prompt delivery.

Backed by our $2 and $5 product guarantees.

And brought to you by salesmen who take a vital interest in your business.

If your business could use a shot in the arm, we invite you to tap our resources.

Contact your NIBCO professional today.

NIBCO INC. • PO Box 1167 • Elkhart, IN 46515

More than just a source. A resource.

SUCCESSFUL PERSON PROFILE

Dale F. Larson

Group President, World Milling Industries
Continental Grain Company
Chicago, Illinois

What can you say about an individual with an agricultural background who demonstrates exceptional business skills? Dale Larson, as general manager of the Wayne Feeds Division of Continental Grain, brought the "value-added" and "market-systems" concepts of American industry to the farm market.

It's ludicrous to suggest that business skills are the total solution to the declining return on investment of the country's farmers. However, it is a necessary and mandatory component of the solution to those difficulties. During a period of tough farm economics, Larson is a man who brought expertise, empathy, and problem-solving skills to the agricultural environment. All parties involved—Continental Grain, the Wayne Feeds distributors, and the farmer—benefited.

Larson implemented a strategy of customer focus throughout his organization to help execute positive change. In early 1987, at a farmer feed dealer meeting in Iowa, discussion focused on methods to recover and improve their businesses. After much discussion, a Wayne Feeds dealer stood up and said, "Our slogan at Wayne Feeds is: 'We won't ask for your business, unless we can help improve it.'" That's Dale Larson's philosophy filtering through to the field, and it works! The process continues with his very able replacement, "Murph" Henderson, as Larson moved to his present position of group president, World Milling Industries.

While earning a bachelor of science degree in agricultural education and completing the Columbia University executive program, Larson personally financed a large portion of his education. He was a high-school Future Farmer of America officer, active in both the Lions Club and Jaycees, and was an officer of his church.

That sound, "rooted" background created a person who views all relationships—manager/subordinate, company/customer, peer/associate—as potential win/win relationships. Of equal importance, however, Dale Larson willingly and intelligently recognizes the need for disciplining non-performance where necessary. Larson is the type of leader our country's universities were designed to create.

LARSONISMS

"People who fail either acquiesce to others too often or not enough."

"Even adverse change must be viewed to find positive impact."

"At times, people who are disorganized perform well. However, most mortals need some organization in their life to make progress and to provide stability and order for others."

"In the past, we were manufacturing-focused. We've made progress toward becoming market-oriented. We, however, still tend to try to become all things to all people, and there is room for improvement."

CHAPTER 12

HOW DO MY PEOPLE SEE ME?

---

*"Knowledge may give weight, but accomplishments give luster,
and many more people see than weigh."*

Lord Chesterfield

The answers you give to the following three questions will directly relate to the degree you're able to meet the challenge to achieve. Answers to these questions will assist you in judging your ability to lead and direct others, and altering your behavior, if necessary.

1. How does my staff see me?
2. How do I see my boss?
3. How do my children see me?

In examining these three questions I will use four models or identities that serve as answers, including the "non-manager," "policeman or policewoman," "superman/woman," and "coach."

The Non-Manager

Whether you are an independent business person, a manufacturer's representative in business for yourself, or a retailer, the same questions must be answered: "How do you see your supplier or your franchisor? How do you perceive your vendor 'rep' or any other individual who is in an advisory role to your business?"

My consulting activities have demonstrated that a majority of the work force today perceives supervisors as "non-managers."

This is paralleled by the attitudes of entrepreneurs toward advisors. When I suggest to entrepreneurs that their perception of the advisor as a non-manager is not conducive to achieving, excelling, and getting ahead in business, they are shocked and indignant.

I ask if their image of a mentor as a non-manager doesn't bother them, and they say "no," because such an image clearly suggests that the mentor should not be disciplining their non-performance. Yet whenever you're in an environment where there are no disciplines for non-performance, you will always have declining standards. Teenaged children are a perfect example. Set a curfew of 10:30 p.m. For the first four to six weeks, the children will follow that policy. Shortly after, they'll begin to test the system. During the seventh week that young person is going to waltz in at 11:00 p.m. If not disciplined, he or she will arrive home after midnight the next night.

When you're in an environment undisciplined for non-performance, you will always have declining standards. At home, in business, in government, around the world, the individual who avoids discipline has great difficulty becoming a "10" in business.

If you are an independent entrepreneur, hope that one of your purveyors has enough guts to discipline your non-performance. Without such an advisor or mentor, you're going to wake up after several years unable to compete in business.

If you work in a corporation and your boss doesn't provide discipline, this lack of correction in your career will become very noticeable. You and I cannot and will not achieve if we see our boss as a non-manager or as someone who should not discipline our non-performance.

What are your standards today? Have they improved or have they deteriorated because you refuse to accept the guidance of a mentor or manager?

Some years ago, we studied professional selling skills and the continuity of those abilities in the careers of 150 different salespeople. At the top of the list were IBM representatives—very skilled, proud, and disciplined. On the bottom of the list were independent manufacturers representatives.

In general, independent representatives complained about supplier inadequacies, felt wronged, and were undisciplined. Moreover, they had the poorest selling skills. For the most part, they were overpaid relative to the degree of difficulty in their job. These sales representatives didn't take sufficient responsibility for the sales effort. They no longer prepared itineraries or work plans, and they seldom incorporated selling tools in their verbal presentations. They could not tell us the specific amounts of time they had designated for calling on new accounts, and they had discarded most of the other basic selling skills. In an environment where there was no discipline for non-performance, they had declining standards for selling skills and sales productivity.

The Policeman or Policewoman

Often, managers perceive their role as policing; consequently, subordinates become less than fully communicative. You must avoid being seen as a policeman. It negates any chance of meaningful communication. In fact, all communication stops.

For years, our firm has been marketing and management consultant to the radio industry, which loses the vast majority of its salespeople within a year and a large percentage of the remainder in the second year. Although the issue is slightly more complicated than this discussion would indicate, one very common but harmful practice is insisting that all the salespeople show up each morning at the office or station.

In addition, activity-call reports—a listing of where the salesperson has been—are required. Some stations also have quotas for the number of calls per day. All of these "activity measurements" have long been considered policing systems; consequently, all honest communication ceases. It's certainly one of the reasons the turnover of salespeople is so high!

Similar policing activity occurs between franchisee and franchisor, manufacturer and dealer, and representative firm and supplier. As a result, open communication simply does not exist in almost every case because the "doer" perceives the "mentor" to be a spy.

Early in my career, I had the opportunity to avoid playing policeman in a position that traditionally supported the role. Ezra Barber represented Mobil Oil Company as a distributor in the Hohenwald, Tennessee, area. I had the standard responsibility of selling him oils, lubes, tires, batteries, and accessories. After months of doing business with Ezra, on one particular visit he offered me a seat near his desk and handed me his profit-and-loss statement. No Mobil distributor had ever shared such information with me.

I must have looked dumbfounded because it was my experience that distributors were secretive about their revenues and profits and *never* disclosed that data to the oil company. Ezra Barber shared that information. Apparently my empathy, expertise, and problem-solving skills precipitated an "evolution" in our relationship. Ezra felt I could help; I was no longer perceived as an oil-company policeman or spy.

Because of Ezra's trust, I had to become more skilled in serving him. And our communication became more open and energizing.

The Superman/woman Syndrome

The third identity is the image of the mentor or manager as a superhuman problem-solver. The "Superman/woman syndrome" is a business cancer in the marketplace. Recall Clark Kent, who worked as a mild-mannered reporter for the *Daily Planet* in Metropolis. Two hooded crooks rob a bank. The tellers and president stand frozen as the crooks gather up the money and dash out the door. As soon as they're gone, the bank president picks up the phone and calls Clark Kent. Shortly after, Superman flies out the nearest *Daily Planet* window, finds the crooks, and promptly puts them in jail. And what are the police doing? They're playing poker, because they no longer need to implement their "crook-catching" skills.

Usually, in the business world, there's a sales manager who handles all the major accounts, a supervisor who handles all the customer complaints, and a production manager who repairs the equipment. However, if these people try to use Superman's method of operating, they will find it to be counterproductive to the interest of the business as a whole. Over the long term, Superman will not make a significant contribution because he doesn't understand that people learn by doing!

I recall an area manager who worked for me in Rochester, New York. At the time, Tom Murphy was a young, aggressive, performance-motivated manager of five field salespeople. Tom was so motivated to achieve he just couldn't learn to leave the actual selling to his representatives. On one occasion, Tom burst into my office and proudly declared that he had just sold a truckload of car tires. Even though we needed the revenue and the unit sales, we couldn't continue to compete if the entire district marketing effort was dependent on one or two area managers.

I looked at Tom very seriously. First, I thanked him for the dollar volume, and I told him the district appreciated the business. Second, I asked Tom by what date I could expect his people to have similar selling skills. Finally, I said, "Tom, I was not aware that you were so anxious to be a salesperson. You know I have the authority to make you one."

Still another example is the business career of Jack Phillips. Jack is an aggressive, talented business person living in central Wisconsin. Today, he is a self-employed manufacturer's representative with several lines of recreational products and sporting goods. Jack and I were in college together and stayed in touch for over 20 years. His career, which had great potential, was short-circuited because Jack Phillips was a classic Superman.

Phillips started out as a top salesperson for Rawlings Sporting Goods in St. Louis. Eventually, he was promoted to national sales manager. He was subsequently terminated because he couldn't allow his salespeople to handle their own accounts. It seemed as if Jack worked 24 hours a day and participated in every sale Rawlings made. However, his sales team was near revolt. It peaked one day in Chicago when Jack jumped into a presentation being made to Sears, Roebuck & Co. by one of his salespeople. When Jack took over the sale (for the seemingly thousandth time), his sales representative walked out.

Jack Phillips visited my office that day, a disillusioned and shaken man. Shortly thereafter, he and Rawlings parted company

Fortunately, Tom Murphy reviewed his job description that detailed the responsibility of the business leader to get things done through other people. Jack Phillips did not.

To achieve, excel, and get ahead in business mandates that we develop skills well beyond the technical abilities upon which we founded our business, or the "doing" skills we demonstrated in the corporation in order to be promoted. People learn by doing. Putting a Superman in a leadership role only guarantees mediocrity from other people in the overall performance of the business.

Coach

As a parent, a mentor, a purveyor, or a manager, the best identity you can have—the identity by which others know you—is that of a "coach." This is the target of the business professionals who are going to attain their lifetime career goals. As leaders, when we see our roles as that of a coach, career advancement and enhancement almost always results.

Coaches formulate and develop plans. Coaches accept the risks of leadership. Coaches are constantly dealing with the need to organize the department, the business, or themselves.

In addition, coaches accept the accountability and the responsibility to control and staff the business with their best possible players.

You have great influence on how you're seen, and the choice is yours. If you truly want to achieve, excel, and get ahead in business, you must be perceived as, and be, a coach.

The person who succeeds in business and life will possess the following characteristics:

- Maintain promotable posturing, preparing himself for success.
- Maintain a continuing challenge.
- Develop excellence standards.
- Set mandatory goals.
- Make change an ally.
- Master team orchestration.
- Execute effectively.

- Develop organization skills.
- Stay customer-focused.

All of the above factors, enhanced by a stimulating environment and supported by effective coaching, open the gates to a lifetime of achievement, because success is not a goal—success is a result!

SUCCESSFUL PERSON PROFILE

W. J. (Jim) Ellison

President/Owner
Ellison Machinery Company
Sante Fe Springs, California

"We strive to use high standards as a means of differentiating our company and for building reasons for our customers to select our products and services," says Jim Ellison, president and owner of Ellison Machinery Company. It's apparent that Ellison, who grew up in a family-owned machine-tool business, has conceptualized that a business is far beyond the product itself.

His Los Angeles office serves as headquarters for several businesses that Jim and his partners own and operate throughout the United States and Japan. He is a director on the boards of a computer company and a major bank. He also lectures at the UCLA Graduate School of Management while serving as a quality role model to his industry.

I've worked for and with this gentleman. Jim Ellison should be packaged and distributed at today's business schools as an example of an effective executive. He is warm but disciplined; flexible yet goal-oriented. Though he is motivated to achieve, he maintains a lifestyle that indicates there is more to life than work. He parallels an earlier successful-person profile, Dick Farmer, in that both accepted the reins of the family business and made it much better than it was when they took over.

A former president of the American Machine Tool Distributors Association, Ellison is candid enough to comment, "Even now there are times when I wonder if life wouldn't have been more simple if I had stayed small and relied solely on my own sales skills." Thankfully, Jim Ellison didn't decide to "stay small," because his integrity, leadership, management skills, and coaching posture have benefited a broad range of other people. Jim Ellison leads with extreme capability.

ELLISONISMS

"Challenge comes from redirecting your energies from that of a doer to that of a successful coach."

"I would guess that as much as 90 percent of our people problems come from failing to get them properly situated in their new position."

"It is not only possible to make change a positive, it is a necessity."

"Our business revolves around goal-setting. It is the beginning of every business plan; it is the basis by which the health of the relationship between management and employees hinges. It gives purpose to our work. Goal-setting allows us to focus our energies on what the important issues are and allows us to support one another in meeting our commitments."

"A team psychology is born out of sharing from the top down. There is a feeling that the glory of the win is the property of the team and no single individual."

BIBLIOGRAPHY

Books

Brown, Dr. William. *Welcome Stress-It Can Help You Be Your Best.* Minneapolis: CompCare Publications, 1983.

Davidson, Jeffrey P. *Marketing to the Fortune 500.* Homewood, IL: Dow Jones-Irwin, 1987.

Hanan, Mack. *Consultative Selling.* 3rd Edition, New York: AMACOM, 1983.

Hartley, Robert F. *Marketing Mistakes.* Revised edition. New York: John Wiley and Sons, 1986.

Lakein, Alan. *How to Get Control of Your Time and Your Life.* New York: New American Library, 1973.

McCormack, Mark H. *What They Don't Teach You at Harvard Business School.* New York: Bantam Books, 1984.

Articles

"A & P Counts the Cost of its Pyrrhic Victory." *Business Week,* April 28, 1973.

Beveridge, Don W., Jr. "Keep Your Managers Out of the Sale." *Sales and Marketing Management,* October 8, 1984.

Crissos, Joan. "Burger King Chairman Moving Up." *Miami Herald,* April 16, 1987.

Huser, Marianne. "House-to-House Car Salesman, Another Foreign Import." *Daily News,* October 27, 1985.

Kirstof, Nicholas D. "Harley Davidson Roars Back." In "Business Day," *New York Times,* October 3, 1985.

Mescon, Dr. Michael, and Dr. Tim Mescon. "What Makes A Leader?" *Delta Airline's Sky,* August, 1985.

Meyer, David, and Herbert M. Greenberg. "What Makes a Good Salesman?" *Harvard Business Review,* July-August, 1964.

"Post Office Licking Image." *USA Today,* November 1, 1985.

"Toyota's Fast Lane." *Business Week,* November 4, 1985.

"War in the Supermarkets," *Time,* August 14, 1972.

Whiteside, David E., and James B. Treece. "GMC and FANUC: An Unlikely Pair but a Winner." *Business Week,* July 21, 1986.

Index